Call to Faith

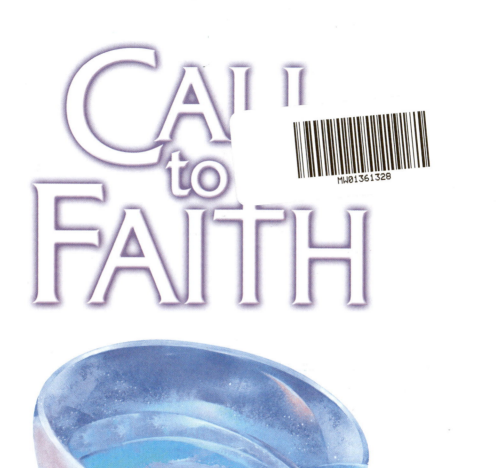

GRADE 5
School

Curriculum Division

www.osvcurriculum.com

The Subcommittee on the Catechism, United States Conference of Catholic Bishops, has found this catechetical series, © 2009 Edition, to be in conformity with the *Catechism of the Catholic Church*.

Nihil Obstat
Rev. Richard L. Schaefer

Imprimatur
✝ Most Rev. Thomas Wenski
Bishop of Orlando
December 14, 2007

The Imprimatur is an official declaration that a book or pamphlet is free of doctrinal or moral error. No implication is contained therein that anyone who granted the Imprimatur agrees with the contents, opinions, or statements expressed.

© by Our Sunday Visitor Curriculum Division, Our Sunday Visitor, 2009 Edition.

All rights reserved. No part of this publication may be reproduced or transmitted in any form or by any means, electronic or mechanical, including photocopy, recording, or any information storage and retrieval system, without permission in writing from the publisher.
Write:
Our Sunday Visitor Curriculum Division
Our Sunday Visitor, Inc.
200 Noll Plaza, Huntington, Indiana 46750

Call to Faith is a registered trademark of Our Sunday Visitor Curriculum Division, Our Sunday Visitor, 200 Noll Plaza, Huntington, Indiana 46750.

For permission to reprint copyrighted materials, grateful acknowledgment is made to the following sources:

Confraternity of Christian Doctrine, Washington, D.C.: Scriptures from the *New American Bible*. Text copyright © 1991, 1986, 1970 by the Confraternity of Christian Doctrine. All rights reserved. No part of the *New American Bible* may be used or reproduced in any form, without permission in writing from the copyright owner.

The Copyright Company, Nashville, TN: Lyrics from "Alleluia No. 1" by Don Fishel. Lyrics © 1973 by Word of God Music. International Copyright secured.

Hope Publishing Co., Carol Stream, IL 60188: Lyrics from "Baptized in Water" by Michael Saward. Lyrics © 1982 by Jubilate Hymns, Ltd.

Hyperion: "On Being a Champion" from *Journey Through Heartsongs* by Mattie Stepanek. Text copyright © 2001 by Mattie Stepanek.

The English translation of the Psalm Responses from *Lectionary for Mass* © 1969, 1981, 1997, International Commission on English in the Liturgy Corporation (ICEL); the English translation of the Act of Contrition from *Rite of Penance* © 1974, ICEL; the English translation of the Prayer to the Holy Spirit, *Angelus, Salve, Regina,* and *Memorare* from *A Book of Prayers* © 1982, ICEL; excerpts from the English translation of *Rite of Christian Initiation of Adults,* © 1985, ICEL; excerpts from the English translation of *The Roman Missal* © 2010, ICEL. All rights reserved.

Liturgy Training Publications, 1800 North Hermitage Avenue, Chicago, IL 60622, 1-800-933-1800, www.ltp.org: From "Prayer for Our Lady of Guadalupe" (Retitled: "Prayer for Our Lady of Guadalupe Day") and "Meal Prayer for Early Spring" (Retitled: "Grace at Mealtime") in *Blessings and Prayers through the Year: A Resource for School and Parish* by Elizabeth McMahon Jeep. Text © 2004 by Archdiocese of Chicago.

Additional acknowledgments appear on page 326.

Call to Faith School Grade 5 Student Book
ISBN: 978-0-15-902286-3
Item Number: CU1382

5 6 7 8 9 10 11 12 015016 16 15 14 13 12
Webcrafters, Inc., Madison, WI, USA; September 2012; Job# 102485

Grade 5 Contents

SEASONAL LESSONS & CELEBRATIONS 6
- **Ordinary Time:** The Rosary 8
- **Advent:** Be Ready! 12
- **Christmas:** Feasts of the Season 16
- **Ordinary Time:** Image of Christ 20
- **Lent:** The Forty Days 24
- **Triduum:** New Life in Christ 28
- **Easter:** It Is Jesus! 32
- **Pentecost:** Called to Serve 36

UNIT 1
REVELATION 40
- Chapter 1: Longing for God 41
- Chapter 2: Worshiping God 51
- Chapter 3: Signs of God's Presence 61
- Faith in Action! 71

UNIT 2
TRINITY 76
- Chapter 4: The Mystery of God 77
- Chapter 5: Prayer and Worship 87
- Chapter 6: Doing Good 97
- Faith in Action! 107

UNIT 3
JESUS CHRIST 112
- Chapter 7: The Image of God 113
- Chapter 8: Proclaim the Kingdom 123
- Chapter 9: New Life 133
- Faith in Action! 143

UNIT 4
THE CHURCH 148
- Chapter 10: A Sign to the World 149
- Chapter 11: The Teaching Church 159
- Chapter 12: Called to Holiness 169
- Faith in Action! 179

UNIT 5
MORALITY 184
- Chapter 13: The Mystery of Evil 185
- Chapter 14: Reborn in Christ 195
- Chapter 15: Forgiveness and Healing 205
- Faith in Action! 215

UNIT 6
SACRAMENTS 220
- Chapter 16: Gathered for Mass 221
- Chapter 17: The Liturgy of the Word 231
- Chapter 18: The Liturgy of the Eucharist . 241
- Faith in Action! 251

UNIT 7
KINGDOM OF GOD 256
- Chapter 19: Answering God's Call 257
- Chapter 20: The Last Things 267
- Chapter 21: Come, Lord Jesus 277
- Faith in Action! 287

CATHOLIC SOURCE BOOK 292
- Scripture 292
- Creed 295
- Liturgy 299
- Morality 304
- Prayer 308
- Words of Faith 320
- Index 324

BEGINNING THE YEAR.................... 1

- About You
- About Your Faith
- About Your Book
- Prayer of Welcome

SEASONAL LESSONS & CELEBRATIONS 6

▶ **Ordinary Time: The Rosary............. 8**
RITUAL ACTION FOR CELEBRATION:
Say "Yes", Bowing to the Cross

▶ **Advent: Be Ready! 12**
RITUAL ACTION FOR CELEBRATION:
Pray with the O Antiphons

▶ **Christmas: Feasts of the Season....... 16**
RITUAL ACTION FOR CELEBRATION:
Honoring the Scriptures

▶ **Ordinary Time: Image of Christ........ 20**
RITUAL ACTION FOR CELEBRATION:
Blessing with Holy Water

▶ **Lent: The Forty Days................. 24**
RITUAL ACTION FOR CELEBRATION:
Penitential Act

▶ **Triduum: New Life in Christ 28**
RITUAL ACTION FOR CELEBRATION:
Washing of Hands

▶ **Easter: It Is Jesus! 32**
RITUAL ACTION FOR CELEBRATION:
The Lord's Prayer and Sign of Peace

▶ **Pentecost: Called to Serve............ 36**
RITUAL ACTION FOR CELEBRATION:
Signing of Hands

UNIT 1
REVELATION............................ 40

Chapter 1 Longing for God................ 41
- True happiness can come only through communion with God.
- Religion expresses our relationship with God through beliefs, prayers, and practices.
- Listening for God

SCRIPTURE
The Woman at the Well
John 4:7–29

Chapter 2 Worshipping God............. 51
- Humans share in the Creator's loving plan by caring for creation.
- God's providence is his care and plan for all of creation.
- Stewardship of God's creation

SCRIPTURE
Glory to God
Psalm 98:4–9

Chapter 3 Signs of God's Presence 61
- God communicates through signs.
- Through the signs and symbolic actions of the sacraments, God's life becomes truly present in your life.
- Recognize God's signs

SCRIPTURE
The Burning Bush
Exodus 3:1–15

Faith in Action!...................... 71
Catholic Social Teaching:
Care for God's Creation

Unit 1 Review....................... 74

iv

UNIT 2
TRINITY 76

Chapter 4 The Mystery of God 77
- The Trinity is the central mystery of Christian faith and life.
- Virtue is the habit of doing good. The theological virtues of faith, hope, and love are gifts from God.
- Virtues in Action

SCRIPTURE

The Baptism of Jesus
John 1:32–34

Chapter 5 Prayer and Worship 87
- Prayer and worship are ways to show love for God and to thank him for his blessings.
- When we pray and worship, God fills us with joy, strength, and hope.
- Body Language for Prayer

SCRIPTURE

A Day of Joy
2 Samuel 6:1–15

Chapter 6 Doing Good 97
- The Great Commandment states that you will love the Lord, your God, with all your heart, soul, and mind.
- The cardinal virtues play a central role in helping people lead morally good lives.
- Decision-making Tips

SCRIPTURE

The Great Commandment
Mark 12:28–34

Faith in Action! 107
Catholic Social Teaching:
Life and Dignity of the Human Person

Unit 2 Review 110

UNIT 3
JESUS CHRIST 112

Chapter 7 The Image of God 113
- The Incarnation is the belief that the Son of God became human in order to save all people.
- Jesus is both human and divine, truly God and truly human.
- Titles of Jesus

Chapter 8 Proclaim the Kingdom 123
- God's kingdom is present and grows in the Church and its sacraments until God's reign comes in fullness at the end of time.
- Jesus proclaimed the kingdom of God through his actions and parables.
- Understanding Parables

SCRIPTURE

The Parable of the Sower
Luke 8:5–8

Chapter 9 New Life 133
- Through the sacraments, Christ unites his followers to his passion, death, Resurrection, and Ascension.
- Jesus Christ is the Redeemer of the human race.
- Images of the Paschal mystery

SCRIPTURE

The Resurrection of Jesus
Luke 24:5–9

Faith in Action! 143
Catholic Social Teaching:
Rights and Responsibilities of the Human Person

Unit 3 Review 146

UNIT 4
THE CHURCH 148

Chapter 10 — A Sign to the World 149
- As members of the Church, we are all united in living out the mission of Christ.
- The Church's unity is expressed in the images of the Body of Christ and the People of God.
- Images of the Church

SCRIPTURE
Built of Living Stones
1 Peter 2:4–5

Chapter 11 — The Teaching Church 159
- The Apostles proclaimed God's good news and brought the reign of God toward its fullness.
- Under the guidance of the Holy Spirit, the pope and the bishops continue the Apostles' mission to teach.
- Church Vocabulary

SCRIPTURE
Teach All Nations
Matthew 28:19–20

Upon This Rock
Matthew 16:15–19

Chapter 12 — Called to Holiness 169
- Mary and the saints provide the Church with models of holiness.
- Canonization declares that a model Christian is enjoying eternity with God.
- Praying the Rosary

SCRIPTURE
The Handmaid of the Lord
Luke 1:30–31, 38

Faith in Action! 179
Catholic Social Teaching: The Dignity of Work and the Rights of Workers

Unit 4 Review 182

UNIT 5
MORALITY 184

Chapter 13 — The Mystery of Evil 185
- Evil is the result of humans turning away from God's goodness.
- God sent his Son to redeem people from the power of sin and evil.
- Prayer of Lamentation

SCRIPTURE
New Life in Christ
Romans 5:19

Chapter 14 — Reborn in Christ 195
- The process of becoming Catholic is called the Rite of Christian Initiation of Adults.
- The Sacraments of Initiation are Baptism, Confirmation, and Eucharist.
- Tools for Growing in Faith

SCRIPTURE
Living for God
Romans 6:10–11

Chapter 15 — Forgiveness and Healing 205
- The Church receives God's forgiveness through the Sacraments of Healing.
- The Sacrament of Reconciliation includes contrition, confession, penance, and absolution.
- Examine your Conscience

SCRIPTURE
The Two Sons
Luke 15:11–32

Faith in Action! 215
Catholic Social Teaching: Solidarity of the Human Family

Unit 5 Review 218

UNIT 6
SACRAMENTS 220

Chapter 16 Gathered for Mass 221
- The wheat bread and grape wine become the Body and Blood of Jesus in the Sacrament of the Eucharist.
- In the liturgical assembly, the Holy Spirit's grace of faith strengthens the community.
- Forms of Parish Service

SCRIPTURE
Rejoice Always
1 Thessalonians 5:14–18

Chapter 17 Liturgy of the Word 231
- The word of God is conveyed through Scripture and Tradition.
- Jesus is truly present in the word as it is proclaimed in the liturgy.
- Reflect on God's word

SCRIPTURE
Let the Word of Christ Dwell in You
Colossians 3:16

Chapter 18 Liturgy of the Eucharist 241
- In Sunday worship and daily living, the community shows that the Eucharist is the source and the summit of the Catholic Church.
- The Eucharist closely unites Christ's followers to him and to one another.
- Live the Eucharist

SCRIPTURE
The Last Supper
Matthew 26:26–28

Faith in Action! 251
Catholic Social Teaching:
Call to Family, Community, and Participation

Unit 6 Review 254

UNIT 7
KINGDOM OF GOD 256

Chapter 19 Answering God's Call 257
- The vocations of ordained and married people build the reign of God and serve others.
- The Sacraments of Service are Holy Orders and Matrimony.
- Explore the Religious Life

SCRIPTURE
Laborers for the Harvest
Matthew 9:35–38

Chapter 20 The Last Things 267
- Faith in the Resurrection is the source of hope in eternal life and happiness with God in heaven.
- The last rites of the Church include prayer, the Sacraments of Healing, and the Eucharist.
- The Journey Through Grief

SCRIPTURE
The Judgment of the Nations
Matthew 25:31–40

Chapter 21 Come, Lord Jesus 277
- The Church's mission is to bring the good news to all people everywhere.
- Every baptized person has the responsibility of sharing the good news.
- Themes of Catholic Social Teaching

SCRIPTURE
Fulfilled in Your Hearing
Luke 4:16–21

Faith in Action! 287
Catholic Social Teaching:
Option for the Poor and Vulnerable

Unit 7 Review 290

Catholic Source Book

Scripture
- Gospel Formation 292
- Canon 292
  - Scripture and Tradition 292
- How Scripture Is Used in the Liturgy 293
  - The Liturgy of the Word 293
  - Sacramental Symbols 294

Creed
- We Believe 295
  - The Holy Trinity 295
  - God the Father 295
  - God the Son 296
  - God the Holy Spirit 296
- The Church 297
  - Mary 297
  - The Saints 298
  - Everlasting Life 298

Liturgy
- Sacraments 299
  - The Sacraments of Initiation 299
  - The Sacraments of Healing 299
  - The Sacraments of Service 300
- Liturgical Year 300
  - The Liturgy of the Hours 300
  - Music in the Liturgy 300
  - Order of Mass 301
  - Liturgical Vestments 302
  - Holy Days of Obligation 302
  - Fasting and Abstinence 303
  - Liturgical Environment 303

Morality
- Law 304
  - The Ten Commandments, The Great Commandment 304
  - Precepts of the Church 304
- The Beatitudes 305
- Works of Mercy 305
  - Gifts and Fruits of the Holy Spirit 305
- Human Dignity 306
  - Grace, Sin 306
- Conscience 307
  - Examination of Conscience and Virtue 307

Prayer
- Sign of the Cross
- The Lord's Prayer
- Hail Mary
- Glory to the Father
- Act of Faith
- Act of Hope
- Act of Love
- Act of Contrition
- Prayer to the Holy Spirit
- *Angelus*
- Morning Prayer
- Grace at Mealtime
- Evening Prayer
- Prayer Before Meditation
- God's Presence
- Prayer for Our Lady of Guadalupe Day
- Litany of St. Joseph
- How to Pray to the Rosary
- The Mysteries of the Rosary
- Eucharist Prayer
- The Way of the Cross
- Gloria
- *Memorare*
- Hail, Holy Queen
- Holy, Holy, Holy Lord (English / Latin)
- *Agnus Dei* (Lamb of God) (English / Latin)

Words of Faith 320

Index 324

About You

Let Us Pray

Leader: Gracious God, we celebrate your love.
"It is good to give thanks to the LORD
to sing praises to your name, Most High . . ."
Psalm 92:2

All: Gracious God, we celebrate your love.
Amen.

Activity — Let's Begin

A New Year What do you think fifth grade will be like? Do you wonder about new friends, new classes, and new teachers? You'll learn new things and grow in new ways. Some things will remain the same. Jesus will continue to invite you to be his friend and his follower. Along with your classmates, you'll have many chances to respond to Jesus. Start by sharing something about yourself.

WHAT DO YOU LIKE TO DO...

after school?	on the weekends?	during the summer?

About Your Faith

Your friends and classmates are not the only ones on this journey of faith with you. Your family and parish guide you and help you grow as a Catholic. Together you can read the Bible, discuss your beliefs, and serve those in need. This year you'll learn more about the Church's teachings and the call to be Christ to one another.

Activity — Share Your Faith

Reflect: What does the Catholic Church celebrate?

Share: In small groups discuss what and how the Church celebrates.

Act: Write one new way you can take part in how the Church celebrates.

_____

_____

_____

_____

© Our Sunday Visitor Curriculum Division

About Your Book

Your book contains many things that will help you learn and grow as a Catholic. You will find Scripture, stories about saints and real life people, pictures of Church celebrations, and much more.

Activity Connect Your Faith

Go on a Scavenger Hunt To get to know your book better, look for the specific features listed below. Write down where you find each of them.

SCRIPTURE The Burning Bush _____

BIOGRAPHY Frederick Douglass _____

Words of Faith Liturgy _____

People of Faith Saint Marguerite Bourgeoys _____

Let Us Pray Celebration of the Word _____

A Call to Faith

Gather

Pray the Sign of the Cross together.

Leader: Blessed be God.

All: **Blessed be God for ever.**

Leader: Let us pray.

Bow your heads as the leader prays.

All: **Amen.**

Listen to God's Word

Reader: A reading from the holy Gospel according to Luke.

Read Luke 5:1–11.

The Gospel of the Lord.

All: **Praise to you, Lord Jesus Christ.**

Dialogue

Why do you think Simon and the others followed Jesus?

How have you followed Jesus?

Prayer of the Faithful

Leader: Lord, we want to follow you as Simon and his companions did. We need your strength and guidance. Please hear our prayers.

Respond to each prayer with these words.

All: **Lord, hear our prayer.**

Answer the Call

Leader: Jesus calls each of you to follow him. You can live by his teachings of love and compassion. Your words and actions can show that you believe.

Jesus wants you to help others learn about him so that they can become followers, too.

Silently reflect on Jesus' call. Then come forward as your name is called. The leader will mark your forehead with the Sign of the Cross.

Leader: (Name), may your actions show the world that you believe in and follow Jesus.

All: **Amen.**

Go Forth!

Leader: Let us go forth to bring the good news of Jesus to all around us.

All: **Thanks be to God.**

Sing together.

We are called to act with justice,
we are called to love tenderly,
we are called to serve one another;
to walk humbly with God!

"We Are Called" © 1988, 2004, GIA Publications, Inc.

Remembering Jesus

The Church prays in many ways. One of the most important ways the Church prays is in its liturgy, or its official public prayer. During the year the Church has many feasts and seasons. These times are marked by the celebration of liturgy. This is why the Church year is called the *liturgical year*.

These seasons and feasts of the liturgical year recall the birth, life, death, Resurrection, and Ascension of Jesus. The liturgical year also honors Mary and the saints. Different seasons focus on different aspects of Jesus. However, in every season the Church remembers all the gifts that come from God the Father, Son, and Holy Spirit.

The liturgy includes different words and actions. These words and actions help us respond to God's life and love. Here are some of them.

Words and Actions

The Bible is reverenced by bowing and sitting before it in silence.
The Cross is reverenced by kneeling in front of it or kissing it.
The sign of Christ's peace is offered by a handshake or other gesture.
The Sign of the Cross is marked on foreheads, hearts, and lips.
Holy water is used as a reminder of Baptism.

During the year, your class will use these words and actions to celebrate the different seasons.

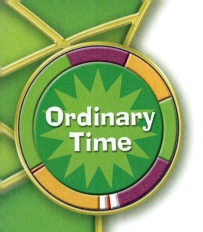

Ordinary Time

The Rosary

Throughout the Church year, the Church honors Mary with many feasts and celebrations. The entire month of October is dedicated to Mary as Our Lady of the Rosary. Many parishes have special Rosary prayer times or services during the month of October.

Yes to God

Catholics have been praying the Rosary for hundreds of years. One reason the Rosary is associated with the month of October is that Christian forces won an important battle on October 7, 1571. They believed that praying the Rosary helped them attain victory. The Church celebrates the Feast of Our Lady of the Rosary on October 7.

In 1917 three young children who lived in Fatima, Portugal, had a special experience of Our Lady. The Blessed Virgin Mary appeared to them several times from May through October. On her last visit in October, she told them to pray the Rosary each day so that there would be peace in the world. She also told them to encourage others to pray the Rosary often.

The message the children of Fatima received asked them to make others aware of the world's need for prayer. Like Mary, these children said "yes" to God. Few people will have apparitions of Mary, but God speaks to those who are open to hearing his voice.

❓ **How do you think the children of Fatima felt when Mary appeared to them?**

The Children of Fatima

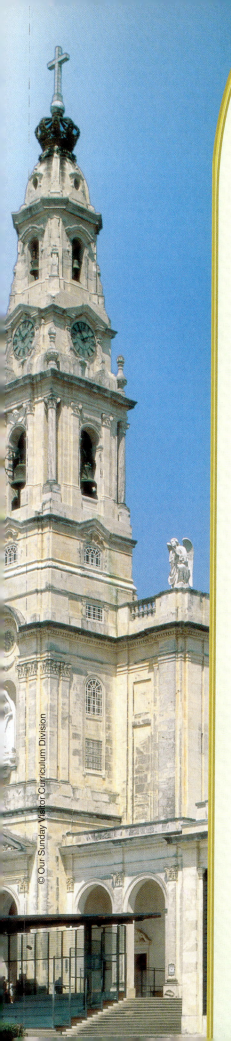

Celebrate Mary

Gather

Pray the Sign of the Cross together.

Leader: Blessed be God.

All: **Blessed be God for ever.**

Leader: Let us pray.
Bow your heads as the leader prays.

All: **Amen.**

Listen to God's Word

Leader: A reading from the holy Gospel according to Luke.
Read Luke 1:26–38.
The Gospel of the Lord.

All: **Praise to you, Lord Jesus Christ.**

Dialogue

How do you listen to God's voice?
What makes it difficult at times to say yes to God?

Say "Yes"

Leader: As Mary and the young children in Fatima said "yes", so you, too can say "yes" to God.

Come forward as your name is called. Bow to the cross and say aloud "I say "yes", my Lord."

Sing together the refrain.

I say "Yes," my Lord. I say "Yes," my Lord.
I say "Yes," my Lord, in all the good times,
   through all the bad times,
I say "Yes," my Lord to ev'ry word you speak.

"I Say 'Yes,' Lord/Digo 'Si,' Senor" © 1989, GIA Publications, Inc.

Prayer of the Faithful

Leader: Let us pray.

God our Father, Mary said "yes" to your plan for her.

We ask your blessing and Mary's intercession for the needs we put before you now.
Respond to each prayer with these words.

All: **Hear us, O Lord.**

Leader: Let us raise our prayers up to the Father in the words Jesus taught us.

All: **Our Father . . .**

Go Forth!

Leader: May the Lord bless us and keep us.

All: **Amen.**

Leader: May the Lord's face shine upon us.

All: **Amen.**

Leader: May the Lord look upon us with kindness, and give us peace.

All: **Amen.**

Leader: Let us go forth to share God's story with all those we meet.

All: **Thanks be to God.**

GIA Publications, Inc.

Pray to Say "Yes"

Mary is honored above all other saints. When the angel Gabriel told Mary that she would be the mother of Jesus, Mary believed and accepted God's plan. Her *yes* sets the example for all believers. Praying the Rosary and meditating on the mysteries as you pray can help you say "yes" to God. Pray the Rosary often, and continue to listen for God's voice.

❓ **In what ways is God calling you to believe?**

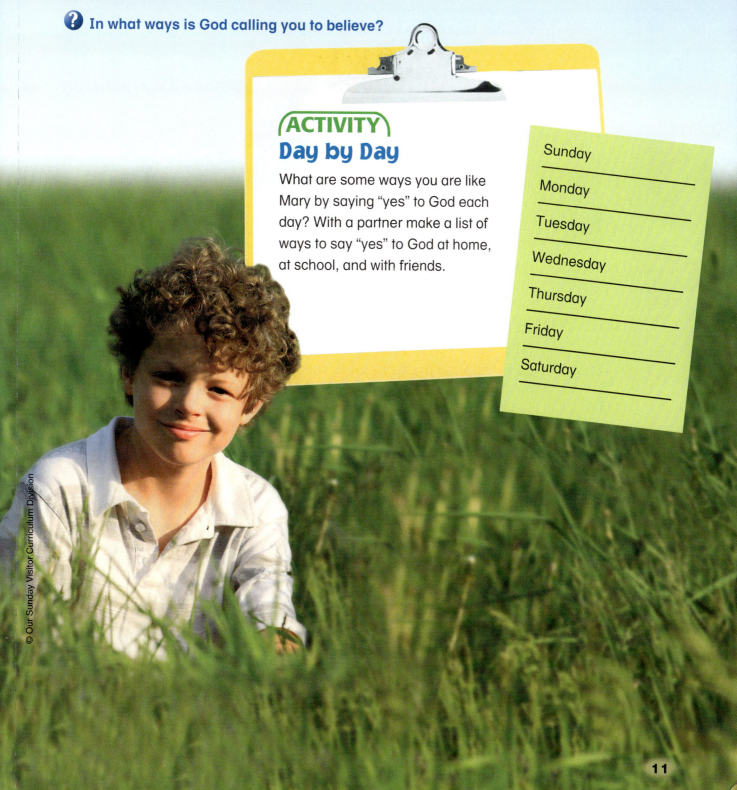

ACTIVITY
Day by Day

What are some ways you are like Mary by saying "yes" to God each day? With a partner make a list of ways to say "yes" to God at home, at school, and with friends.

Sunday
Monday
Tuesday
Wednesday
Thursday
Friday
Saturday

Advent

Be Ready!

The Season of Advent is a four-week period of preparation before the Feast of Christmas. During Advent you listen to readings from Scripture that help you prepare to celebrate Jesus' birth at Christmas. The Church's traditional color for this season is purple. Purple reminds you to change your ways in order to prepare for the coming of Christ.

The O Antiphons

Advent wreaths and calendars are some of the signs of this season. The Church also uses special prayers and devotions throughout Advent to help you prepare for Jesus' second coming.

One of the special prayers the Church often uses is an ancient Advent prayer called the O Antiphons. An *antiphon* is a verse, usually taken from the Bible, that is recited or sung at a liturgy. The Advent antiphons are called the O Antiphons because each one begins with the word "O"; for example, "O sacred Lord of ancient Israel." These ancient preparation prayers called on the Messiah to save the people as God has promised. Each antiphon uses a name of the promised Messiah found in the Old Testament. Christians believe that Jesus is the promised Messiah. The commonly used Advent song, "O Come, O Come, Emmanuel," is a sung version of the O Antiphons.

❓ **What are some other titles for Jesus that remind you of his saving love?**

O Wisdom

O Lord and Ruler

Celebrate Advent

Gather

Pray the Sign of the Cross together.

Leader: Our help is in the name of the Lord.

All: **Who made heaven and earth.**

Sing together.

O come, O come, Emmanuel,
And ransom captive Israel,
That mourns in lonely exile here
Until the Son of God appear.

Refrain
Rejoice! Rejoice! Emmanuel
Shall come to you, O Israel.

"O Come, O Come, Emmanuel" © 1975, GIA Publications, Inc.

Leader: Let us pray.
Bow your heads as the leader prays.

All: **Amen.**

Listen to God's Word

Reader: A reading from the holy Gospel according to Mark.
Read Mark 13:33–37.
The Gospel of the Lord.

All: **Praise to you, Lord Jesus Christ.**

Dialogue

How might you "be alert" to welcome Jesus?

Why do you think it is important to prepare for Jesus' coming?

Take a moment of silence to let the word of God speak to your heart and mind.

Prayer of the Faithful

Leader: Let us pray.

God our Father, you sent us your Son Jesus to show us who you are. Hear the prayers we offer you now. *Respond to each prayer with these words.*

All: Hear our prayer, O Lord.

Pray with the O Antiphons

Spend a few moments in silence before the Advent wreath. Then listen carefully as the leader reads aloud each of the O Antiphons. Reflect on how Jesus fulfills each promise for the Messiah.

Leader: Let us pray words of praise to God, who has done great things for us.

Glory to the Father, and to the Son, and to the Holy Spirit:

All: as it was in the beginning, is now, and will be for ever. Amen.

Go Forth!

Leader: Let us go forth to prepare our minds and hearts to welcome Christ into our lives.

All: Thanks be to God.

Sing together.

O come, O Wisdom from on high,
Who orders all things mightily;
To us the path of knowledge show,
And teach us in her ways to go.

Refrain
Rejoice! Rejoice! Emmanuel
Shall come to you, O Israel.

"O Come, O Come, Emmanuel" © 1975, GIA Publications, Inc.

Waiting in Joy

During Advent the Church anticipates with great joy the return of Jesus at the end of time. You are called to spend time in prayer and meditation. At Mass you listen to Scripture readings that tell you who Jesus is. With your faith community, you recall that you are connected to those who have come before you in faith.

❓ **What are some ways you feel united to all followers of Christ?**

ACTIVITY
Advent Antiphons

Write your own Advent antiphon this week. Begin your antiphon with your favorite title for Jesus. The title may be one that is used by the Church or a new title that you create for Jesus. Pray your antiphon every day during Advent.

Christmas

Feasts of the Season

Christmas, or the Feast of the Nativity, is a major feast in the Church's liturgical year. This feast is too important to be celebrated for only one day. Instead, the Church celebrates an entire Christmas Season, marked by the celebration of several feasts. With each celebration you learn more about Jesus, God's greatest gift.

The Christmas Season begins with the celebration of Jesus' birth on the eve of Christmas, December 24. On the Sunday after Christmas, the Church celebrates the Feast of the Holy Family. Catholics honor Mary, the Mother of God, on January 1. On the Solemnity of the Epiphany, the Church tells the story of the Magi and their gifts for the Christ Child. Finally, the Church celebrates Jesus' baptism in the Jordan River, where Jesus is declared the beloved Son of God.

The Holy Family

On the Feast of the Holy Family, the Church celebrates in a special way the love and unity of Jesus, Mary, and Joseph. Mary and Joseph were devout Jews who followed Jewish law. They accepted Mary's special role as Mother of the Son of God. When Jesus was born, they brought him to the Temple to present him to the Lord. As Jesus grew, he prayed and celebrated the great Jewish feasts with his family. The Holy Family is a model of respect and peace for all families.

❓ **Why are families important?**

Celebrate the Holy Family

Gather

Pray the Sign of the Cross together.

Sing together.

He came down that we may have love;
He came down that we may have love;
He came down that we may have love,
Hallelujah for ever more.

"He Came Down" © 1990, GIA Publications, Inc.

Leader: Blessed be the name of the Lord.

All: **Now and for ever.**

Leader: Let us pray.
Bow your heads as the leader prays.

All: **Amen.**

Listen to God's Word

Honoring the Scriptures

Leader: Lord, open our minds so that we may understand your word.

All: **Lord, open our hearts so that we may live by your word.**

Stand silently as some class members carry the Bible to the prayer table. When the Bible is placed on its stand, take turns respectfully bowing in front of it.

Reader: A reading from the holy Gospel according to Luke.
Read Luke 2:22, 29–40.
The Gospel of the Lord.

All: **Praise to you, Lord Jesus Christ.**

Dialogue

In what way did Simeon and Anna surprise Mary and Joseph?

In what ways can you give thanks to God the Father for the redemption won by his Son, Jesus?

Prayer of the Faithful

Leader: Let us pray.

God our Father, we ask you to listen to our prayers, which we offer now as gifts to you.
Respond to each prayer with these words.

All: **Lord, accept our prayer.**

Leader: Glory to the Father, and to the Son, and to the Holy Spirit:

All: **as it was in the beginning, is now, and will be for ever. Amen.**

Go Forth!

Leader: Let us go forth to show respect and love for our families.

All: **Thanks be to God.**

Sing together.

He came down that we may have love;
He came down that we may have love;
He came down that we may have love,
Hallelujah for ever more.

"He Came Down" © 1990, GIA Publications, Inc.

Families of Love

Mary and Joseph did not always understand Jesus, but they continued to trust in God and love their Son. Trust in God and respect for one another are very important in families. You can honor your parents and guardians in my ways. You can obey them, do kind things for them, and appreciate the sacrifice they make. Sharing what we have with other family members is another way to show love for God and one another.

? **What are some ways your family can follow the example of the Holy Family?**

ACTIVITY
Make a Banner

In groups talk about ways families can grow closer and stronger. Come up with specific things you can do to be more respectful at home. Make a list of things younger children can do, too. Create a "Respect Banner" and present it to a class of younger students.

Image of Christ

Ordinary Time

Ordinary Time provides an opportunity to celebrate the feasts of many saints. Most of these saints lived ordinary lives. What makes them special is that as they grew in friendship with Jesus their lives reflected the image of Christ to others. One of these saints is Saint Katharine Drexel. Her feast day is celebrated on March 3.

Saint Katharine Drexel

Katharine was born into a wealthy U.S. family in 1858. She had a good education and traveled often. Her family taught her that wealth should be used to help others who were poor or needed education. As a young woman, Katharine inherited large sums of money. She used it to support missionaries who ministered to Native Americans. In 1887 Katharine asked Pope Leo XIII to send more missionaries. The Pope challenged Katharine to become a missionary herself.

Katharine founded the Sisters of the Blessed Sacrament to work with Native and African Americans. The Sisters set up a system of Catholic schools for African Americans and fifty Native American missions. Katharine Drexel also founded the first university for African Americans in New Orleans, Louisiana.

Katharine Drexel reached out to people in need. She showed others the face of Christ through her devotion to those who were poor and undereducated. You can do the same in very ordinary ways. Every action you take out of love shows the image of Christ to others.

❓ In your parish and school, who shows Christ's image to you?

Celebrate God's Image

Gather

Sing together.

Baptized in water, Sealed by the Spirit,
Cleansed by the blood of Christ our King:
Heirs of salvation, trusting his promise,
Faithfully now God's praise we sing.

"Baptized in Water" © 1999, GIA Publications, Inc.

Leader: Our help is in the name of the Lord.

All: **Who made heaven and earth.**

Leader: Let us pray that we may become more like Christ.
Bow your heads and pray silently.

All: **Amen.**

Listen to God's Word

Reader 1: A reading from the Letter to the Galatians.
Read Galatians 3:26–29.
The word of the Lord.

All: **Thanks be to God.**
Stand.

All: **Alleluia. Alleluia.**

Reader 2: A reading from the holy Gospel according to John.
Read John 17:18–26.
The Gospel of the Lord.

All: **Praise to you, Lord Jesus Christ.**

Dialogue

What does it mean to be "clothed in Christ"?

What do the Scripture passages inspire you to do in your life?

Prayer of the Faithful

Leader: Let us pray for the needs of the Church, the world, and our community.

Respond to each prayer with these words.

All: **O Lord, hear our prayer.**

Blessing with Holy Water

Leader: This water reminds us of our Baptism. It is a sign of the new life that is given us.

Sing together.

Baptized in water, Sealed by the Spirit,
Dead in the tomb with Christ our King:
One with his rising, Freed and forgiven,
Thankfully now God's praise we sing.

"Baptized in Water," Michael Saward© 1982, Jubilate Hymns, Ltd.

Leader: Let us put on Christ by signing ourselves with the cross.

Come forward, dip your hand into the water and make the Sign of the Cross on your forehead.

Go Forth!

Leader: Let us go forth and show Christ's love to everyone we meet this week.

All: **Amen.**

Sing together.

Baptized in water, Sealed by the Spirit,
Marked with the sign of Christ our King:
Born of one Father, We are his children,
Joyfully now God's praise we sing.

"Baptized in Water," Michael Saward© 1982, Jubilate Hymns, Ltd.

That Others May See

You were created in God's image and baptized into the Body of Christ, the Church. This was the beginning of your faith journey. Each time you act out of kindness toward another person, each time you forgive someone, and each time you choose to obey God's laws, you deepen your relationship with God. The image of Jesus shines forth in you for others to see and believe.

❓ **What actions can you take that show forth the image of Christ to the world?**

KATHARINE

ACTIVITY

Write a Poem

Think of ways in which you can show forth the image of Christ. Write a poem using each letter of Katharine's name to begin a sentence or phrase that tells an action you can take.

Lent

The Forty Days

For six weeks before Easter, the Church observes the Season of Lent. This season offers the Church community an opportunity to turn away from any selfish ways of living and turn toward God. Lent prepares you to celebrate Easter with great joy!

Turn Back to God

During Lent the Church asks its members to pray, to fast, and to give alms. Through prayer you can ask God to show you how to make your relationships with him and others stronger. Fasting leaves you with a sense of hunger and an emptiness. This helps you see that God alone can satisfy all your needs. Giving alms means to give some of what you have to those who are in need. Almsgiving as a work of mercy may consist of feeding those who are hungry, clothing those who do not have proper clothing, and giving drink to those who are thirsty. Sometimes you might give money or time.

Whatever form of love and charity you choose, there should be some kind of sacrifice involved. This is a reminder that during Lent, you are showing your dependence on God and that all things come from God and are meant to be shared with others.

❓ **How can you rely on God during the season of Lent?**

Celebrate Lent

Gather

Pray the Sign of the Cross together.

Leader: O Lord, open my lips.

All: That my mouth shall proclaim your praise.

Leader: Let us pray.

Bow your heads as the leader prays.

All: Amen.

Penitential Act

Move into a circle and kneel.

Leader: Let us now ask God and one another to forgive us.

All: I confess to almighty God
and to you, my brothers and sisters,
that I have greatly sinned,
in my thoughts and in my words,
in what I have done
and in what I have failed to do,

Gently strike your chest with a closed fist.

through my fault, through my fault,
through my most grievous fault;

Continue:

therefore I ask blessed Mary ever-Virgin,
all the Angels and Saints,
and you, my brothers and sisters,
to pray for me to the Lord our God.

Sing together the refrain.

Hold us in your mercy.

"Hold Us In Your Mercy" © 1993, GIA Publications, Inc.

Listen to God's Word

Reader: A reading from the holy Gospel according to Luke. *Read Luke 19:1–10.*
The Gospel of the Lord.

All: **Praise to you, Lord Jesus Christ.**

Take a moment of silence to let the word of God speak to your heart and mind.

Dialogue

What part of the Zacchaeus story do you like the best? Why?

How did Zacchaeus show that he truly wanted to turn his life toward God?

Leader: With trust we call upon the Lord.

All: **Our Father . . .**

Go Forth!

Leader: Let us go forth to live in God's grace.

All: **Thanks be to God.**

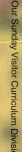

God's Loving Power

God's love for you is far greater than any wrong you can commit. God will always welcome you and give you forgiveness when you are truly sorry. As Zacchaeus learned, God's forgiveness brings the strength to help make up for any harm that may have been caused. With God's help, you can become more loving toward God, yourself, and others.

❓ **What kinds of actions do you want to ask God's help in changing?**

ACTIVITY
Lenten Poster

Decide on one action of prayer, fasting, and almsgiving you will do during Lent to better prepare yourself for the joy of Easter. Create a poster that reminds you of your decision, and hang it in your room.

Triduum

New Life in Christ

After Lent the Church celebrates its three holiest days, known as the Triduum. During these three days—starting with the Mass of the Lord's Supper on Holy Thursday evening and ending with evening prayer on Easter Sunday—the Church remembers that Jesus crossed over from death to new life. You recall your own passing over through Baptism from the power of sin and everlasting death to new life in Christ.

Three Holy Days

The Mass of the Lord's Supper on Holy Thursday is the first plunge into the mystery of salvation. The first Eucharist looked forward in expectation to Jesus shedding his blood for the forgiveness of sins. In the Eucharist you are brought back to God through Christ's sacrifice on the cross.

With the gift of the Holy Eucharist, Jesus showed you how to love. When Jesus washed the feet of his Apostles at the Last Supper, Jesus showed his followers how to serve one another. The Church remembers these actions and their meanings in the ritual of foot washing on Holy Thursday.

As the Triduum continues, you recall Jesus' suffering and death on the cross. Good Friday is the most solemn day in the Church year. During Good Friday liturgy, you thank Jesus for his great sacrifice.

Holy Saturday is a day of silent prayer as the Church waits for the joy of Resurrection. At the Easter Vigil the third sacred day begins. This day begins the special celebration of Jesus' Resurrection. It is your celebration of new life.

 How does your parish celebrate Triduum?

Celebrate Love

Gather

Pray the Sign of the Cross together.

Leader: God, come to my assistance.

All: **Lord, make haste to help me.**

Leader: Glory to the Father, and to the Son, and to the Holy Spirit:

All: **as it was in the beginning, is now, and will be for ever. Amen.**

Leader: Let us pray.
Bow your heads as the leader prays.

All: **Amen.**

Listen to God's Word

Reader: A reading from the holy Gospel according to John.
Read John 13:1–15.
The Gospel of the Lord.

All: **Praise to you, Lord Jesus Christ.**

Dialogue

How does Jesus show his love?

What does "washing others' feet" mean to you?

29

Washing of Hands

Leader: I give you a new commandment: love one another. As I have loved you, so you also should love one another.

John 13:34

Process to the prayer table. Sing as you and your classmates take turns washing the hands of the person next to you.

Sing together the refrain.

Love one another. Love one another,
as I have loved you.
Care for each other. Care for each other,
as I care for you.

"Love One Another" © 2000, GIA Publications, Inc.

Prayer of the Faithful

Leader: Let us pray. God, our Father, hear our prayers for those who are not free this day.

Respond to each prayer with these words.

All: **Lord, hear our prayer.**

Leader: Let us pray together the prayer that Jesus gave us.

All: **Our Father . . .**

Go Forth!

Leader: Let us go forth to love and serve one another, as Jesus has taught us.

All: **Thanks be to God.**

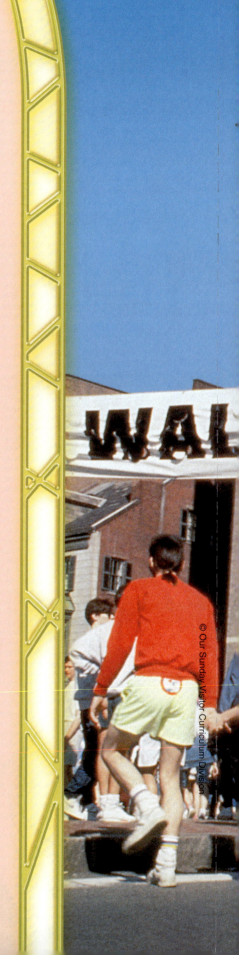

Serving One Another

Washing one another's hands or feet is a symbol of serving one another as Jesus asked his Apostles to do. We continue to serve others and follow Jesus every day when we show patience, forgiveness, and care. Serving others is a way to share in the new life that Jesus offers his followers.

❓ **Who do you know that serves others? How is that person a role model to others?**

ACTIVITY

A Sign of Service

What are some signs of serving one another today? Write down some signs of service that you see in your family, in your neighborhood, and in your school. How does this service show love for God and others?

Easter

It Is Jesus!

The celebration of Easter begins during the celebration of the Triduum—the three holiest days of the Church year. The third day of the Triduum is the day the Church celebrates Jesus' Resurrection from the dead. This great feast is called Easter. On this day Christians proclaim that Jesus is alive forever!

In the Breaking of the Bread

Jesus' disciples were very downcast and frightened. How could they go on? They thought Jesus was dead forever.

As two of Jesus' disciples were walking home from Jerusalem, a stranger joined them on the road. He explained the Scriptures to them as they walked along. Although the disciples did not recognize the man, they invited him to stay with them for the night in the town of Emmaus. The stranger agreed. As they shared a meal together, the two disciples recognized the stranger. It was Jesus!

Jesus walks along the road with you, too. Jesus is present in the midst of the assembly gathered for Mass. He speaks God's word to you through the Scripture readings, and he shares himself with you in the Eucharist. Your eyes are opened to see that it is Jesus, the Risen Lord, who is sharing this special meal with you.

❓ **What can you do to help others recognize Jesus' presence in their lives?**

Celebrate Easter

Gather

Sing together.

Sing a new song, Sing of Christ who
  rose from the dead.
Alleluia! Alleluia! Sing a new song.

Alleluia! Sing and dance a song of joy!
Christ now lives among us. Alleluia!

All God's children, Hearts and souls we live in joy!
Give thanks to the Lord as Children of God.

"Sing a New Song" © 2000, GIA Publications, Inc.

Pray the Sign of the Cross together.

Leader: Light and peace in Jesus Christ Our Lord, alleluia.

All: **Thanks be to God, alleluia.**

Leader: Let us pray.
Bow your heads as the leader prays.

All: **Amen.**

Listen to God's Word

Reader: A reading from the holy Gospel according to Luke.
Read Luke 24:13–35.
The Gospel of the Lord.

All: **Praise to you, Lord Jesus Christ.**

Dialogue

Why do you think the disciples didn't recognize Jesus when he walked with them on the road?

What is one way you recognize Jesus in your life?

The Lord's Prayer and Sign of Peace

Leader: Let us call on our Loving Father as Jesus taught us.

All: **Our Father . . .**

Leader: May the God of life and hope fill our hearts and lives.

All: **Amen.**

Leader: Let us offer to each other a sign of the peace of Christ.

Offer one another a sign of the peace of Christ.

Go Forth!

Leader: May the Lord bless us and keep us.

All: **Amen.**

Leader: May the Lord's face shine upon us.

All: **Amen.**

Leader: May the Lord look upon us with kindness, and give us peace.

GIA Publications, Inc.

All: **Amen.**

Leader: Let us leave this place strengthened to recognize Jesus' presence, alleluia, alleluia.

All: **Thanks be to God, alleluia, alleluia.**

Jesus Is Present

In the Easter Season you come to a deeper realization that Jesus is alive and present. You can recognize Jesus just as the disciples recognized him at Emmaus. Jesus is present in the Scriptures and most especially in the Eucharist. Jesus comes to you every day in people and in prayer.

❓ **Where will you look for Jesus this week?**

ACTIVITY
Act It Out

Imagine that the story of the disciples on the road to Emmaus took place today. What would keep the disciples from recognizing Jesus? What distractions might they have today? Where would they be going? How would they travel? With a group plan a modern-day Emmaus skit and act it out for the class.

Called to Serve

The Church community celebrates the coming of the Holy Spirit on Pentecost Sunday, fifty days after Easter. The Church recalls the coming of God's Spirit upon the first followers of Jesus. Each year, those gathered pray that the Holy Spirit will continue to enliven the Church. The priest wears red vestments on this feast as a symbol of the gifts of the Holy Spirit.

The Holy Spirit Strengthens God's People

On the first Pentecost the early Church community received the gift of the Holy Spirit. The first Christians were strengthened to live as followers of Jesus. With the Holy Spirit's help, they were able to serve people in need.

The Holy Spirit gives you the strength to serve others, too. God the Holy Spirit empowers you to live a good Christian life. The Holy Spirit helps the Church community remember the teachings of Jesus, especially his command to serve one another. At Baptism and Confirmation you are anointed with holy oil. Anointing with oil is an ancient custom. In the time of Jesus, anointing someone with oil was a sign that he or she had been given a very important mission. It was also a sign of healing.

When you are anointed with oil in the Sacraments of Baptism and Confirmation, you are entrusted with a share in Jesus' mission. Jesus asks you to continue to be a sign of the kingdom of God that he came to establish. An important part of Jesus' mission is loving service to others.

 When have you called on the Holy Spirit for strength and guidance?

Celebrate Pentecost

Gather

Sing together.

Send down the fire of your justice,
Send down the rains of your love;
Come, send down the Spirit, breathe life
  in your people,
and we shall be people of God.

"Send Down the Fire" © 1989, GIA Publications, Inc.

Pray the Sign of the Cross together.

Leader: Come, Holy Spirit, fill the hearts of your faithful;

All: **And kindle in them the fire of your love.**

Leader: Send forth your Spirit and they shall be created.

All: **And you will renew the face of the earth.**

Leader: Let us pray.
Bow your head as the leader prays.

All: **Amen.**

Listen to God's Word

Reader: A reading from the Acts of the Apostles.
Read Acts 2:1–11.
The word of the Lord.

All: **Thanks be to God.**

Take a moment of silence to let the word of God speak to your heart and mind.

Dialogue

Why do you think the images of wind and flames are used to describe the coming of the Holy Spirit?

How might a young person like you experience God's Spirit?

Signing of Hands

Take a few quiet moments now to pray to the Holy Spirit. Ask the Spirit of God to give you the strength you need to be a faithful follower of Jesus. One by one the leader will mark your hands with the Sign of the Cross.

Leader:	(Name), may your hands willingly serve all those in need.
All:	**Amen.**
Leader:	Let us offer a prayer of praise to God—Father, Son, and Holy Spirit.
All:	**Glory to the Father . . .**

Go Forth!

Leader:	Let us go forth to serve others through the power of the Holy Spirit.
All:	**Thanks be to God.**

Courage to Serve

The Holy Spirit gives you the gifts of strength and courage so that you can be a faithful follower of Jesus. Through your service, others will come to know God. Without the Holy Spirit's presence in your life, you could not share the good news with others.

❓ **What other gifts of the Holy Spirit would strengthen you as a follower of Jesus?**

ACTIVITY

Share Your Time

Together with your family or a group of friends, decide this week how you will serve others through a special project. You might decide to volunteer at a soup kitchen or food pantry or to work with others to clean up a neighborhood park or lot.

Unit 1
Revelation

In this unit you will…

learn that we come to know who God is from both within ourselves and from outside of ourselves. God puts longings in our hearts for him, and our response is faith. One way we discover God is by reflecting on all the good gifts of his creation. We use his gifts in the sacraments, where God is present to us. We respond to God's invitation to know him and feel his presence by our worship and participation in the sacraments.

Faith in Action!

**Catholic Social Teaching Principle:
Care for God's Creation**

Chapter 1: Longing for God

Let Us Pray

Leader: Gentle Father, lead us to you.
"My soul rests in God alone,
   from whom comes my salvation."
Psalm 62:2

All: Gentle Father, lead us to you. Amen.

Activity

● **The Latest Thing** Tomás lay on the floor watching TV. "Be the first in your neighborhood to have one!" the voice on the commercial cried. "It's the latest thing in video games! You'll have hours and hours of fun—no more boring afternoons! Look for it wherever video games are sold! Don't wait. These are selling out fast!"

Tomás sighed. He was saving his money, but this game was so expensive—he'd never have enough. "One day I'll be rich," he thought, "and I'll never have to wish for anything again!"

Now think about something you are longing for.

When have you received something you really longed for?

_____

_____

What changed after you got it?

_____

_____

✏️ **Make a Wish List** Write a list on a separate sheet of paper of things you want that money cannot buy. Then choose one that you want most of all.

41

What We Want

Focus Why are longings important?

Some people long for things that others take for granted. What would it be like if you could neither see nor hear? Helen Keller knew all about it. Here is her story.

A REAL-LIFE STORY

My Name Is Helen Keller

I was born soon after the Civil War. As a toddler, I got very sick, and the illness left me unable to see or hear. Being cut off from the world frightened me. My family and I could not communicate. I felt hurt, angry, confused, and alone.

When I was six, a new teacher tried to help me by tracing signs on the palm of my hand. I did not understand the signs, but she kept trying.

After weeks without progress, we went to the water pump one day. My teacher put my hand under the spout, and the water ran over my fingers. Into my other hand, she traced the symbols that spell w-a-t-e-r. She did this many times. Suddenly I understood—the letters made up a word, a word that meant the cool something running over my hand.

I couldn't wait to share my joy! My teacher had shown me how to reach the world and express my thoughts and feelings.

❓ **Have you ever been unable to express what you were thinking or feeling? What could have helped you at that time?**

Make Connections

People long for all kinds of things. Some of these things are important, and some are not. Helen Keller longed for something that most humans take for granted—the ability to communicate and to express thoughts and feelings. What a wonderful gift she received when her teacher opened the world of language for her!

There are many layers of longing in the world. You may long for things, as Tomás did, or for the right words to say. You may long to be loved and accepted by others. You may long for good health, or to win a game, or to be chosen for a special honor. All of your longings are part of your desire to be truly happy.

❓ What are the most important things that you would like to have?

The Gift of Longing

Longing is actually a gift in itself; it is planted inside you by God. God wants you to find your way home to him at the end of your life on earth. **Religion** is the way you express your longing for God. Just as Helen Keller's teacher taught her how to express thoughts and feelings, religion gives you a language to express your thoughts and feelings about God.

Religion is the group of beliefs, prayers, and practices through which people express longing for God.

Activity — Share Your Faith

Reflect: Think about some of the ways you express your thoughts and feelings about God.

Share: Discuss some of those ways with a partner.

Act: Make a chart showing how you express your thoughts and feelings about God and what they mean to you.

Action	Meaning for me
Sign of the cross	Father Son holy spirit
the cross	Jesus
singing	worshiping
charity	giving to others

Explore

What God Gives

 **Focus** Who alone can satisfy your longing?

Helen Keller's teacher knew what Helen really wanted. Here is a story in which Jesus offers a woman even more than she thought she needed. Read to learn how Jesus surprises her.

SCRIPTURE John 4:7–29

The Woman at the Well

The Samaritan woman, tired and hot, trudged along with her water jars. At the well, she noticed a Jewish stranger. Contrary to custom and much to her surprise, the man spoke directly to her and asked her for a drink. He then said, "If you knew the gift of God and who is saying to you, 'Give me a drink,' you would have asked him and he would have given you living water."

She asked what this "living water" might be and where she could get some. The stranger, who was Jesus, replied that he did not mean ordinary water. The water he spoke of was God, who wants everyone to worship him in the Spirit and in truth. The woman said, "I know that the Messiah is coming, the one called the Anointed; when he comes, he will tell us everything." Jesus answered, "I am he, the one who is speaking with you."

At that, the woman forgot about the water for which she had come. This news of "living water" was more important. She ran to tell everyone about the stranger. She asked, "Could he possibly be the Messiah?"

Based on *John 4:7–29*

? What message did Jesus want to give the woman?

? Why did Jesus choose the image of water for his teaching?

44

God Satisfies You

When you long for God, only the living water of his grace will satisfy you. Jesus knows that deep in the human heart is a longing that only God can fill. The longing for God is more powerful than your thirst for water on a hot, dusty day. The Samaritan woman's response to Jesus shows the beginning of her faith.

Faith is a supernatural gift from God. Faith enables you to believe that God is with his people, even though you cannot see him. Faith is also a human action by which you choose to respond to God's presence in your life. You received the gift of faith in the Sacrament of Baptism. In the waters of Baptism, you became a child of God and a member of the Body of Christ.

Faith and Baptism are necessary for salvation for all who have heard the good news of Jesus. If infants die without Baptism, the Church trusts in God's merciful love to bring them to salvation. Those who have not heard the gospel can be saved if they are doing their best to follow God's will. For a catechumen, the desire for the sacrament and repentance for sins is enough for salvation.

Helping Faith Grow

Baptism is the beginning of your faith journey. Your faith continues to grow and develop. In this life, you come to know God through creation, through the Bible, and, most of all, through Jesus. You are helped by your parents and the Church community. Your faith grows through praying, reading Scripture, and being active in your parish. Like the Samaritan woman, you are called to share your growing faith and joy with others.

Words of Faith

Grace is God's free, loving gift of his own life and help. It is participation in the life of the Holy Trinity.

Faith is both a gift given by God and your free choice to seek God and believe in him.

Activity — Connect Your Faith

Share Your Joy Create headlines that describe your faith to others.

_____

_____

_____

_____

45

How We Find God

 **Focus** How do you seek God?

We help satisfy our longing for God by searching for him in prayer and Scripture. If we are willing to listen, God will speak to us and help us follow him.

No matter where you decide to pray or read the Bible, your effort will bring you closer to God. However, some places help you be a better listener.

Listening for God

Church The parish church is the house of God. Even when the community is not worshiping there, Christ is present. Go there and tell him everything in your heart. Read what he has said in Scripture, and then be still and listen for his answer.

Outdoors Jesus often chose to pray outdoors. There he felt close to the Father, who had created all the world's beauty. In good weather, being out in the natural world can lead you to a spirit of grateful praise.

Home Sometimes it is best to go to a separate room and close the door when you want to talk to God. If your bedroom is not quiet enough, you may be able make a prayer space in another part of your home.

❓ What would help you be a better listener when you pray?

Activity: Live Your Faith

Organize Your Classroom for Prayer In a small group, brainstorm what things might be included for your prayer space. Here are some ideas:
- a table or shelf with a Bible
- a cross
- an icon or a holy picture
- a candle and some baptismal water for blessing yourselves
- a book for writing petitions

Make a list below of the prayer space items that will be needed.

_____   _____
_____   _____
_____   _____
_____   _____
_____   _____

Decide what your contribution will be. Be practical about your decision, and choose something that you are sure you can bring.

My contribution to the prayer space will be

Celebrate

Celebration of the Word

 Let Us Pray

Gather and begin with the Sign of the Cross.

Leader: Brothers and sisters, let us praise our God, who meets our deepest longings.

All: **Praised be God forever.**

Reader: A reading from the Second Letter of Peter.

Read 2 Peter 1:2–3.

The word of the Lord.

All: **Thanks be to God.**

Leader: Lord God, as we come together to continue our journey of faith this year, we thank you for your love for us. We delight in you. Teach us how to seek you, for in you all our happiness will be found.

All: **Great is your power, O God, and of your wisdom there is no end.**

Leader: Let us pray.

Bow your heads as the leader prays.

All: **Amen.**

Sing together.

Fill us with your love, O Lord, and we will sing for joy!

"Psalm 90", *Lectionary for Mass,* © 1969, 1981, and 1997, ICEL

CHAPTER 1 Review

A Work with Words Complete each sentence with the correct word from the Word Bank.

WORD BANK
Messiah
faith
religion
grace
Baptism
creation

1. _____ allows you to seek God and believe in him.
2. The woman at the well realized that Jesus was the _____.
3. The gift of God's own life and help is _____.
4. You became a member of the Church through _____.
5. _____ allows people to express their longing for God.

B Check Understanding Match each description in Column 1 with the correct term in Column 2.

Column 1

_____ 6. helps you on your faith journey
_____ 7. a gift planted inside us by God
_____ 8. can improve your prayer
_____ 9. learned to communicate through the sense of touch
_____ 10. one of the ways in which we come to know God in this life

Column 2

a. creation
b. Helen Keller
c. parish community
d. a quiet place
e. longing

UNIT 1: CHAPTER 1

Family Faith

Catholics Believe

- True happiness can come only through communion with God.
- Religion expresses our relationship with God through beliefs, prayers, and practices.

SCRIPTURE

Read *Hebrews 3:1–6* to learn more about the importance of reflecting on Jesus' call.

GO online www.osvcurriculum.com
For weekly scripture readings and seasonal resources

Activity

Live Your Faith

Listen to Feelings How and when does your family listen best?

- Have a family listening session.
- Invite each member of your family to share.
- Ask each person to tell something that he or she would like the whole family to know.
- Don't interrupt while the person is talking!
- Be aware that sometimes "heart feelings" take a little more time to express.

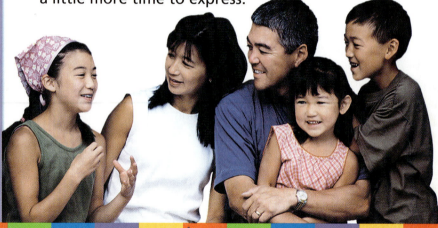

People of Faith

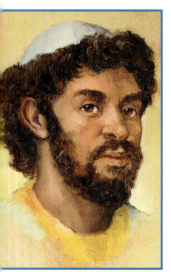

▲ Saint Augustine 354–430

Augustine was a brilliant young man of North Africa. He searched for truth, but at first the philosophies he explored only confused him. Finally, he found fulfillment in the Christian faith. Augustine became a monk and a priest and later was named bishop of Hippo, a city near his hometown. He became a great teacher and writer of the Church. He summarized the story of his life by saying to God, "You have made us for yourself, and our hearts are restless until they rest in you." Saint Augustine's feast day is August 28.

Family Prayer

Saint Augustine, pray for us that we may follow your example of tirelessly searching for God. May God give us the grace to use our minds as you did to love and understand the mystery of God's creation as much as we are able. Amen.

In Unit 1 your child is learning about REVELATION.
See *Catechism of the Catholic Church* 27–28 for further reading on chapter content.

© Our Sunday Visitor Curriculum Division

Chapter 2 Worshipping God

 **Let Us Pray**

Leader: Open our lips in praise, O Lord.
"Bless the Lord, my soul!
Lord, my God, you are great indeed!"
Psalm 104:1

All: Open our lips in praise, O Lord. Amen.

 **Activity** — Let's Begin

Thankfulness e e cummings was a poet who experimented with language to help people look at the world in a new way. Here is one of his prayers of thanksgiving to God.

i thank You God for most this amazing
day: for the leaping greenly spirits of trees
and a blue true dream of sky; and for everything
which is natural which is infinite which is yes

A selection from the poem by e e cummings

Now think about the reasons every day offers to thank God.

Put your thanks to God in a poem as e e cummings did.

_____
_____
_____
_____

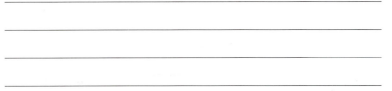 **Make a List** Write on a separate sheet of paper all the things in nature that remind you of God, and explain why.

Explore

Respect God's Work

Focus How does work give glory to God?

As you will discover in this story, appreciation and praise for God's creation can lead to care and action.

A REAL-LIFE STORY

CHICO MENDES AND THE RAIN FOREST

When he was nine, Chico Mendes began working with his father as a *seringueiro*, or rubber tapper, in the rain forest of Brazil. The family was very poor. Chico Mendes worked hard for many years among the rubber trees in the forest. He gathered liquid that would be turned into rubber and sold all over the world. He learned how the trees grew and how to care for them. He knew that his family's survival depended on a healthy rain forest.

In their everyday care for these trees, *seringueiros* come to understand the complex web of life within the rain forest. The Brazilian rain forest has been called the lungs of the world. Its 3 million square miles of plants cleanse the air. The rain forest is also home to thousands of plants and animals found nowhere else on earth. Many of the most important medicines on which modern doctors depend come from rain forest plants. Most important to the *seringueiros*, the trees they tend will produce rubber for as long as 200 years if they are well cared for and respected.

? How did Chico Mendes care for God's creation?

? What blessings come from the rain forest for people everywhere?

The Forest in Danger

When local ranchers decided to burn down areas of the rain forest to make room for raising cattle, Chico Mendes was alarmed. He knew that this destruction would endanger the environment. So he organized the *seringueiros* to hold peaceful protests to keep the trees from being destroyed. The group petitioned the government to protect the rain forest.

During the 1980s, people from around the world who were concerned about the rain forest began to hear about Mendes's work. He was invited to come to Washington, D.C., to speak to Congress. He was honored by the United Nations. As a result, some areas of Brazilian land were set aside as reserves.

Because of the efforts of Chico Mendes and the other *seringueiros,* a priceless natural resource was saved from destruction.

Activity: Share Your Faith

Reflect: Think about the fact that God has created both a rain forest that can produce good things, such as fresh air and medicines, and humans, who have the power to protect or destroy the forest.

Share: With a partner, discuss what this says about God's loving plan for creation.

Act: What do you want to say to God about his plan for creation? Write your responses below.

_____
_____
_____
_____
_____

Praise God's Work

Focus How are stewardship and God's providence connected?

The rain forest and all other wonders of creation never cease to praise their Creator. The world was made for the glory of God, and all creation gives the Creator praise. In return, God in his **providence** cares for all that he has created.

SCRIPTURE

Psalm 98:4–9

Glory to God

Shout with joy to the Lord, all the earth;
    break into song; sing praise.

Sing praise to the Lord with the harp,
    with the harp and melodious song.

With trumpets and the sound of the horn
    shout with joy to the King, the Lord.

Let the sea and what fills it resound,
    the world and those who dwell there.

Let the rivers clap their hands,
    the mountains shout with them for joy,

Before the Lord who comes,
    who comes to govern the earth,

To govern the world with justice
    and the peoples with fairness.

Psalm 98:4–9

? What are some ways that God in his providence is caring for creation?

Work and Worship

Whenever you choose to care for creation, you help the world achieve its purpose: to praise God and to show God's goodness. In fact, caring for creation is a way of praising God through your actions.

In God's plan, the goodness of creation unfolds through time. All humans have a choice to help or harm the world during their lives. You are the crown of God's creation, created in his image and likeness. Jesus invites you and all other people to reflect God's image by practicing **stewardship** of God's creation.

❓ **What are some practical actions that are examples of stewardship?**

Creation and the Sacraments

When Jesus wanted to create ways for humans to celebrate his presence after he returned to his Father, he thought of the works of his Father's creation. Jesus used gifts from God, such as water, oil, wheat, and grapes, to perform his saving works. When these created things are used in the sacraments, they remind you of God's creative power and make God's power present now. Strengthened by the sacraments, you can go out to continue Jesus' work in the world. Work and worship become one.

Words of Faith

Providence is God's loving care for all things. It is God's will and plan for creation.

Stewardship is the human response to God's many gifts. It includes respect for all life and the responsible care of creation.

Activity — Connect Your Faith

See Signs of God's Love How are each of these gifts of creation used in the sacraments as signs of God's presence? Write your answer next to each picture.

holy water

body of christ

wine

Explore

You Are God's Creation

 **Focus** What is your role in the stewardship of God's creation?

When you care for any part of God's creation, you are sharing in his plan. What you do will echo his glory! Here are some ways to make sure that your stewardship of God's creation will be successful.

10 Steps to Successful Stewardship

1. Choose a small project that will improve the environment. Find something nearby so that you can see results. Perhaps you know some older people who can't get to a recycling center.

2. Work for changes that will last. If you can discover the cause of the problem, work on that.

3. Work with others who have experience. Often you can volunteer your time to groups. They will teach you what needs to be done.

4. Respect the feelings, rights, and property of others. Another person may not agree with your opinions.

5. Be aware of how your actions will affect others. Remember that you are helping solve a problem, not blaming anyone.

6. Create feelings of cooperation and goodwill. Always ask for permission, and thank those who help you.

7. Ask yourself questions like these: How does this help? How does this hurt?

8. Finish what you start. You will gain respect and more cooperation in the future.

9. Follow up and evaluate. Plan a way to learn whether your action accomplished its purpose.

10. Ask God to bless what you have done.

? Have you followed any of these steps in the past for a project?

? Which of these steps would make your efforts more productive?

Activity — Live Your Faith

Learn and Do Chico Mendes worked to save the rain forest. Every area has priceless ecosystems that are necessary for the survival of all creatures: prairies, wetlands, rivers and lakes, deserts, and old-growth forests. With a partner, brainstorm and use the Internet or other resources to learn more about the ecosystems in your area. What is being done to preserve and restore them?

Ecosystem	What is being done to preserve and restore the system?

What can you do to help?

_____
_____
_____

I, _____, promise to help this ecosystem: _____
by _____
_____.
I will complete my commitment by _____.
Signature

Psalm of Praise

 Let Us Pray

Gather and begin with the Sign of the Cross.

Leader: Sisters and brothers, let us give thanks to God who made the universe.

Reader 1: We see your glory in the heavens above.

All: **Praise to you, Creator God!**

Reader 2: The moon and stars you have put in place.

All: **Praise to you, Creator God!**

Reader 3: You made the birds in the sky and all the ocean creatures.

All: **Praise to you, Creator God!**

Reader 4: You have made humans little less than a god.

All: **Praise to you, Creator God!**

Leader: God, you have given us every good thing. Teach us your tender care for creation!

All: **Amen.**

Based on *Psalm 8*

Sing together.

Proclaim to all the nations the marvelous deeds of the Lord!
Proclaim to all the nations the marvelous deeds of the Lord!

"Psalm 96", *Lectionary for Mass*, © 1969, 1981, and 1997, ICEL

CHAPTER 2
Review

Check Understanding Fill in the circle next to the correct response.

1. You share in God's _____ by caring for creation.
   - ○ power to create
   - ● plan
   - ○ sacraments
   - ○ judgment
   - ○ knowledge

2. When you care for creation, you are _____.
   - ● praising God
   - ○ being selfish
   - ○ committing a sin
   - ○ earning money
   - ○ interfering

3. You should care for yourself and others because you are made _____.
   - ○ to do the dishes at home
   - ● in God's image
   - ○ with one purpose only
   - ○ of flesh and blood
   - ○ humble by it

4. God's loving plan for creation is called _____.
   - ○ grace
   - ○ providence
   - ● stewardship
   - ○ divine blueprint
   - ○ destiny

5. Responsible care for creation is _____.
   - ○ a sacrament
   - ○ providence
   - ○ loyalty
   - ● stewardship
   - ○ pride

6. For his efforts to save the rain forest, Chico Mendes was honored by _____.
   - ○ President Reagan
   - ○ the bishop of Brasília
   - ○ the Nobel Prize
   - ● the Green Party
   - ○ the United Nations

7. Successful stewardship involves _____.
   - ○ power over others
   - ○ working alone
   - ○ being careless
   - ● respect and cooperation
   - ○ profiting from nature

8. The rain forest of Brazil was threatened by _____.
   - ● cattle ranchers
   - ○ flooding
   - ○ timber harvesting
   - ○ strip mining
   - ○ erosion

9. God makes his power present in the sacraments through _____.
   - ● our work
   - ○ stewardship
   - ○ created things
   - ○ his mercy
   - ○ our intention

10. Chico and his fellow *seringueiros* work in the rain forest to harvest _____.
    - ○ wheat
    - ○ fruit
    - ○ orchids
    - ● rubber
    - ○ quinine

59

UNIT 1: CHAPTER 2
Family Faith

Catholics Believe

- Humans share in the Creator's loving plan by caring for creation.
- God's providence is his care and plan for all of creation.

SCRIPTURE

Read *Psalm 145:1–21* to learn more about the goodness of God the Creator.

 www.osvcurriculum.com
For weekly scripture readings and seasonal resources

Activity
Live Your Faith

Help the Environment Write the words Reduce—Reuse—Recycle on a card, and attach the card to the refrigerator. These words remind you to care for the earth by producing less trash, reusing what you can, and recycling as much as possible. This week

- make a list of what you can do to reduce, reuse, and recycle.
- pray about your options.
- choose a few items from the list to work on this week.

People of Faith

▲ Saint Benedict
480–550

As a young man, **Benedict** decided to become a hermit (one who lives alone by choice) and live in silence and prayer. But people wanted to be near him and learn from him about how to become holy. In time, Benedict devised a way by which people could live prayerfully in community. His plan, called the Rule of Saint Benedict, balances prayer, study, work, and rest. Benedict also taught his followers to welcome all strangers as they would welcome Christ. Benedictine communities around the world are still known for their welcoming spirit. Benedict's feast day is July 11.

Family Prayer

Saint Benedict, pray for us that we may live in harmony with others and with the world. Help us balance work and prayer so that the time we have will be spent pleasing our almighty Father. Amen.

© Our Sunday Visitor Curriculum Division

In Unit 1 your child is learning about REVELATION.
See Catechism of the Catholic Church 302, 303, 307, 339, 2415 for further reading on chapter content.

Chapter 3 Signs of God's Presence

Let Us Pray

Leader: All-powerful God, we see you in your works.
"The heavens declare the glory of God;
the sky proclaims its builder's craft."
Psalm 19:2

All: All-powerful God, we see you in your works. Amen.

Activity — Let's Begin

● **Reminders** Sandy's father is in the military and has to be away for long periods on special assignments. Sometimes when she is especially lonely for him, Sandy gets his bathrobe out of the closet, wraps herself up in it, and sits in his favorite chair, pulling her knees up to her chin. Snuggling in his robe, she feels closer to her dad.

Every day, the many people and events that cross your path can serve as signs. Name some signs of danger that you see at times in your life.

_____

Name some signs of hope in your life.

_____

Name some signs of love in your life.

_____

✏️ **Look Around** Write on a separate sheet of paper signs of safety, learning, or holiness that you find in your school.

61

Explore

Powerful Signs

 **Focus** What are some signs of God's presence?

Yahweh, the name of the God of Israel, means *I AM.*

Some signs help you remember someone or something that you have seen at an earlier time, just as the robe helps Sandy remember her father. But certain signs can remind you of things you cannot see. The most powerful signs remind you of God's presence. God is a mystery. He is pure spirit and cannot be seen or heard directly. So God uses signs to help you understand what he wants you to know. Read to find out how God spoke to Moses long ago.

 SCRIPTURE Exodus 3:1–15

The Burning Bush

It seemed an ordinary day. As Moses tended the flocks of his father-in-law, Jethro, on the mountain, he had no idea that his whole life was about to change. Moses had a lot on his mind. His people, the Hebrews, were enslaved by the Egyptians and were being treated unjustly. Moses himself was hiding because he had killed an Egyptian who was mistreating one of the Hebrews. As Moses arrived at Horeb, the mountain of God, he heard a voice.

Suddenly Moses noticed something mysterious. A nearby bush was in flames—but it wasn't burning up. As Moses moved closer to investigate, the voice called to him, "Remove the sandals from your feet, for the place where you stand is holy ground." God was speaking to Moses from the burning bush!

Moses and God talked. God had heard the cries of the Hebrew people, and he intended to free them. Moses asked God what he should tell people when they asked who had told him all this. God replied, "This is what you shall tell the Israelites: I AM sent me to you." Moses knew that by revealing his name, God was promising to be with his people.

Based on *Exodus* 3:1–15

❓ What did God want Moses to understand when he showed Moses that the burning bush was not consumed by the flames?

62

Signs Point the Way

The burning bush was a sign. A sign is something you can see, hear, smell, touch, or taste. A sign points beyond itself to something more. Thunder is a sign of possible rain. A stop sign is only letters on red-painted metal, but everyone knows that there could be danger if you do not obey the sign. Sign language gives people who cannot hear or cannot hear well a way to communicate.

God uses signs to communicate with people. The wonders of creation and the events of human life contain signs of God's awesome power and nearness. They tell of his eternal goodness, strong justice, and gentle mercy. When Moses first saw the burning bush, he was puzzled and surprised. But this sign of the presence of God was not the end of Moses' encounter—the experience opened the way for Moses to know God better.

At first Moses did not realize that God was with his people in their hardship and distress. But when Moses saw the sign of the burning bush, he began to understand that God was present and wanted to help the Israelites. You may not see, hear, smell, taste, or touch God, but signs can show you that God is with you.

❓ **What are some signs of God's goodness, justice, and mercy?**

Activity — Share Your Faith

Reflect: Think about a place, other than church, where you experience signs of God's presence.

Share: Describe this place to a partner. Is it indoors? Is it light or dark? Can you see the sun rise or set? Can you smell flowers? Can you hear music or bird songs?

Act: Write about one of the signs of God's presence in this place on a separate sheet of paper. If you prefer, draw a picture of the place.

God's Presence in Signs

 **Focus** What are signs of God's covenant?

Throughout history God has communicated his presence and shown his love for people through signs. He commanded the Hebrew people, later known as the Israelites, to eat a special meal on the night before Moses led them out of slavery in Egypt. It was called the Passover meal, and it became a sign of the **covenant**, or sacred agreement, between God and the people he saved.

The Hebrews understood that the meal was a sign of the agreement God had made with them. Because of the meal's importance as a sign, the Hebrews made it a part of their faith and tradition. Jewish people still eat the Passover meal every year.

The New Covenant

Jesus' death and Resurrection became the basis for a new covenant. You hear about this covenant each time you attend Mass. The bread and wine come from wheat and grapes, signs of God's goodness in creation. At the Last Supper, Jesus gave a new and life-giving meaning to the signs of bread and wine by changing them into his Body and Blood. He said that they were to be shared in a meal with those who believe that Jesus fulfilled God's saving promise.

 What is the relationship between the Mass and the Jewish Passover meal?

Sacraments as Signs

All of the ==sacraments== are signs of the new covenant made through the life and sacrifice of Jesus. They point to God and to his love. But sacraments are even more. Christ himself acts in the sacraments, and they become sources of grace. Sacraments are celebrations of God's presence in and with his people.

Jesus himself is truly the Sacrament—the one great universal sign of God's love—because he is the Son of God who became human. In this chart, you can see how Jesus chose powerful signs to show how God is present in important moments of life.

Words of Faith

Covenant is a sacred agreement between God and his people.

Sacraments are effective signs of God's life, given by Christ to the Church.

SACRAMENT	SIGN—SYMBOLIC ACTION	GOD IS PRESENT THROUGH
Baptism	water and words (I baptize you. . .)	new life in Christ
Confirmation	chrism and laying on of hands	strengthening by the Holy Spirit
Eucharist	bread, wine, and the words of consecration, eating and drinking	nourishment by the Body and Blood of Christ
Reconciliation	words of absolution	conversion and forgiveness
Anointing of the Sick	anointing with the oil of the sick	healing and strengthening
Matrimony	mutual consent and total giving of the man and woman to each other in married love	loving union and commitment
Holy Orders	the laying on of hands and the Prayer of Consecration prayed over the man	ordained ministry for God's people

Activity

Connect Your Faith

We Agree To . . .

Make a Contract Brainstorm ideas for a class contract. Include in your agreement what you will do for others over the coming year. Choose a class sign as a way to remind one another to keep the agreement.

Our sign: _____

Explore

Recognize God's Signs

 **Focus** How do you see the signs God sends to you?

Through practice, you can become more attentive to signs of God's will and presence. Here is an exercise to strengthen your prayer skill.

A Prayerful Exercise

1 Sit quietly. Remember that God is near. Open all of your senses to signs of his presence.

2 Imagine yourself as a half-finished drawing or piece of sculpture that God is going to complete.

Let God begin to work on you, and imagine the results.

3 Think of your desire to be with God.

Repeat God's name "I AM" in your mind as you call to him.

4 Let God speak to you. Listen with your heart and mind.

5 End this time of listening by thanking him for always being with you. Say "Amen."

© Our Sunday Visitor Curriculum Division

❓ Write a note to yourself about what you became aware of during the exercise.

❓ How will you act on that awareness?

Activity: Live Your Faith

Record Your Relationship with God In your class, begin new prayer books. Gather as a group to brainstorm questions to put in the books. Here are some suggestions to get you started:

What are some blessings that you have received?
_____
_____
_____
_____

When have you forgiven and reconciled with someone?
_____
_____
_____
_____

What new things have you learned recently about Scripture?
_____
_____
_____
_____

What other things could you enter in your prayer book?
_____
_____
_____
_____

Celebrate

Prayer of Petition

 **Let Us Pray**

Gather and begin with the Sign of the Cross.

Leader: Gracious God, we come together now to pray in the name of your Son.

Reader 1: God our Father, we thank you for the goodness of creation, for the blessing of your covenant, and for the signs of your presence in the world. Most of all, we thank you for your Son, Jesus. Help us know you better every day.

All: **Hear our prayer, O Lord.**

Reader 2: God our Father, open our eyes to see your hand at work in the beauty of human life. Help us cherish the gifts that surround us and share your blessings with others.

All: **Hear our prayer, O Lord.**

Reader 3: God our Father, you give us grace through sacramental signs that tell us of the wonders of your unseen power. Help us grow to become signs of your love. We pray, now and always, in the name of your Son, Jesus.

All: **Amen.**

Sing together.

All things bright and beautiful,
All creatures great and small,
All things wise and wonderful,
The Lord God made them all.

"All Things Bright and Beautiful"
Traditional

CHAPTER 3 Review

A **Work with Words** Complete the following statements.

1. Signs point to something you cannot know through your _____.
2. God appeared to Moses in the _____.
3. The one great universal sign of God's love is _____.
4. The Passover meal is a sign of the _____ between God and the Israelites.
5. _____ become the Body and Blood of Christ.

B **Check Understanding** In complete sentences, explain the following:

6. Creation _____
_____
_____

7. Sacraments _____
_____
_____

8. Signs of Confirmation _____
_____
_____

9. God's presence in the Anointing of the Sick _____
_____
_____

10. A way to improve or strengthen your prayer skill _____
_____
_____

UNIT 1: CHAPTER 3
Family Faith

Catholics Believe

- God communicates through signs.
- Through the signs and symbolic actions of the sacraments, God's life becomes truly present in your life.

SCRIPTURE

Read *Matthew 1:21–23* to learn the meaning of Jesus' name.

www.osvcurriculum.com
For weekly scripture readings and seasonal resources

Activity
Live Your Faith

Research Look up the meaning of each family member's first name. Then ask each family member to say how he or she is or can be a sign to others of what the name means.

People of Faith

▲ Saint Hildegarde of Bingen 1098–1179

Hildegarde was an abbess, the head of a large religious community in Bingen, Germany. At a time when few women could read or write, Hildegarde was well educated. Her curiosity and her love for God's creation led her to study the natural world. She wrote and illustrated books on gardening and herbal medicine. People in need of healing and spiritual guidance often traveled to the abbey to meet with Hildegarde. She composed music and created paintings inspired by her vision of creative love. We celebrate her feast day on September 17.

 Family Prayer

Saint Hildegarde, pray for us that we may discover the many signs of God's love within the world around us. May we learn to value our own gifts and to use them as you did for the greater honor and glory of our Creator. Amen.

© Our Sunday Visitor Curriculum Division

In Unit 1 your child is learning about REVELATION.
CCC See *Catechism of the Catholic Church* 774, 1084, 1147, 1152 for further reading on chapter content.

DISCOVER

Catholic Social Teaching:
Care for God's Creation

Faith in Action!
CATHOLIC SOCIAL TEACHING

In this unit you learned that one way you come to know God is through creation. When you choose to care for creation, you praise God. You are a steward of his creation.

Care for Creation

God calls you to protect and preserve all that he has created. He gives you the responsibility of stewardship. You are trusted not to upset or destroy the balance in nature. The earth is for your use today, but you must care for it so that future generations will be able to enjoy life.

The universe provides energy. Without natural gas, coal, oil, and the energy from the sun, wind, and water, our world would be a dark, cold, and isolated place. In the past, industrialized nations used a tremendous amount of energy with little regard for its replacement. Humans must not waste energy and must work to find new sources.

Catholics are called to take an active role in programs and projects that protect and preserve creation.

❓ What does the text above tell us about God's creation?

❓ Why is it important to be involved in caring for natural resources?

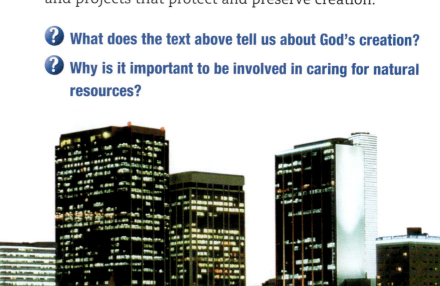

71

CONNECT

With the Call to Justice

The Energy Patrol

In Pennsylvania the Sulzberger Middle School became a Green School. Students and adults worked together to raise awareness of how their school used energy.

Signs were put up everywhere in the building. A group called the Energy Patrol charged ten cents every time a class didn't switch the lights off, close the windows, or pull down the shades. This worked so well that after a little while, no fines needed to be given out! The Energy Patrol also worked to develop a system to recycle waste from the building. This plan worked so well that the school collected 120 pounds of cans in just six months.

Some of the activities were fun as well as successful. As a way to get their message across, students used puppets to create an energy video. The school also held a Trash Fashion Show. The models wore clothes made of things that could be recycled.

The program at Sulzberger Middle School was so successful that the school used only 43 percent as much energy as it had used the previous year. The students and staff worked hard to conserve energy by doing small things that made a big difference. The school earned a third place Earth Apple Award.

? **Why do you think the Energy Patrol was so successful in saving energy at Sulzberger Middle School?**

The Alliance to Save Energy has a project called *Green Schools.* The program encourages students to develop action plans in their schools to conserve energy. Let's see how one school did that.

Reach Out!

SERVE Your Community

Design a Project

As you have seen, small changes can make a big difference in preserving resources. Think of a way that your class could make a difference by working together.

With a partner, respond to the following items. Then plan a project together.

What are some of the ways your school may be wasting energy or resources?

_____
_____

Write one way of wasting energy that you could change.

_____

What would have to happen at school to stop this problem?

_____
_____
_____

What would it take to make students and teachers want to take the action needed?

_____
_____
_____

How would you organize the class to make this happen?

_____
_____
_____

Make a Difference

Take on a Class Project After students explain their suggestions, vote on one project that your class will do to help conserve energy.

Write here the names of the members of your group and what you will do.

_____
_____
_____
_____

73

UNIT 1 REVIEW

A **Work with Words** Complete each sentence with the correct term from the Word Bank.

1. Sacraments, _____, and creation are all signs of God's _____.

2. _____, reading or listening to _____, and the guidance of your parish community help you build up your faith.

3. People show good _____ of creation by _____ glass, paper, and plastic instead of throwing away these things.

4. Using _____ sparingly rather than wasting it and planting _____ rather than cutting them down are ways to show respect for God's gift of our environment.

5. Living water and the burning bush are _____ of God's presence because God _____ through them.

WORD BANK

signs
pictures
faith
recycling
trees
grace
water
communicate
works
prayer
stewardship
Scripture

B **Check Understanding** Write answers to the question on spaces 6 through 9. Find and circle these answers in the word search. The remaining letters form a message. Write the message on the spaces for number 10.

G	J	E	S	U	S	U	S	E	R
D	R	T	H	E	S	E	G	E	I
F	T	A	S	F	R	O	T	M	C
R	L	E	P	A	T	A	I	O	N
T	O	I	P	E	W	E	R	F	O
R	M	H	O	I	S	S	S	A	V
I	N	G	W	O	R	K	S	R	N
W	H	E	A	T	F	E	F	M	W

What gifts did Jesus use for signs of his sacraments?

6. _____   8. _____

7. _____   9. _____

10. __ __ __ __ __ __ __ __ __ __ __ __ __ __
    __ __ __ __ __ __ __ __ __ __ __ __ __ __
    __ __ __ __ __ __ __ __ __ __ __ __ __.

74

Match each description in Column 1 with the correct term in Column 2.

Column 1

_____ 11. longed for the ability to communicate because of blindness and deafness

_____ 12. a gift from God and your free choice to seek God and believe in him.

_____ 13. through their efforts, a priceless natural resource was saved from destruction

_____ 14. God's loving care for all things, God's will and plan for creation

_____ 15. effective signs of God's life, given by Christ to the Church

Column 2

a. providence

b. Helen Keller

c. sacraments

d. faith

e. *seringueiros*

C **Make Connections** Write a response to each question or statement.

16. "Remove the sandals from your feet, for the place where you stand is holy ground." How do you imagine this place affected Moses' attitude toward God?

_____

_____

17. Give an example of how you practice stewardship.

_____

_____

18. What are signs of a loving union and commitment between married people?

_____

_____

19. Describe an example of how longing for something caused you to try harder or work longer than you might have otherwise.

_____

_____

20. Jesus promised the woman at the well "living water." He meant water for the soul. How would his words also emphasize the need for people to protect the environment?

_____

_____

Unit 2
Trinity

In this unit you will...

learn about the many ways you experience the mystery of God. When we follow the First Commandment, we live in relationship with the Blessed Trinity. We respond to God's love with prayer, with worship, and with practicing virtues in our everyday life.

Faith in Action!

**Catholic Social Teaching Principle:
Life and Dignity of the Human Person**

Chapter 4: The Mystery of God

Let Us Pray

Leader: Almighty and powerful God, we are in awe of you.

"Again his voice roars—
  the majestic sound of his thunder.
He does great things beyond our knowing;
  wonders past our searching out."

Job 37:4–5

All: Almighty and powerful God, we are in awe of you. Amen.

Activity — Let's Begin

How Great Thou Art

O Lord my God, when I in awesome wonder
Consider all the worlds Thy hands have made,
I see the stars, I hear the rolling thunder,
Thy power throughout the universe displayed!
Then sings my soul, my Savior God, to Thee;
How great Thou art, how great Thou art!

A selection from lyrics by Stuart K. Hine

What are some things that remind you of the greatness of God?

To describe God, write a word or phrase that begins with each of the letters in the word below.

G _____
R _____
E _____
A _____
T _____

• **God in Nature** Draw something in nature that shows God's greatness.

More Than Can Be Known

 **Focus** What gift did Patrick bring to the Irish people?

We can't always see God's plan for us. Blessings often come in the form of hardships. The following story shows how this was true for one Christian.

BIOGRAPHY

Kidnapped

Patrick, the son of a Roman official, lived on the western coast of Britain. While working on his father's farm one day, he was seized by a group of raiders and sold as a slave.

Patrick was taken away to Ireland, a place completely new to him. Again he worked on a farm, but now he had no warm clothing to wear and almost nothing to eat. He had no family and no friends. Angry with God, Patrick thought only of his misery. Why had God allowed this terrible thing to happen?

❓ **What is a word or symbol that describes what you would think or feel at such a time?**

The Mystery Unfolds

As time went by, Patrick began to realize that despite his harsh life, the lives of his Irish masters were even harder because they did not know Jesus. They did not know the Christian faith, which is full of hope and love. Patrick began to pray with all his heart, turning his life and his future over to God. After six years, he escaped and made the long, hard journey home. His parents were overjoyed to see him. They hoped that he would never leave them again.

But Patrick kept thinking about the Irish people he had left. He never stopped wondering about the mystery of his life and what good might come from his time among these people. One night he dreamed that they were calling him. All at once it became clear to him that because he knew their language, he could bring them the Christian faith. Although the studies were hard for him, Patrick prepared to become a priest. In time, he became a bishop and returned to Ireland. When the Irish people heard Patrick speak, great numbers of them asked to be baptized. Because of his great holiness and love for God, the Church made Patrick a saint.

Experience taught Patrick that the mysteries in human life draw people toward the **mystery** of God, who is so much more than they can ever grasp.

? What are some things about your own life that cause you to wonder as Patrick did?

Words of Faith

A **mystery** is a truth of faith that you cannot fully understand but that you believe because God has shown it to people in Scripture, in the life of Jesus, or in the teachings of the Church.

Activity: Share Your Faith

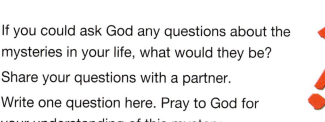

Reflect: If you could ask God any questions about the mysteries in your life, what would they be?

Share: Share your questions with a partner.

Act: Write one question here. Pray to God for your understanding of this mystery.

_____

_____

The Mystery Beyond Words

 **Focus** Who is the Holy Trinity?

Like Patrick, people today wonder about the mystery of God and the way God works in their lives. God wants to be known, yet he is greater than anyone can tell or understand.

From earliest Old Testament times, the Israelites learned through revelation that God is one, unfailing in truth and love. Jesus revealed a deeper level of this mystery, showing that the one God is three Persons: Father, Son, and Holy Spirit—the **Holy Trinity**. Patrick emphasized and honored the Trinity in all his teaching. Jesus and his followers invite you into a deeper understanding of the mystery of the God you cannot see.

SCRIPTURE John 1:32–34

The Baptism of Jesus

John the Baptist testified that Jesus was the Son of God, sent by the Father and filled with the Holy Spirit:

"I saw the Spirit come down like a dove from the sky and remain upon him. I did not know him, but the one who sent me to baptize with water told me, 'On whomever you see the Spirit come down and remain, he is the one who will baptize with the holy Spirit.' Now I have seen and testified that he is the Son of God."

John 1:32–34

Whenever the Church baptizes, the names of the three Persons in the Holy Trinity are used. Those who are baptized enter into the very life of God, who is love. All of the Sacraments offer a share in God's life and into the mystery that is God—Father, Son, and Holy Spirit.

❓ **What are some ways in which you experience the love of the Holy Trinity in your life?**

The Baptism of Christ, Currier and Ives

Living Your Faith

The Sign of the Cross helps you recall that the Trinity is with you, protecting and guiding you to live as Jesus did. When you renew your baptismal promises, you are reminded that the Trinity gives you new life that never ends.

The first commandment is this: I am the Lord your God; you shall not have strange gods before me. This commandment calls you to believe in God, to hope in him, and to love him above everything else. In obeying this commandment, you live in relationship with the Trinity.

A **virtue** is a habit of doing good. The virtues of faith, hope, and love are called theological virtues because they are gifts from God.

- Faith is the virtue by which you freely choose to respond to God's invitation and say "yes" to all that he has revealed.
- Hope is your desire and expectation that God will grant you eternal life with the Trinity and give you the grace to attain it.
- Love, or charity, is the virtue by which you love God above all things and others for the love of God.

All people are made in the **image of God** because they are created by God. If you try, you can see traces of the Trinity reflected in every person. When people love one another, they reflect the communion of the three Persons in one God.

Words of Faith

The **Holy Trinity** is the mystery of one God in three Persons: Father, Son, and Holy Spirit.

A **virtue** is a habit of doing good that helps you grow in love for God.

Image of God means the divine likeness in each person, the result of being created by God.

❓ How do some of the people you know show themselves as images of God?

Activity — Connect Your Faith

Discover Symbols of the Trinity Legend says that Patrick used the shamrock as an image for the Trinity. How could the shamrock be useful in explaining the Trinity? What other images would help explain the Trinity? Draw one or more of them in this space.

Your Response to God's Love

 **Focus** How do you respond to the love God shows you?

The theological virtues of faith, hope, and love are actions that people do and see others doing every day. Here are some everyday examples of faith, hope, and love.

Virtues in Action

Faith	Hope	Love
• Peter goes through the process of becoming a Christian. • Amanda makes the Sign of the Cross each day when she wakes up. • Carlos attends a Bible study.	• Elena goes to Mass with her family on the anniversary of her grandfather's death. • Tony gathers with other people of his parish to pray for peace. • Shantelle asks God to show her how to deal with her temper.	• Meg helps the teacher of a first-grade religion class every Saturday. • Andrew helps serve dinner at a homeless shelter. • José volunteers at a nursing home after school.

❓ How have you responded to God in faith, hope, and love?

Activity: Live Your Faith

Bring It to Life In a small group, brainstorm four examples of people practicing the virtues of faith, hope, and love. Jot down each idea below.

Faith
_____
_____
_____
_____

Hope
_____
_____
_____
_____

Love
_____
_____
_____
_____

Act It Out Make up a short skit or pantomime that shows each of the three virtues, and present the skit to the rest of the class.

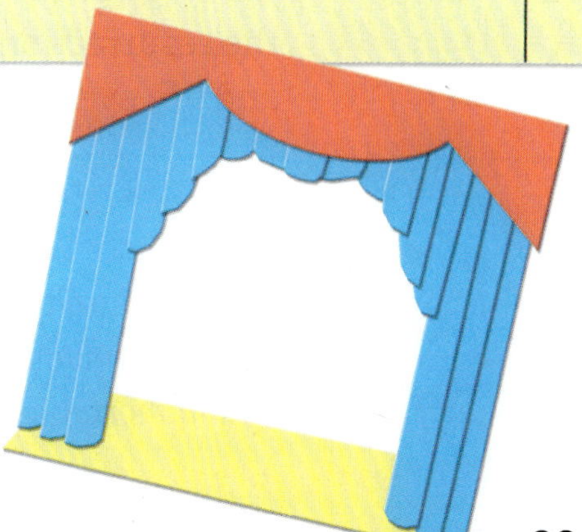

Celebrate

Apostles' Creed

 Let Us Pray

Gather and begin with the Sign of the Cross.

Leader: Let us affirm what we believe.

After each reader, say: I do believe!

Reader 1: I believe in God,
the Father almighty,
Creator of heaven and earth,
and in Jesus Christ, his only Son,
our Lord,

At the words that follow, up to and including the Virgin Mary, *all bow.*

Reader 2: who was conceived by the
Holy Spirit,
born of the Virgin Mary,
suffered under Pontius Pilate,
was crucified, died and was buried;
he descended into hell;
on the third day he rose again
from the dead;

Reader 3: he ascended into heaven,
and is seated at the right hand
of God the Father almighty;
from there he will come to judge
the living and the dead.

Reader 4: I believe in the Holy Spirit,
the holy catholic Church,
the communion of saints,
the forgiveness of sins,
the resurrection of the body,
and life everlasting. Amen.

 O most holy Trinity,
Undivided unity;
Holy God, mighty God,
God immortal be adored!

"Sing Praise to Our Creator," Omer Westendorf, © 1962 World Library Publications, Inc.

Check Understanding Circle True if a statement is true, and circle False if a statement is false. Correct any false statements.

1. Faith in God means that God is not a mystery.
   True   False   _False_

2. The mystery of God in three Persons is called the image of God.
   True   (False)   _True_

3. Jesus reveals to people the God they cannot see.
   (True)   False   _True_

4. Those who are baptized are baptized into the very life of God.
   (True)   False   _____

5. The theological virtues are feelings that give us comfort.
   True   (False)   _____

Circle the letter of the choice that best completes the sentence.

6. A virtue is a __c__.
   a. bad habit
   b. prayer prayed during Mass
   c. habit of doing good
   d. symbol

7. The theological virtue which expresses your expectation that God will grant you eternal life is __d__.
   a. patience
   b. image
   c. love
   d. hope

8. A truth of faith that God has shown in Scripture, in the life of Jesus, or in the teaching of the Church is called __d__.
   (a.) Gospel
   b. stewardship
   c. covenant
   d. mystery

9. The divine likeness in each person, the result of being created by God, is known as _____.
   (a.) the image of God
   b. virtue
   c. the first commandment
   d. faith

10. The mystery beyond words is _____.
    (a.) the Trinity
    b. virtue
    c. the Corporal Works of Mercy
    d. creation

85

UNIT 2: CHAPTER 4

Family Faith

Catholics Believe

- The Trinity is the central mystery of Christian faith and life.
- Virtue is the habit of doing good. The theological virtues of faith, hope, and love are gifts from God.

SCRIPTURE

Read *1 Corinthians 13:1–13* to learn how Saint Paul describes love.

Activity
Live Your Faith

Make a Symbol Love is one of the virtues talked about in this week's lesson. Love is the glue that holds a family together. The love within a family is meant to reflect the love of the Holy Trinity. Create a symbol that represents how your family shows God's love to others. If someone in your family is skilled with art or fabric, you can help that person make a more permanent symbol to display in your home.

GO online www.osvcurriculum.com
For weekly scripture readings and seasonal resources

▲ Saint Athanasius
c. 295–373

People of Faith

Athanasius became the bishop of Alexandria in Egypt at the age of thirty. He lived at a time when many people were supporting a false teaching that Jesus was not really the Son of God. As bishop, Athanasius defended the doctrine of the Trinity. Because of his outspokenness, he was sent into exile—not once, but five times over the course of his life. During these times he lived in hardship but spent his time writing, praying, and encouraging other Christians. The Church celebrates his feast day on May 2.

Family Prayer

Saint Athanasius, pray for us that we may know and love the Father, Son, and Holy Spirit as you did. May we also follow your example and uphold our convictions even when it is difficult to do so. Amen.

In Unit 2 your child is learning about the Trinity.
See *Catechism of the Catholic Church* 234, 1812, 1813 for further reading on chapter content.

Chapter 5: Prayer and Worship

 **Let Us Pray**

Leader: Make us humble before you, O God.

"Enter, let us bow down in worship; let us kneel before the LORD who made us."

Psalm 95:6

All: Make us humble before you, O God. Amen.

Activity

● Give Thanks

Dear Aunt Gina,

Thanks—You really are the best! I can't thank you enough for that great ski sweater you made for me. . . .

When someone gives you a gift, what do you do? Say thank you? Give that person a hug or a kiss? Write a note? Well, God loves you more than anybody else does. Every good thing you have and are is a gift from God.

Now think about what gifts of God you are most grateful for today.

What gifts has God given to everyone in the world?

_____

_____

_____

Suggest a way to show gratitude to God.

_____

 **Compose a Prayer** Write a prayer of thankfulness on a separate sheet of paper to recite at a prayer service.

87

Explore

God with Us

 **Focus** How did David praise and honor God?

David was the second king of Israel. He was a soldier who often led Israel to victory against its enemies. He was also a poet and a musician. Many of the psalms are attributed to him. In the story that follows, David brings the Ark of the Covenant to Jerusalem.

SCRIPTURE 2 Samuel 6:1–15

A Day of Joy

David's armies had carried the Ark of the Covenant—a box containing the tablets of the Law—into battle as a sign of God's presence. Now David brought the Ark to Jerusalem, where it would signal God's presence to all the people.

To celebrate the Ark's arrival, David organized a great procession and invited musicians and singers to take part. Singing with joy, the people followed the Ark through the streets. David led the procession, dressed not as a soldier or a king but in the simple clothes of a priest of the Lord—and he danced with abandon before the Lord!

Based on 2 Samuel 6:1–15

- What do you think was in David's heart as he danced before the Ark?
- When have you felt so happy that you wanted to dance?

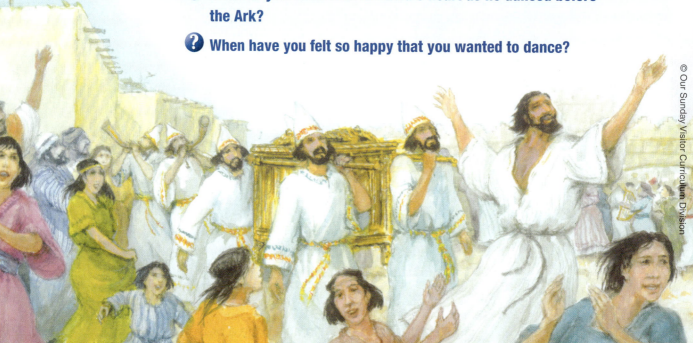

The Church Prays and Worships

From the earliest days of the Christian community, the followers of the Risen Christ gathered for prayer and worship. Like David, they praised God with great faith and joy.

SCRIPTURE

"Every day they devoted themselves to meeting together in the temple area and to breaking bread in their homes. They ate their meals with exultation and sincerity of heart, praising God and enjoying favor with all the people."

Acts 2:46–47

Words of Faith

Prayer is talking to and listening to God. Prayer can be private or public; spoken, sung, or silent; formal or spontaneous.

Responding to God's Love

Prayer and worship are ways to respond to God's love as King David did. The Bible is filled with stories of Jesus at prayer. Today, you can lift your mind and heart to God through prayer. You also honor God through worship, by offering words and actions in public praise and thanks. The Mass is the Church's greatest act of worship. It unites the whole People of God gathered around the table of the Lord Jesus. In the Mass, the Church reads from both the Old and New Testaments, most especially the Gospels, to recall those saving events of God in the Old Testament that found their fulfillment in the mystery of Jesus, the Christ.

Activity — Share Your Faith

Reflect: Think about the psalms that you have read or heard.

Share: With a partner, share the psalms you remember.

Act: A psalm is a song of praise to God. Write a short psalm in this space. Use this form:

1. Invite others to praise God. _____
2. Tell why God is worthy of praise. _____
3. End by making a promise to _____
   God or by asking him for a favor. _____

Holy Work

Focus What is liturgy?

The third commandment is this: Remember to keep holy the Lord's day. This means that faithful people have a duty to pray and to offer **worship** to God on the Lord's day. But that duty is also a joy and a gift. Spending time with someone who loves you, someone whom you love very much, is not a chore.

Worship is a natural response to God's loving goodness. There are times and places for individual acts of prayer, but worship is centered in the community of faith.

The Church's expressions of communal worship are formal practices known as the **liturgy**. In the liturgy, you are participating along with the whole Body of Christ in the saving work accomplished through Jesus' life, death, Resurrection, and Ascension. The Catholic Church's liturgy includes

- the Eucharist, the Church's central sacrament and expression of worship.
- the other sacraments: Baptism, Confirmation, Reconciliation, Anointing of the Sick, Matrimony, and Holy Orders.
- the Liturgy of the Hours, the Church's public daily prayer.

❓ What does it mean to say that the liturgy is a form of work?

❓ When is your work most meaningful for you?

The Trinity at Work

The presence of the Trinity is at the core of the Church's liturgy. Prayers are offered to the Father in Jesus' name. Christ is the one true priest who offers himself through the actions of the priest, the deacon, and the assembly. The Spirit guides and sustains the Church in the way of prayer and worship. Through the liturgy, heaven and earth are joined in one hymn of praise.

The work of the Father, Son, and Holy Spirit is acknowledged in many prayers at Mass. From the Sign of the Cross at the beginning of Mass until the final blessing, the entire liturgy is a celebration of the saving love of the Holy Trinity poured out to all the world. In the Glory to God, the readings, the Creed, the Eucharistic Prayer, and the Great Amen, the Holy Trinity is called upon. And over and over, the people respond: Amen!

Words of Faith

Worship is public adoration and honor shown to God in prayer.

Liturgy is the official public worship of the Church. The word means "the work of the people."

Activity — Connect Your Faith

Explore Prayer In a small group, discuss which experiences of prayer and worship have been best for you. Create a list of good advice you can offer another person on how to deepen his or her prayer life.

Explore

Liturgical Posture and Gesture

 **Focus** How do you pray with your whole self?

God wants you to worship him not only with your mind, but also with your body. Some postures and gestures are used frequently in prayer and worship.

Body Language for Prayer

Standing shows
- your complete attention and commitment
- respect at Mass for the Gospel

Sitting shows
- willingness to rest
- willingness to reflect

Kneeling shows
- humility
- the need for God
- repentance

Hands clasped shows
- concentration in prayer
- sincerity

Hands raised, palms upward shows
- openness to receiving a gift from God
- praise

Hands extended shows
- blessing
- giving of the Spirit

? In what position do you feel most comfortable praying? Why?

Activity

Create a Prayer Service In small groups, outline a prayer service, using postures and gestures. You may use those from the liturgy, but you may also make up your own. For the prayer service you may use a scripture reading, hymns, and prayers you compose yourselves. Indicate which posture or gesture is appropriate for the place in which you have used it, and explain your choice. Then, choose one of the services, and pray it together as a class.

Scripture Reading, Prayer, or Hymn	Posture or Gesture	Appropriate because . . .

93

Celebrate

Prayer of Thanks and Petition

 Let Us Pray

Gather and begin with the Sign of the Cross.

Leader: Loving God, every breath we take—every good thing we are, have, and do—comes from you. Speak to us in your word.

Reader 1: A reading from the Letter to the Philippians.

Read Philippians 4:4–7.

The word of the Lord.

All: **Thanks be to God.**

Leader: Let us offer our thanks and praise to God.

Respond to each petition: Thank you for your blessings, Lord.

Reader 2: For creating us in your image, we pray:

Reader 3: For revealing yourself to us that we might praise you, Father, Son, and Holy Spirit, we pray:

Reader 4: For all those who love and care for us, we pray:

Leader: Lord, we now offer you our prayers of thanksgiving.

Add your individual prayers of thanks.

Leader: Let us pray.

Bow your heads as the leader prays.

All: **Amen.**

Sing together.

Rejoice in the Lord always, again I say, rejoice!
Rejoice! Rejoice! Again I say, rejoice!

"Rejoice in the Lord Always"
Traditional

CHAPTER 5
Review

A **Work with Words** Complete each sentence with the correct term from the Word Bank.

WORD BANK
Liturgy of the Hours
community
rosary
prayer
third
public
second

1. The official _____ prayer of the Church, such as the celebration of the seven sacraments, is called the liturgy.

2. The _____ commandment tells you to offer prayer and worship to God.

3. _____ can be silent or spoken, formal or spontaneous.

4. Worship is centered in the _____ of faith.

5. The Church's daily prayer is called the _____.

B **Check Understanding** Fill in the circle next to the correct response.

6. Worship is public adoration and honor shown to God in _____.
   ○ church   ○ the open   ○ prayer
   ○ song   ○ sincerity

7. Dancing, King David led the procession that brought the _____ into Jerusalem.
   ○ army   ○ harvest   ○ bride
   ○ Ark   ○ Scriptures

8. The Church's greatest act of worship is _____.
   ○ the Mass   ○ Baptism   ○ kneeling
   ○ the Rosary   ○ Christmas

9. The Church's public daily prayer is the _____.
   ○ Mass   ○ Liturgy of the Hours   ○ Scripture
   ○ meal prayer   ○ benediction

10. The Sign of the Cross acknowledges the work of _____.
    ○ the priest   ○ grace   ○ Jesus
    ○ the congregation   ○ the Trinity

UNIT 2: CHAPTER 5
Family Faith

Catholics Believe

- Prayer and worship are ways to show love for God and to thank him for his blessings.
- When we pray and worship, God fills us with joy, strength, and hope.

SCRIPTURE

Read *Psalm 22:23–32* to learn about others who have worshiped God.

GO online www.osvcurriculum.com
For weekly scripture readings and seasonal resources

Activity
Live Your Faith

Welcome When David, the king of Israel, celebrated the return of the Ark of the Covenant to Jerusalem, he invited everyone in the kingdom. Is there someone you know who might appreciate an invitation to worship with you? Invite that person to come to Mass with your family, and then share a meal together.

People of Faith

As early as the fourth century, Christians honored the Roman martyr **Cecilia** as a saint. A legend about Cecilia says that her husband, Valerian, was a martyr, too. Because of their example and words, hundreds of Romans became Christian. The legend also says that Cecilia sang to God on her wedding day, and it is probably for this reason that she is the patron saint of music and musicians. Many music societies are named for Cecilia. Her feast day, November 22, is a traditional time for musical celebrations.

▲ Saint Cecilia
second or third century

Family Prayer

Saint Cecilia, pray for us that we may sing the praises of God and, like you, rejoice in purity of mind and body so that we may one day join you and the other saints and angels with our Father in heaven. Amen.

© Our Sunday Visitor Curriculum Division

In Unit 2 your child is learning about the TRINITY.
CCC See Catechism of the Catholic Church 1077–1083, 2637, 2638, 2648 for further reading on chapter content.

Chapter 6 Doing Good

 **Let Us Pray**

Leader: Gracious God, open our hearts to you.
"I will run the way of your commands,
for you open my docile heart."
Psalm 119:32

All: Gracious God, open our hearts to you. Amen.

Activity  Let's Begin

● **Act with Love** Mr. Switzer shuffled past the boys sitting on the steps and opened the door to the apartment building. He didn't speak to them as he usually did.

"Hi, Mr. Switzer," said one of the boys. "What's new?" The old man turned and gave the boys a half-hearted smile.

"I'm afraid I'm a little sad today, boys," he said. "I've lost my little dog, Spike. He's been sick, you know, and the vet called earlier to say that she couldn't save him."

"That's too bad," said another of the boys. "I'm really sorry." All the other boys said the same thing.

When Mr. Switzer went inside, one of the boys said, "Let's see what we can do about getting Mr. Switzer another dog. He won't know what to do with himself without Spike. That little dog was a real friend to him."

What do you think the boys will do?

With a partner, think of a loving action that you are willing to do and describe it below. When you have done your loving action, your teacher will mark your "promise" with a heart.

My loving action will be:

_____

● **Draw a Character Map** Make a chart of all your interests, talents, good choices, and struggles.

Explore

The Way to Goodness

 **Focus** What does Jesus teach about following God's commandments?

Faith Fact
The Hebrews first used the term *scribe* to refer to those who held government positions or carried out orders issued by the king.

Knowing how to be your best self and how to do good is not always easy. Often you need to ask advice or learn from the examples of others. In Jesus' time, a special group of people called scribes studied the Law of God and helped others understand what God wanted them to do. It was not unusual for Jesus to meet with scribes and join in their debate about points of God's Law. Scribes concerned themselves with minor as well as major matters. We learn from the following story about one particular scribe who asked Jesus a very important question.

SCRIPTURE

Mark 12:28–34

The Great Commandment

One of the scribes, when he came forward and heard them disputing and saw how well [Jesus] had answered them, asked him, "Which is the first of all the commandments?" Jesus replied, "The first is this: 'Hear, O Israel! The Lord our God is Lord alone! You shall love the Lord your God with all your heart, with all your soul, with all your mind, and with all your strength.' The second is this: 'You shall love your neighbor as yourself.' There is no other commandment greater than these." The scribe said to him, "Well said, teacher. You are right in saying, 'He is One and there is no other than he.' And 'to love him with all your heart, with all your understanding, with all your strength, and to love your neighbor as yourself' is worth more than all burnt offerings and sacrifices." And when Jesus saw that [he] answered with understanding, he said to him, "You are not far from the kingdom of God."

Mark 12:28–34

? **What two laws did the scribe name?**

? **How do you keep these two commandments in your own life?**

Worship that Pleases God

In Jesus' time, religious people thought that it was important to worship God with burnt offerings and sacrifices. But Jesus praised the scribe, who understood that a person who shows love for God and neighbor by doing good makes an even greater act of worship.

The first step is understanding that God wants you to love him and love your neighbor. The next step is putting that understanding to work in everyday life. Learning to do this is a lifelong process. You will need to practice. Just as physical exercise builds the strength of your body, so the exercise of doing good builds virtue.

How do you practice doing good?

Words of Faith

The **cardinal virtues** are acquired by human effort and cooperation with God's grace.

The Cardinal Virtues

The four **cardinal virtues** are central to becoming a good person. They provide a foundation for moral living.

Prudence	is knowing what is right and good and choosing it. Prudence helps you "see ahead" to the consequences of actions.
Temperance	is keeping a balance in life. Temperance helps you enjoy all good things in moderation and promotes self-control.
Justice	is giving God and people their due. Justice helps you build up the community by respecting rights and promoting the common good.
Fortitude	is showing courage, especially in the face of evil. Fortitude helps you resist temptation and overcome obstacles to doing good.

Activity — Share Your Faith

Reflect: Think about the ways in which the people in your class or family practice a cardinal virtue.

Share: With a partner, share what people do when they practice one of the cardinal virtues.

Act: Choose one of the cardinal virtues, and with your partner act out a way that each of you could practice the virtue.

Explore

Living the Cardinal Virtues

 **Focus** How does living the cardinal virtues show love for God and others?

Virtues are habits that help you live according to your conscience, the ability you have to know right from wrong. All of the virtues help you act for good. When you do good, you become the person God wants you to be.

Practicing virtue, or living a morally good life, is a way to praise God—but it is also a challenge. Often you see ways to be and act that are not the Christian way. Consider the challenges to virtuous living that these young people face. Imagine what you would do in these situations.

A Prudent Choice?

Jill and Kenzie were in the mall. Kenzie wanted a new CD, but she didn't have the money for it. "So just take it," Jill said. "No one will see you."

"But that's stealing," Kenzie replied.

"Not really," returned Jill. "They overcharge for this stuff, anyway."

? How could the virtue of prudence help Kenzie decide to do the right thing?

With Justice for All

"See the new kid over there?" one of his school friends asked Miguel. "Well, he isn't like us—he sounds funny when he talks. Let's get the other guys and gang up on him. He deserves it." Miguel paused before responding.

? What response would show that Miguel knows about the virtue of justice?

100

It Takes Courage

"Move your arm, Phan," Ty whispered. "I can't see your answers." During recess, Ty had pressured Phan to let him cheat during the test. Phan had not wanted to refuse in front of the other fifth grade boys who were listening. They would all call him chicken if he did not go along with Ty.

❓ **If you were Phan, what would you do to show the virtue of courage?**

Out of Balance

Marisol loved her new computer. She spent hours sending e-mails to her friends and never tired of playing games on the flashing screen. One day her little sister asked, "Why don't you ever play with *me* anymore?" Then their mother gently reminded Marisol of some unfinished craft projects in the basement and a number of neglected chores.

❓ **If you were Marisol, how could you practice temperance?**

Activity — Connect Your Faith

Write Your Own Story In the space, create a problem story in which someone has an opportunity to practice one of the four cardinal virtues. Write your story. Then read it aloud and pose a question to the group.

PRUDENCE

JUSTICE

FORTITUDE

TEMPERANCE

Explore

Moral Decisions

 **Focus** How do you decide what is right and wrong?

Every day you make choices about how to behave. People of faith can turn to the teachings of Jesus and the Church for help in making choices between right and wrong.

Decision-Making Tips

Remember	that you are a child of God. You are not alone in making this decision.
Draw	upon what you have learned at home, at school, and at church about right and wrong behavior. Understand that your decision will be a good one if it is made in agreement with God's commandments, Jesus' law of love, and the teachings of the Church.
Listen	to what your conscience tells you when you have to decide what is right. The Holy Spirit will guide you in forming your conscience.
Pray	to the Holy Spirit for help in doing what your conscience tells you is right.
Focus	on your *motive*—why you want to do one thing or the other. Pay attention to your feelings as well as to your thoughts. Both come into play in making decisions.
Evaluate	the consequences of your decision after you have acted on it. How did what you decided affect those with whom you live, play, and go to school? How did your decision help others experience the goodness of God?

❓ **Think of a bad decision you have made. Can you find the reason it was bad by recognizing that you missed one of the steps above?**

❓ **Think of a good decision you have made. Can you see that you followed some of the steps above?**

Activity: Live Your Faith

Show How to Decide In small groups, think of an example of a moral decision that people your age might have to make. Together, decide how each of the steps should be followed in the situation. Role-play the situation for the rest of the class as an example of how to apply the steps.

Describe the example that you and your group have chosen:

Step:	How to follow it:
1. Remember that you are a child of God.	
2. Draw upon what you have learned. Understand that your decision will be good if it is in agreement with God's commandments.	
3. Listen to what your conscience tells you.	
4. Pray to the Holy Spirit.	
5. Focus on your motive—Pay attention to your feelings as well as to your thoughts.	
6. Evaluate the consequences of your decision after you have acted on it.	

Celebrate

Psalm of Praise

 **Let Us Pray**

Gather and begin with the Sign of the Cross.

Leader: God, come to my assistance.

All: **Lord, make haste to help me.**

Group 1: Happy those whose way is blameless,
who walk by the teaching of the LORD.

Group 2: Happy those who observe God's decrees,
who seek the LORD with all their heart.

Group 1: May my ways be firm
in the observance of your laws!

Group 2: Then I will not be ashamed
to ponder all your commands.

All: **I will praise you with sincere heart.**

Psalm 119:1–2, 5–7

Reader: A reading from the Letter to the Philippians.
Read Philippians 1:3–6.
The word of the Lord.

All: **Thanks be to God.**

Leader: We pray for the needs of the
Church and the world.

All: **We ask your blessing, Lord.**

Leader: Let us pray.
Bow your heads as the leader prays.

All: **Amen.**

 Sing together.

Amen si – a – ku – du – mi – sa.
Amen si – a – ku – du – mi – sa.
Amen ba - wo, Amen ba - wo,
Amen si - a - ku - du - mi - sa.

"Amen Siakudumisa" South African traditional

CHAPTER 6
Review

A **Check Understanding** Circle the choice that best completes each sentence.

1. By doing good, you (learn to be a scribe, become your best self, avoid having to listen to your conscience).

2. Loving your neighbor means that you (remind people to be good to you, get people to do whatever you want, care for others and live virtuously).

3. Practicing virtue is (a way to praise God, a sign that you can't make up your mind, a sacrament).

4. Avoiding situations that could influence you to make wrong choices is a way you can practice the cardinal virtue of (temperance, justice, prudence).

5. Virtues are acquired through (human effort and God's grace, human effort alone, God's grace alone).

B **Make Connections** Write a brief response to each statement or question.

6. Give an example of how a student might show temperance on the playing field.

   _____
   _____

7. How have you been prudent at home or in school?

   _____
   _____

8. What is the benefit of the cardinal virtues?

   _____
   _____

9. How might justice be part of making a moral decision?

   _____
   _____

10. Explain the "listen" step in decision making.

    _____
    _____

UNIT 2: CHAPTER 6

Family Faith

Catholics Believe

- The Great Commandment states that you will love the Lord, your God, with all your heart, soul, and mind.
- The cardinal virtues play a central role in helping people lead morally good lives.

SCRIPTURE

Read *Isaiah 56:1–2* to learn more about the rewards that await those who act justly.

www.osvcurriculum.com
For weekly scripture readings and seasonal resources

Activity
Live Your Faith

Volunteer Practice the cardinal virtue of justice. Most neighborhoods and parishes have meal programs. Your town may have a homeless shelter. Find a program in which you can volunteer as a family or with one other family member, and take time to do it. Talk about how you could help change conditions in your community so that more people might have what they need.

People of Faith

▲ Saint Thomas More
c. 1477–1535

Sir Thomas More had a wonderful family, a brilliant career, and the friendship of the king of England, Henry VIII. But then the king demanded that the English people cut their ties with Rome and accept him as the head of the Church in England. More resigned his office. He could not cut himself off from the Catholic Church. He knew the meaning of fortitude. Angered, the king had More beheaded. Thomas More became a saint and a martyr because he obeyed his conscience. His feast day is June 22.

Family Prayer

Saint Thomas More, pray for us that we may act as our conscience directs us and always obey our heavenly King before all other powers and authority. Amen.

© Our Sunday Visitor Curriculum Division

In Unit 2 your child is learning about the TRINITY.
See Catechism of the Catholic Church 1805–1809, 2055 for further reading on chapter content.

DISCOVER

Catholic Social Teaching:

Life and Dignity of the Human Person

Faith in Action!
CATHOLIC SOCIAL TEACHING

In this unit you learned that all persons are made in the image of God. He has commanded you to recognize his image in others and to love your neighbor as yourself. One way to do that is by practicing the cardinal virtue of justice.

Life and Dignity

The Church teaches that the commandments forbid sins against the dignity and rights of human beings. This means that people may not be abused. They must be free to follow God's will for them and to make choices about how they will live. Human dignity requires Christians to love others as they love themselves. All people are equally deserving of the benefits of God's creation.

Many citizens of the United States live comfortably. They have dreams and ambitions for the future. They pray and worship whenever they like. But there are those who can't take any of these things for granted. In the world today, as many as 27 million people are being held as slaves. They cannot go to school, and so they have no hope for a better life. They cannot even choose to worship God. They have no one to protect them from danger in the work their owners force them to do.

❓ **Why is it the responsibility of Christians to help those who are treated unjustly and without dignity?**

CONNECT
With the Call to Justice

S.T.O.P.

Ms. Vogel is a fifth-grade teacher in Colorado. Five years ago, when her history class was studying American slavery, she read a newspaper article about slavery in the Sudan to her students. They were shocked to realize that slavery still exists and that children no older than themselves are kidnapped and sold as slaves.

So Ms. Vogel's students decided to do something about it. They learned that slaves in the Sudan could be bought back for about $50 to $100. The students founded an organization called S.T.O.P. (Slavery That Oppresses People). They saved what money they had or received in order to buy freedom for the slaves. In the first year the students won freedom for two slaves in the Sudan. S.T.O.P. began to attract attention. Many other classes and schools around the country began their own campaigns. By 2001 over $70,000 had been raised, and 2,000 slaves had been freed. By 2003, S.T.O.P. had helped free 45,000 slaves.

S.T.O.P. and Ms. Vogel have received many awards for their work, among them the Anne Frank Award and the Martin Luther King Humanitarian Award. Some members of the class, along with Ms. Vogel, even went to Rome to meet with the pope about ending slavery. But the most important reward they have received is the knowledge that they are helping bring people held as slaves into a new life of freedom.

It may be difficult to imagine that slavery exists in the world today, and yet many people still suffer as slaves. Let's learn how some fifth graders are helping to end slavery by practicing the virtue of justice.

❓ Why do you think the students in Ms. Vogel's class decided to do something about slavery?

❓ What did you learn about Ms. Vogel's students that could apply to you or to your class?

© Our Sunday Visitor Curriculum Division

Reach Out!

SERVE Your Community

Reflect

It is not easy to make changes in the world. But if Catholics sit by and do nothing, they are ignoring God's call to love others and help those in need. Take some time to think very carefully about what slavery really is.

Read and reflect on *Matthew 25:31–40*. What does this passage say to you about how human beings should treat one another?

_____

_____

Slavery means that you have no choice. Of the choices you do have, which is most important to you?

_____

_____

What would you most like to have a choice about?

_____

_____

Physical slavery is not the only way in which people are slaves. Make a list of things, such as peer pressure, that control the choices people make.

_____

_____

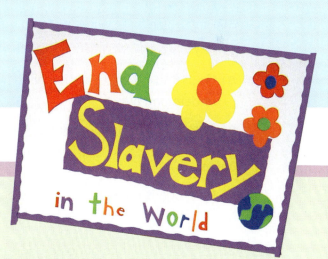

Make a Difference

Do Something About It   As a class, decide on and plan one thing that you can do to increase awareness of one kind of slavery. This may include starting a daily or weekly prayer time. You might also establish a publicity campaign about slavery or suggest a fund-raising activity. You might also consider making posters.

Describe what your contribution to this activity will be.

_____

_____

© Our Sunday Visitor Curriculum Division

UNIT 2 REVIEW

A **Work with Words** Solve the puzzle, using the clues provided.

Across

5. Prayer and _____ are ways to respond to God's love as King David did.

7. We worship the Trinity in the Church's _____.

8. God is called a _____ because humans never completely know and understand him.

9. The "Glory to God," or doxology, praises the _____.

Down

1. Fortitude is showing _____, especially in the face of evil.

2. King David wrote a particular prayer of praise called a _____.

3. _____ are habits of doing good that help humans grow in love of God.

4. The _____ to worship God on the Lord's day is also a _____ and a gift.

6. _____ is talking and listening to God.

8. Humans can pray by playing _____.

B Check Understanding Match each description in Column 1 with the correct term in Column 2.

Column 1

_____ 11. a box containing the tablets of the law

_____ 12. means "work of the people"

_____ 13. says that faithful people have a duty to pray and to offer worship to God on the Lord's day

_____ 14. divine likeness in each person

_____ 15. "Hear O Israel! The Lord our God is Lord alone! You shall love the Lord your God with all your heart, with all your soul, with all your mind, and with all your strength."

Column 2

a. image of God

b. Ark of the Covenant

c. the first commandment

d. liturgy

e. the third commandment

C Make Connections Write a response to each statement.

16–17. Choose the theological virtue you understand most clearly, and in a few sentences explain:

What it means

How you practice it

_____

_____

_____

18–20. Describe a moral decision you have made. Be sure to cover these steps:

Listen

Focus

Evaluate

_____

_____

_____

_____

_____

Unit 3
Jesus Christ

In this unit you will...

learn that Jesus is the perfect image of God because he is God. In Jesus we are given the greatest sign of God's presence. Jesus teaches about the kingdom of God through parables and shows us the kingdom in his miracles. We continue to know God's presence, and to experience the Paschal mystery of Jesus through the seven sacraments.

Chapter 7

Chapter 8

Chapter 9

Faith in Action!

Catholic Social Teaching Principle: Rights and Responsibilities of the Human Person

Chapter 7: The Image of God

 **Let Us Pray**

Leader: All-knowing God, teach us your works.
"You formed my inmost being;
  you knit me in my mother's womb.
I praise you, so wonderfully you made me;
  wonderful are your works!"

Psalm 139:13–14

All: All-knowing God, teach us your works. Amen.

Activity — Let's Begin

Everybody Says

Everybody says / I look just like my mother.
Everybody says / I'm the image of Aunt Bee.
Everybody says / My nose is like my father's.
But I want to look like me.

Dorothy Aldis

Think of a special person whom you want to be like.

What qualities of that person do you already have?

_____
_____

What qualities of that person would you like to have in the future?

_____
_____

Write a Narrative On a separate sheet of paper, describe a "typical" day ten years in your future.

Explore

Seekers of God

 **Focus** What do the gifts of the magi tell you about Jesus?

This is a story about people who looked for signs of God and found a newborn king in a surprising place.

A SCRIPTURE PLAY

The Magi

Scene 1

Narrator: Long ago in kingdoms of the East, three wise men searched for God's truth by studying the skies.

Caspar: Have you ever seen anything like this star?

Melchior: No, it's amazing. Where exactly is it? What does it mean?

Balthasar: Caspar! Melchior!

Caspar: Balthasar! What are you doing here?

Balthasar: I was going to ask you the same question, friend!

Melchior: Caspar has come to see me about a great star. We have been following its movements.

Balthasar: I saw the same star. I have charted all the constellations that meet at this one point in the sky. Look! *[He unrolls a chart and points to several stars and planets.]* These stars stand for kingship; and this one, rising, stands for birth!

Caspar: God may be saying that a great king has been born.
Melchior: We must go now to take gifts to this king and give honor to him.

Scene 2
Narrator: Guided by the star, the magi traveled far from home, finally arriving in Judea.
Balthasar: This is an out-of-the-way place! Where are we now?
Caspar: Melchior, are we really going to find a king in such humble surroundings?
Melchior: Caspar, you know how God works.
Balthasar: The first rays of the morning sun don't show the full light of day, but you know it is coming. I predict that this child's life and death will be extraordinary. So I brought him myrrh—fragrant oil to anoint for burial.
Melchior: That is why I brought the gift of frankincense so to worship his divinity.
Caspar: I brought gold because this child is a king.
Balthasar: Come, let us enter here beneath the stars.

The magi enter and silently place their gifts before the child.

Narrator: Far from their own countries and culture, the magi found a Jewish baby whose greatness would change the world.

❓ There is a saying: "Wise people still seek him." When or how do you seek God?

Activity — Share Your Faith

Reflect: Your good works are your gifts for Jesus. Think about some of the good things you have done in your life.

Share: Share with a partner two of the good things you have done.

Act: Write your two examples below, and add a third good work that you will do this week.

_____
_____
_____

Explore

In God's Image

 **Focus** What does it mean to be an image of God?

The magi saw a human baby who they thought would be the king of the Jews. But Jesus is even greater than the wise men could have known. He is both God and man, and he came to earth not only for the Jewish people, but for all people.

The mystery of how the Son of God, the second Person of the Blessed Trinity, took on a human nature is called the **Incarnation**. The word *incarnation* means "coming into flesh."

The Church calls the Incarnation a mystery because it can be understood only through faith. In faith Christians believe that Jesus is both fully **divine** and fully human at the same time. Jesus is both true God and true man. Jesus is the perfect image of God because he is God. Sometimes he is called the sacrament of God because he makes God truly present among us. To meet Jesus is to meet God.

The name *Jesus* means "God saves." Jesus saved all people from the power of sin and everlasting death, and so he is rightly called the Savior of the world.

❓ **What are some things you have learned about God through the teachings of Jesus?**

Madonna and Child, Lorenzo di Credi

God's Image in You

Jesus reveals God fully. In his ministry, Jesus set out to love, heal, and forgive—to show that God is with his people. All people are made in the image of God because they are created by God. If you try, you can see traces of the Trinity reflected in every person. When people love one another, they reflect the communion of three Persons in one God.

❓ How do some of the people you know show that they are images of God?

❓ What do you learn about God through them?

Signs of God's Love

You are created in God's image. But original sin blurred that image. In the Sacrament of Baptism you are united to Christ and are fully restored to God's image. You are given God's very life and the grace to be a living image of Christ every day.

Every time you offer help, every time you are a good listener, every time you forgive someone, every time you look for the good in others, you are following Jesus' example and are being a sign of God's love to the world. Your dignity as a child of God becomes clearer the more you become like Jesus. The more you cooperate with God's grace and the more you care for others, the more you reflect God's image. Jesus is the image of God, and, in a very real way, so are you.

Words of Faith

The **Incarnation** is the mystery that the Son of God took on a human nature in order to save all people.

Divine means God, like God, or of God. Sometimes God is referred to as *The Divine*.

Activity — Connect Your Faith

Show the Face of God Imagine that you are directing a film showing how young people reflect God's image. On a separate sheet of paper, illustrate a scene that you have decided to include in the film.

Titles of Jesus

◎ Focus Who is Jesus?

When you call Jesus *Savior*, you affirm the good news that Jesus came to save all people and give them everlasting life. Jesus has been given many titles, and each one teaches something about who he is. You may have heard Jesus referred to as the Lamb of God, the Good Shepherd, or the Son of Man.

The Many Faces of Christ

Read the following scripture passages to learn some of the titles given to Jesus. Reflect on them, and see how they expand your understanding of who Jesus is. Remember, Christians use some titles from the Old Testament as titles for Jesus. Write the title of Jesus on the line after the scripture reference.

Matthew 1:23

_____

Mark 1:1

_____

Luke 2:11

_____

Isaiah 9:5

_____

❓ **What human qualities do these titles suggest?**

❓ **What divine qualities do they suggest?**

❓ **What title would you give Jesus as your personal friend?**

Activity

Make a Mural Think of titles of Jesus that you have found in Scripture or that you have made up. Then choose the one that best describes how you think of Jesus. Draw a picture illustrating your choice in the space below, and write the title on the banner. Make a mural of all of the pictures drawn in the class.

Celebration of the Word

 **Let Us Pray**

Gather and begin with the Sign of the Cross.

Leader: Lord Jesus, we thank you for coming among us to show us who God the Father is. Thank you for becoming like us so that we can become more like you. Open our hearts now to listen to God's word.

Reader 1: A reading from Paul's Letter to the Colossians.

Read Colossians 2:6–10.

The word of the Lord.

All: **Thanks be to God.**

Sing together the refrain after each reader's part.

Come, O Lord, change our hearts!
Emmanuel, God is with us.

Advent Gathering: "Make Ready the Way/Come, O Lord"
© 1997, David Haas, GIA Publications, Inc.

Reader 2: Praise to you, Emmanuel, God with Us, for you show us the compassion and love of God.

All: **Praise to you, Prince of Peace, for you offer peace to every heart and every place.**

Reader 3: Praise to you, Good Shepherd, for you guide us to safety and you lay down your life for your sheep.

All: **Praise to you, Savior of the World, for you did not abandon us to the power of sin, but came among us to save us and set us free.**

Leader: Let us pray.

Bow your heads as the leader prays.

All: **Amen.**

The Good Shepherd,
Philippe De Champaigne

CHAPTER 7
Review

A **Work with Words** Match each description in Column 1 with the correct term in Column 2.

Column 1

_____ 1. This term describes Jesus, the second Person of the Holy Trinity, who became a human being to offer salvation to all people.

_____ 2. This is the mystery by which the second Person of the Holy Trinity took on human nature.

_____ 3. This means God, like God or of God.

_____ 4. Their story indicates that Jesus' message of salvation is for all people.

_____ 5. This fully restores you to God's image and gives you his very life.

Column 2

a. Incarnation
b. magi
c. Sacrament of Baptism
d. divine
e. Savior

B **Make Connections** Write a brief response to each question or statement.

6. Explain the meaning of the gifts that the magi brought.
   _____

7. Why is Jesus the "perfect image of God"?
   _____

8. What is the connection between the Trinity and Jesus' command to love?
   _____

9. How do you become a sign of God's love to the world?
   _____

10. Name the title of Jesus that is most meaningful to you, and explain why.
    _____
    _____
    _____
    _____

UNIT 3: CHAPTER 7
Family Faith

Catholics Believe

- The Incarnation is the belief that the Son of God became man in order to save all people.
- Jesus is both human and divine, truly God and truly human.

✝ SCRIPTURE

Read *Colossians 1:15–20* to find a poem about the image of Christ.

GO online www.osvcurriculum.com
For weekly scripture readings and seasonal resources

Activity
Live Your Faith

Pray with an Image What images of Jesus do you have in your home and in your parish? Images could include a picture, an icon, or a crucifix. Ask each family member to name his or her favorite image and explain why it is a favorite. Use an image of Jesus as the center of a family prayer this week.

People of Faith

Baptized Vicenta, but known in religious life as **María de la Encarnación del Corazón de Jesús** (Mary of the Incarnation of the Heart of Jesus), this courageous sister was the first Guatemalan woman to be named "Blessed." Political unrest and religious persecution often made María Encarnación a refugee, but she accomplished much good despite many hardships. She reformed her order, founded schools and orphanages, and established the first women's college in Costa Rica. Her feast day is April 18.

▲ Blessed María Vicenta Rosal Vásquez 1820–1886

Family Prayer

Blessed María, pray for us that we may live in imitation of Jesus, as you did, and that the people of Guatemala may continually receive the blessings of your intercession with our Father in heaven. Amen.

© Our Sunday Visitor Curriculum Division

In Unit 3 your child is learning about Jesus Christ.

CCC See Catechism of the Catholic Church 461–464, 470, 483 for further reading on chapter content.

Chapter 8: Proclaim the Kingdom

Let Us Pray

Leader: Show us your ways, O Lord.

"Guide me in your truth and teach me, for you are God my savior."

Psalm 25:5

All: Show us your ways, O Lord. Amen.

Activity

Let's Begin

● **A Good Story** What kinds of stories do you like? Check your favorite kinds from this list.

- ☐ mysteries
- ☐ adventure stories
- ☐ fables
- ☐ fantasy
- ☐ true stories
- ☐ folktales
- ☐ biographies
- ☐ stories about history

Think about one of your favorite stories.

Why do you like it?

_____

Where have you learned your favorite stories?

_____

With whom do you share your favorite stories?

_____

● **Draw and Tell** Draw a scene from your favorite story, and then use your drawing to tell the story to a partner.

123

Explore

The Power of Stories

 **Focus** How did Jesus teach about the kingdom?

Some amazing things can happen when people tell stories. Martin Buber was a Jewish philosopher in the twentieth century. In his writings, he describes a time when his grandfather showed the power of a good story.

"A story must be told in such a way that it constitutes help in itself. My grandfather was lame. Once he was asked to tell a story about his teacher. And he related how his teacher used to hop and dance while he prayed. My grandfather rose as he spoke, and he was so swept away by his story that he began to hop and dance to show what the master had done. From that hour he was cured of his lameness. That's how to tell a story."

❓ **What is Martin Buber trying to teach about good storytelling?**

Paths to Understanding

When Jesus told his followers stories of the **kingdom of God**, wonderful things happened. As they listened to Jesus, people understood better what they had to do to enter God's kingdom. Many decided to change the way they lived. Then, as they shared Jesus' stories with others, their faith became stronger.

Because Jesus was a great teacher, he understood that people remember important ideas better when they are expressed in an interesting way. That's why Jesus used stories to spread his message and to invite people into God's reign of justice, love, and peace.

❓ **How can retelling Jesus' stories help your faith grow stronger?**

Examples

Jesus told many stories that are known as ==parables==. A parable is a story that makes a comparison by using examples from everyday life to bring to light something that is hidden. Here is one example that Jesus used to show what it means to be open to the word of God so that you can enter his kingdom.

SCRIPTURE
Luke 8:5–8

The Parable of the Sower

A sower went out to sow. As he sowed, some seed fell on the path, and birds came and ate it. Some seed fell on rocky ground, where it had little soil. It sprang up at once because the soil was not deep; but when the sun rose, the seed was scorched, and it withered for lack of roots. Some seed fell among thorns, and the thorns grew up and choked it. But other seed fell on rich soil, and produced fruit, as much as a hundredfold. Whoever has ears ought to hear.

Based on *Luke 8:5–8*

- In this parable, who is the sower?
- What do the seeds represent?
- What can help the seed grow and bear fruit?

Words of Faith

The **kingdom of God** is God's reign of justice, love, and peace. Jesus came to bring the kingdom of God, which is both present now and yet to come.

Parables are stories that make comparisons in order to teach something. Jesus used parables to teach about the kingdom of God.

Activity

Reflect: Read about other images for the kingdom of God in *Matthew 13:44–50*.

Share: Choose one of the images, and discuss with a partner why you chose it.

Act: On a separate sheet of paper, write a saying that will help others know what the kingdom of God is like. Then sketch the image you have chosen.

Signs and Wonders

Focus What are signs of the kingdom of God?

Jesus proclaimed the kingdom of God in many ways. He preached the good news. He told stories and parables about the kingdom. He also performed signs and wonders, or **miracles**, as ways of showing that God's kingdom was being established. These miracles included casting out demons and curing people who were sick.

Jesus himself was a proclamation of the kingdom. He welcomed sinners and ate with them, showing that forgiveness is part of the kingdom. He paid attention to children, to women, to lepers, to those from other lands, and to others who were often ignored. He showed that everyone is invited into God's kingdom, which will come in fullness at the end of time when Christ returns in glory.

Through his stories and signs, Jesus taught that God's kingdom is not a faraway, imaginary land. It is real, and it is here with you now. However, not everyone lives in the way that God intends. Whenever you cooperate with God's grace by loving, acting justly, or making peace, you help the reign of God come in its fullness.

❓ **What are some ways that Jesus proclaimed the kingdom of God?**

❓ **What person do you know who is doing Jesus' work today?**

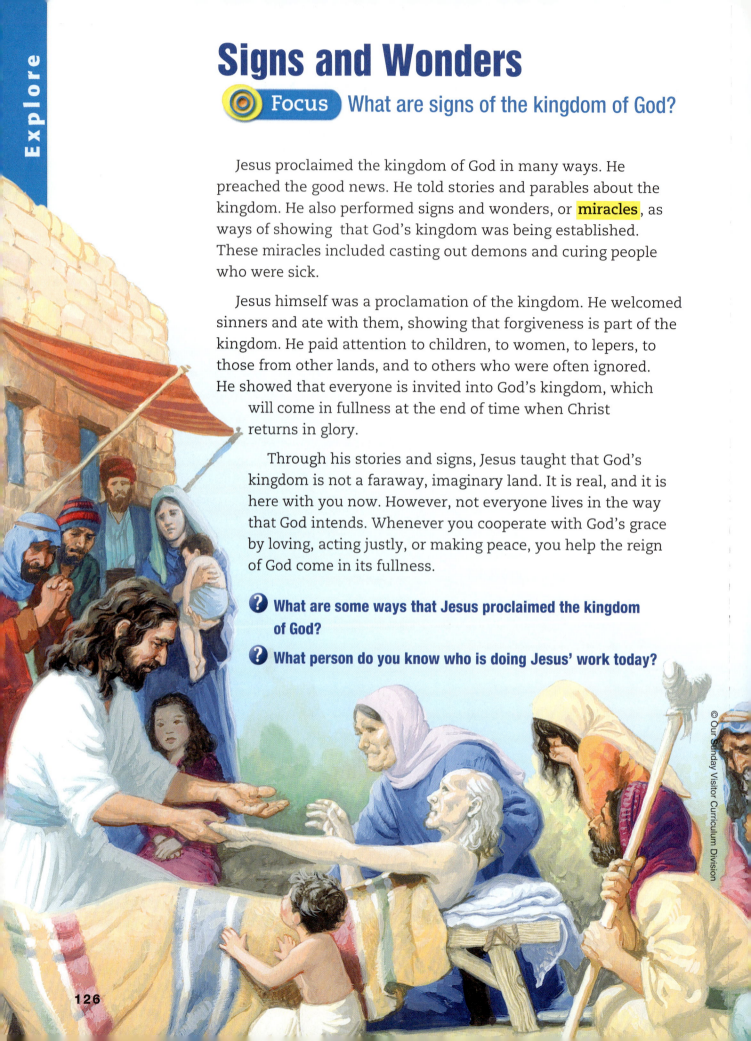

Sacramental Living

Jesus Christ is present in the world today, working signs and wonders. The Church and its sacraments keep the words and actions of Jesus present in your life. The sacraments have the power to change the way in which you relate to God and others.

You can be changed as you gather with the Church community to hear the word of God and experience the power of the Holy Spirit through the words and actions of the sacraments. The Scripture readings you hear and the prayers you pray invite you to become a part of God's kingdom.

You can be changed at Eucharist when, through the actions of the priest, you and the assembled community offer praise and thanksgiving to God for the gift of his Son. When the priest says at the end of Mass, "Go in peace to love and serve the Lord," he is sending you in the name of Jesus to be a sign of Jesus to the world.

When you have sinned, God calls you to experience **conversion**. With God's help you can change your heart and place your sin before him. In the Sacrament of Reconciliation, you receive God's grace and forgiveness through the ministry of the Church. You are renewed and strengthened to live a moral life that draws you ever closer to God and into service for his kingdom.

Words of Faith

The **miracles** of Jesus are signs and wonders of the divine power that help you see the presence of the kingdom of God.

Conversion is the process of turning away from sin and toward God and his ways. It is a response to God's love and forgiveness.

Activity: Connect Your Faith

Keep an Open Heart Around the outside of the heart, write some things that keep you from hearing the message of Jesus. Inside the heart, write a few words that tell which story of Jesus has helped you understand his message most clearly.

Explore

Understanding Parables

 **Focus** How can you understand what a parable means?

To understand the message of the parables Jesus told, you need to consider how parables work. Here are some points to look for.

Answers a Question
A parable may give **an answer to a question,** such as "Who is my neighbor?" or "How often must I forgive?" The answer to the question is what the parable is intended to teach.

Compares Two Things
Jesus' parables often begin with the words "The kingdom of heaven is like . . ." The parable **compares two things.**

Uses Examples from Everyday Life
The setting and characters of a parable are taken from **everyday life.** The places and people in a parable were familiar to the people listening to Jesus. For example, many of the parables of Jesus are about people who work in fields or on farms. That is because many people in Jesus' time did such work. Many of those references are known by people today, too.

Reveals a Hidden Truth
Often, a parable has a surprise ending. The parable **reveals a hidden truth.** This is the surprise.

Prompts Decision or Action
A parable challenges its listeners to **decide or act.** "What will *you* do now?" is the question the parable leaves you to answer. The question is understood rather than stated.

❓ **What is your favorite parable?**

❓ **What can you learn from this parable by reading it carefully?**

Activity — Live Your Faith

Plan a Parable Drama Working in a small group, read the parable that your teacher assigns to your group from the following passages.

Matthew 13:47–48   Matthew 20:1–16   Matthew 25:1–13
Luke 8:16–17   Luke 10:29–37   Luke 14:15–24

After you have read the parable, decide how to dramatize it.

WHO? _____
_____

WHAT? _____
_____

WHEN? _____
_____

WHERE? _____
_____

WHY? _____
_____

What's your part?
_____
_____

Explain how your parable fits the characteristics on the previous page.
_____
_____
_____
_____

Tell the class how the parable is an example of the characteristics on the previous page.

Celebrate

Celebration of the Word

 Let Us Pray

Gather and begin with the Sign of the Cross.

Leader: Brothers and sisters, Jesus invites us into God's kingdom of justice, love, and peace. Let us pray.

O God, open our hearts to hear your word of life, and help us respond to it in action. We ask this through Christ our Lord.

All: **Amen.**

Reader: A reading from the prophet Isaiah.

Read Isaiah 55:10–11.

The word of the Lord.

All: **Thanks be to God.**

Sing together.

Bring forth the Kingdom of mercy,
Bring forth the Kingdom of peace;
Bring forth the Kingdom of justice,
Bring forth the City of God!

"Bring Forth the Kingdom", Marty Haugen © 1986, GIA Publications, Inc.

Leader: Let us pray.

All raise hands and pray the Lord's Prayer.

Leader: Now let us go in peace.

All: **Thanks be to God.**

CHAPTER 8
Review

A **Work with Words** Complete each sentence with the correct term from the Word Bank.

WORD BANK
conversion
kingdom of God
miracles
parables
philosopher
sower
moral life

1. The _____ of Jesus are signs and wonders of the divine power that help you see the presence of the reign of God.

2. _____ are stories that make comparisons in order to teach something.

3. _____ is the process of turning away from sin and toward God and his ways.

4. Martin Buber was a _____ who told about how his grandfather benefited from storytelling.

5. The _____ is God's reign of justice, love, and peace.

B **Check Understanding** Fill in the circle next to the correct response.

6. The mighty deeds of Jesus, the signs of the kingdom, are called _____.
   ○ parables   ○ feats   ○ miracles
   ○ sacraments   ○ mysteries

7. Through his stories and actions, Jesus invited people into the _____.
   ○ temple   ○ kingdom of God   ○ inn
   ○ Trinity   ○ desert

8. The _____ of the Church continue to pass on the words and actions of Jesus and point to the kingdom of God.
   ○ virtues   ○ prophets   ○ sacraments
   ○ rulers   ○ writings

9. Telling a story is a good way to _____.
   ○ rest   ○ learn   ○ love God
   ○ make friends   ○ teach

10. Jesus did all of these to tell about the reign of God except _____.
    ○ tell parables   ○ set an example   ○ work miracles
    ○ preach   ○ fast

UNIT 3: CHAPTER 8
Family Faith

Catholics Believe

- God's kingdom is present and grows in the Church and its sacraments until God's reign comes in fullness at the end of time.
- Jesus proclaimed the kingdom of God through his actions and parables.

SCRIPTURE

Read *Matthew 6:25–34* to learn how to seek the kingdom of God.

www.osvcurriculum.com
For weekly scripture readings and seasonal resources

Activity
Live Your Faith

See God at Home Create a kingdom collage for your refrigerator or kitchen bulletin board. During the week, collect photos and stories from newspapers and magazines that show evidence of the reign of God in the world. If a member of the family does something that reveals God's goodness, add a photo or a few words about him or her to the collage.

People of Faith

▲ Saint Marguerite Bourgeoys 1620–1700

Marguerite Bourgeoys is a hero of early Canadian history. In 1653, inspired by a desire to serve God, she left France to become the first schoolteacher in a tiny French settlement. In a stable that was both her school and her home, she taught the children of colonists and of Native Americans. She also taught young women the skills needed for living in the Canadian wilderness. Because of her love for people and her readiness to help them, she was called "Sister Marguerite" by those she served. Her feast day is January 12.

Family Prayer

Saint Marguerite, pray for us that we may proclaim Jesus with our words and actions. May we follow your example of service to those who have the greatest need and the least power. Amen.

© Our Sunday Visitor Curriculum Division

In Unit 3 your child is learning about JESUS CHRIST.

CCC See *Catechism of the Catholic Church* 546–547, 567, 763–769 for further reading on chapter content.

Chapter 9 New Life

 **Let Us Pray**

Leader: Eternal God, we want to walk your path.

"I shall walk before the Lord
in the land of the living."
Psalm 116:9

All: Eternal God, we want to walk your path. Amen.

 Activity

● **Endings** Nobody looks forward to suffering. Everyone who enjoys life would like it to go on and on. Yet, even in the midst of life, you experience different kinds of suffering and death all the time. You may know the suffering that comes from failure or from being left out. You may experience a kind of death if you move to another town or say good-bye to a good friend. You may even have been separated from someone you love because of death.

Now think about a situation of suffering or death you have witnessed or experienced in your own life.

How were you affected by the experience?

_____
_____

Who or what helped you get through the experience?

_____
_____

✏️ **Say Good-bye** Imagine that your best friend is moving away. Write a letter on a separate sheet of paper, telling your friend what you will miss most.

A Valiant Witness

 **Focus** How did Archbishop Romero witness to Jesus' message of love for all?

Faith Fact
Oscar Romero began studying for a vocation to the priesthood at the age of thirteen.

In El Salvador, a country in Central America, no one expected the quiet Archbishop Oscar Romero to become a champion of those who were poor. But the situation of the people he served was so desperate that he dedicated himself to helping them.

BIOGRAPHY

The Shepherd Speaks Out

Those who worked for justice in El Salvador were often attacked by bands of armed men called "death squads." One day a Jesuit priest and two other people working among those who were poor were murdered by one of the death squads. Archbishop Romero protested the killings and led a peaceful march to take back the town from the army that had overrun it.

Many times the archbishop was told that his life was in danger, but he never stopped speaking out for justice. He said, "If they kill me, I shall rise again in the Salvadoran people."

❓ What do you think the archbishop meant by his statement?

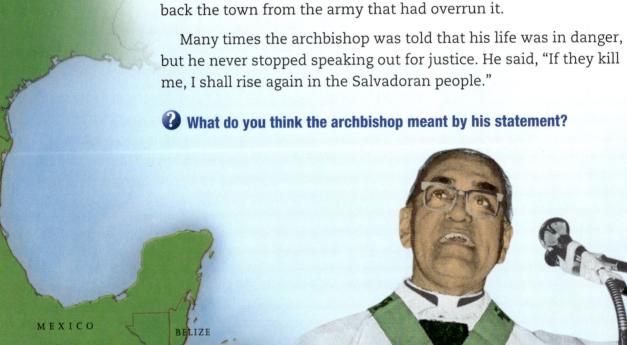

From Death to New Life

Archbishop Romero used his radio program to beg members of the death squads to lay down their weapons. In his last public address, he called on the government to stop the violence. The day after he made this appeal, he was shot dead as he stood at the altar celebrating Mass.

The funeral on March 30, 1980, became the occasion for the largest popular demonstration ever seen in El Salvador. The struggle of the Salvadoran people for justice began to gain more international attention. Archbishop Romero's insights were appreciated in a new way because he had given his life for the people. His words and witness, his life and death, continue to inspire those who work for justice in El Salvador and around the world.

Archbishop Romero believed in Jesus and his message of love so strongly that nothing could keep him from speaking that message, not even fear of death. Death had no power over him because he knew that he would live forever with God.

Activity — Share Your Faith

Reflect: Think about the courage Archbishop Romero showed when he led the protest.

Share: With a partner, list times when young people today show courage.

Act: Write three sentences stating how the story of Archbishop Romero is a reflection of something that Jesus taught.

_____
_____
_____
_____

© Our Sunday Visitor Curriculum Division

Explore

Sacramental Sacrifice

 **Focus** What is the Paschal mystery, and how is it celebrated?

Because of original sin, life on earth includes suffering and death. The good news is that Jesus broke the power of evil by choosing to suffer and die on the cross. He is the Redeemer of the human race, bringing it back from the slavery of sin and everlasting death. The Gospel of Luke tells us that the Resurrection was first discovered and announced by several women who were followers of Jesus.

 SCRIPTURE Luke 24:5–9

The Resurrection of Jesus

They [the angels] said to [the women], "Why do you seek the living one among the dead? He is not here, but he has been raised. Remember what he said to you while he was still in Galilee, that the Son of Man must be handed over to sinners and be crucified, and rise on the third day." And they remembered his words. Then they returned from the tomb and announced all these things to the eleven and to all the others.

Luke 24:5–9

The Paschal Mystery

The Resurrection is the cornerstone of the Paschal mystery. The Paschal mystery refers to the Passion, death, Resurrection, and Ascension of Jesus. Because of it, Christians live in hope. You participate in the Paschal mystery. You are united to this mystery through the grace of the Holy Spirit that you first received in the Sacrament of Baptism and that you celebrate in the Sacrament of Eucharist.

Death is not the end but the beginning of life forever with God. Every Sunday is a day of joy as the Church remembers the Resurrection of Jesus. Because of the Resurrection, Christians believe that Jesus will one day return in glory.

Resurrection of Christ, Mathis Gruenewald

The Celebration of the Mystery

Each of the sacraments celebrates, in some way, the Paschal mystery of Jesus' dying and rising to new life. Each sacrament offers a new way of looking at the mystery of your life. Jesus, who died and was raised, is at work in and through the sacraments.

Words of Faith

The **Paschal mystery** is Christ's work of redemption through his Passion, death, Resurrection, and Ascension.

BAPTISM
You die with Christ in the waters of Baptism, and then you are raised to the new life of grace.

CONFIRMATION
You die to selfishness and live in compassion as the Holy Spirit moves you to acts of charity and service.

HOLY ORDERS
You die to selfishness in your own will and needs and are raised to a new life of ordained ministry to God's people.

EUCHARIST
This sacrificial meal is the greatest celebration of the Paschal mystery. You enter into Jesus' saving death and Resurrection. You are raised and sent forth to serve God as Jesus did.

MATRIMONY
You rise to new life in a family as you become one with another.

RECONCILIATION
You die to sin and are raised to new life in forgiveness and community.

ANOINTING OF THE SICK
You become one with Jesus' suffering and death and rise to renewed health or pass over to eternal life.

Activity: Connect Your Faith

Role-Play the Resurrection Story With your group, act out the story of the discovery of Jesus' Resurrection as recorded in *Luke 24:1–12*. When you have finished the role-play, imagine that you are one of the first disciples and write a message to a friend, telling what you have seen and what it means.

_____
_____
_____
_____

Explore

Images of the Paschal Mystery

 **Focus** What images remind you of Jesus' death and Resurrection?

The Paschal mystery is central to the Catholic faith, and the Church uses art and design to illustrate this truth.

Symbols of Victory

Cross and Shroud

In the empty tomb, the disciples found only a burial cloth.

A white cloth hanging over the cross is a symbol of Christ's death and Resurrection.

Paschal Candle

This large candle is a symbol of Christ and the new life of the Resurrection.

The five grains of incense in the candle recall his five wounds.

Risen Christ on the Cross

These crucifixes display the risen Savior.

His arms extend to embrace the world he has redeemed.

Baptismal Font

The vessel of water for Baptism is a symbol of the Paschal mystery.

Through Baptism, you share in the Paschal mystery and receive new life. (See *Romans* 6:4.)

Victorious Lamb

Christ is compared to the Passover lamb, whose blood saved the people.

A victory pennant, held high by the lamb, symbolizes the Resurrection.

? How do these symbols help you think about the Paschal mystery?

Activity: Live Your Faith

Solve the crossword puzzle.

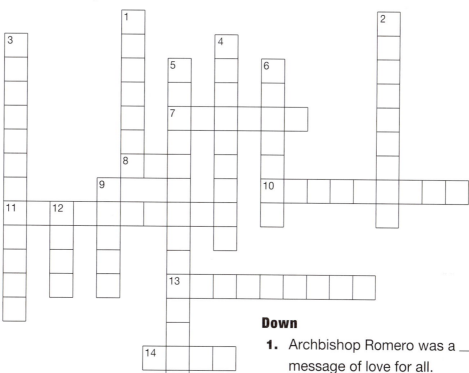

Across

7. The cross represents the death of _____.
8. The Lamb is victorious because Christ has conquered _____.
10. The Paschal mystery is Jesus' Passion, death, Resurrection, and _____.
11. Those who are confirmed join the Risen Christ by dying to selfishness and living in _____ through charity and service.
13. The Sacrament of the _____ of the Sick offers the hope of renewal.
14. The shroud on the cross represents the one found in the empty _____.

Down

1. Archbishop Romero was a _____ to Jesus' message of love for all.
2. The _____ is the greatest celebration of the Paschal mystery.
3. Images of the Paschal mystery strengthen Christians' faith in the _____.
4. Two sacraments of service are Holy Orders and _____.
5. Through Christ's victory, sins are forgiven in the Sacrament of _____.
6. The grains of incense in the _____ candle represent Christ's wounds.
9. The baptismal font contains the _____ through which the Paschal mystery is shared.
12. The Paschal candle burns during every _____ of the Easter season.

As a class, make posters of the images of the Paschal mystery. Place them in a common area of your school, such as a meeting hall or cafeteria. These pictures will speak to your school community about the saving effects of joining the Risen Christ on the cross by dying to selfishness and living in charity and compassion.

139

Prayer of Praise

 Let Us Pray

Gather and begin with the Sign of the Cross.

Leader: Jesus, you are risen from the dead and call us to walk in newness of life. We trust in you. We shall not fear.

Reader 1: We shall not fear the lightning or thunder, the roar of the sea, or the trembling of the earth.

All: Alleluia.

Reader 2: We shall not fear the dark of night, the emptiness of silence, or the times of being alone.

All: Alleluia.

Reader 3: We shall not fear the jeers of our enemies or the smallness and meanness of those who wish us harm.

All: Alleluia.

Leader: Yes, Lord, by embracing death for our sake, you have shown us that death cannot overcome the power of life. By your glorious Resurrection you have conquered sin and death, and you give us the courage to sing:

Sing together.

Alleluia, alleluia, give thanks to the risen Lord.
Alleluia, alleluia, give praise to his name.

"Alleluia No. 1," Donald Fishel, © 1973, Word of God Music.

CHAPTER 9
Review

A **Work with Words** Match each description in Column 1 with the correct term in Column 2.

Column 1

_____ 1. protested killings and was murdered because of his opposition to the death squads

_____ 2. asked the women at the tomb why they were seeking Jesus among the dead

_____ 3. refers to the passion, death, Resurrection, and Ascension of Jesus

_____ 4. rising to new life in a family as you become one with another

_____ 5. the greatest celebration of the Paschal mystery

Column 2

a. Matrimony
b. Paschal mystery
c. Archbishop Oscar Romero
d. Eucharist
e. angels

B **Check Understanding** Cross out any incorrect answers you find in the items below.

6. Christ communicates the saving effects of his Paschal mystery through the sacraments, such as (Baptism, Confirmation, Thanksgiving, Reconciliation).

7. (a baptismal font, bread and wine, the cross and shroud, the Paschal candle) are images of the Paschal mystery.

8. All people need Christ the Redeemer to free them from (bondage to sin, the reign of death, mistakes they have made).

9. Jesus' suffering and death on the cross means that you can (avoid all suffering in this life, live forever with God, share in the Paschal mystery).

10. Jesus' Resurrection is (remembered at Mass every Sunday, less important than other truths of the Catholic faith, a part of the Paschal mystery).

UNIT 3: CHAPTER 9
Family Faith

Catholics Believe

- Through the sacraments, Christ unites his followers to his Passion, death, Resurrection, and Ascension.
- Jesus Christ is the Redeemer of the human race.

SCRIPTURE

Read *Psalm 41:1–4* to see how God responds to people who are concerned about those who are poor.

GO online www.osvcurriculum.com
For weekly scripture readings and seasonal resources

Activity
Live Your Faith

Visit the Sick Loneliness, illness, and disability are found everywhere. Encourage family members to pray each evening for those who need help. Locate someone who could use your help, perhaps in a local care center. Think of ways to bring encouragement and cheer to that person. Consider a visit, a gift, a song, a flower arrangement, or some other sign of interest and caring. Carry out your plan.

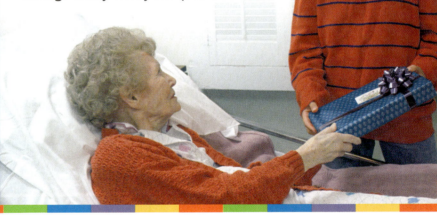

People of Faith

▲ Saint Paul Miki
c. 1564–1597

In the sixteenth century, missionaries took the Catholic faith to Japan. **Paul Miki** was one who accepted Catholic teachings. He joined the Jesuits and became a great preacher, persuading many to become Christians. In 1597, Japan's ruler turned against the Christian mission and executed twenty-six Christians, including Paul Miki. They were tied to crosses and then stabbed. Like Jesus, Paul Miki forgave and prayed for his persecutors while hanging on a cross. His feast day is February 6.

Family Prayer

Saint Paul Miki, pray for us that we may be fearless witnesses to Jesus and may be forgiving of others, as you were. May we follow your example in accepting the cross in imitation of Jesus our Savior. Amen.

© Our Sunday Visitor Curriculum Division

In Unit 3 your child is learning about Jesus Christ.
CCC See *Catechism of the Catholic Church* 515, 571, 618, 628, 654, 655, 1002, 1003, 1010, 1067, 1076, 1085 for further reading on chapter content.

DISCOVER

Catholic Social Teaching:

Rights and Responsibilities of the Human Person

Faith in Action!
CATHOLIC SOCIAL TEACHING

In this unit you learned that God's image appears in many different ways. You have the right to be respected because you are made in the image of God. You have the responsibility to respect the rights of others because they are made in God's image, too.

Respect People's Rights

When you love, act justly, and make peace, you are building the kingdom of God. You are also respecting your own and others' right to live according to God's plan. Although you may not realize it, every day you meet situations that involve the rights of others.

- You respect your classmates' right to privacy when you respect their space and belongings.
- You respect your classmates' right to an education when you participate in class and share your ideas.
- You respect your classmates' right to a safe environment when you settle conflicts peacefully.

Learning to deal with conflict without violence, anger, or bullying is both a right and a responsibility. It is one way to follow God's law of love.

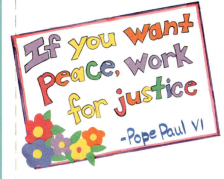

If you want peace, work for justice —Pope Paul VI

❓ **In what ways can you see the rights of others being violated in your school and neighborhood?**

❓ **When is it difficult to see God's image in others?**

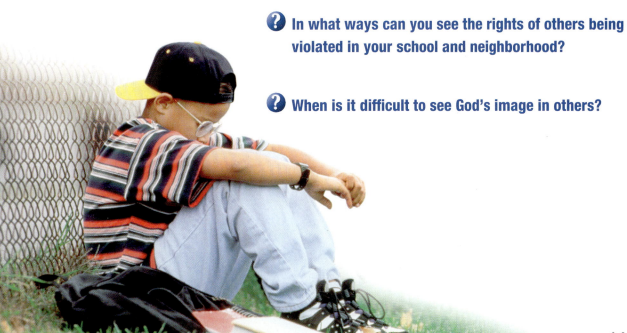

CONNECT
With the Call to Justice

Peace by PEACE

Francelia Butler was a professor who saw that children have problems with conflict, competition, and rivalry. She asked students to invent games that could teach children to cooperate and negotiate instead of fight. In 1990 Professor Butler launched the International Peace Games Festival. More than 2,000 elementary schoolteachers and their students participated in games and workshops to help them understand how to settle fights and arguments peacefully. As a result of Professor Butler's work, peace games festivals have been held throughout the United States.

When Francelia Butler died in 1998, her students created an international student-run organization called Peace by PEACE (Playful Explorations in Active Conflict-resolution Education) to carry on the work that Butler had started. Peace by PEACE trains volunteers to work in schools. They teach students what to do before a fight starts. They help students understand that having conflicts is not wrong, but that problems occur when students don't know how to handle the conflict. These college students understand what it is like to be bullied, and they work very hard to stop bullies from hurting others.

It is difficult to know just how to stop bullying and violence in schools, but many organizations are working to find ways to help. Let's learn about one of them.

❓ **What kinds of things do you think Professor Butler discovered about children?**

Reach Out!

SERVE Your Community

Do It Differently

In the space below, write an example of a time when you felt a lack of respect from others. Describe to a partner how you felt when it happened.

_____
_____
_____
_____

With your partner, role-play the examples in the way you wish they had happened.

Now write an example of a time when you did not treat others with respect. Describe what happened to your partner.

_____
_____
_____
_____

Explain below what you should have done differently.

_____
_____
_____
_____

Make a Difference

Launch a Campaign In small groups, brainstorm ways that you can eliminate bullying in your school. Choose your best ideas, and explain them to the whole class. List ideas that everyone can use to help anyone who is being bullied. Let volunteers role-play ways of handling such situations. Post the ideas in your classroom as a reminder. As a class, pledge to show support for people who are bullied. Find ways to let other classes know what you are doing, and get them involved as well.

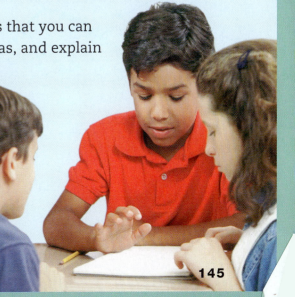

UNIT 3 REVIEW

A **Work with Words** Match each description in Column 1 with the correct term in Column 2.

Column 1

_____ 1. Christ's work of redemption through his Passion, death, Resurrection, and Ascension

_____ 2. By this you die to selfishness and live in compassion as the Holy Spirit moves you to acts of charity and service

_____ 3. Stories that make comparisons in order to teach a lesson

_____ 4. The mystery that the Son of God took on a human nature in order to save all people

_____ 5. God's reign of justice, love, and peace

Column 2

a. kingdom of God

b. parables

c. Incarnation

d. Paschal mystery

e. Confirmation

B **Check Understanding** Complete each sentence with the correct term from the Word Bank.

6. You can be _____ as you gather with the Church community to hear the word of God and experience the power of the Holy Spirit through the words and actions of the sacraments.

7. The Church calls the Incarnation a mystery because it can be understood only through _____.

8. Your _____ as a child of God becomes clearer the more you become like Jesus.

9. Archbishop Romero was a _____.

10. Every _____ is a day of joy as the Church remembers the Resurrection.

WORD BANK

Sunday
dignity
hope
martyr
changed
faith

146

Complete the statement or answer the question with the correct word or phrase.

11. "The Divine" is another way of saying _____.

12. Miracles help you see the presence of _____.

13. From what do you turn away by conversion? _____

14. What was the purpose of the magi's gift of myrrh? _____

15. Who received the first news of the Resurrection? _____

C **Make Connections** Write a response to each statement.

16–18. Explain why Jesus himself was a proclamation of God's kingdom, using the following terms:

forgiveness   signs and wonders   preached

_____
_____
_____
_____

19. Choose one of these images of the Paschal mystery (cross and shroud, Paschal candle, or victorious lamb), and explain what it means.

_____
_____
_____
_____

20. Explain why the story of the sower is a parable.

_____
_____
_____
_____

147

Unit 4
The Church

In this unit you will...

learn about the marks of the Church. As members of the Church we are called to show God to others. Together we continue Christ's mission in the world. We are united by our belief in Christ and by the Holy Spirit. With the guidance of the Holy Spirit, the leaders of the Church continue the Apostles' mission to proclaim the good news and bring the kingdom of God to its fullness.

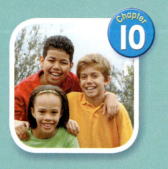
Chapter 10

Chapter 11

Chapter 12

Faith in Action!

Catholic Social Teaching Principle: Dignity of Work and Rights of Workers

Chapter 10: A Sign to the World

 **Let Us Pray**

Leader: Loving Father, unite us in your Son.
"How good it is, how pleasant,
where the people dwell as one!"
Psalm 133:1

All: Loving Father, unite us in your Son. Amen.

 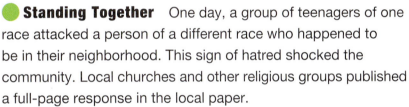

Activity — Let's Begin

● **Standing Together** One day, a group of teenagers of one race attacked a person of a different race who happened to be in their neighborhood. This sign of hatred shocked the community. Local churches and other religious groups published a full-page response in the local paper.

We stand together against every expression of hate. We are committed to building a world where love and respect are shown to all people.

Why is it important for churches and other religious groups to unite in sending a message of justice?

_____
_____
_____

What are some other ways that people could help in such situations?

_____
_____
_____

● **Draw a Picture** You can be a sign of goodwill and harmony. Draw a picture that shows how you can do this.

149

Explore

A New Beginning

 **Focus** Why was the Second Vatican Council important?

The years from 1962 to 1965 were years of a new beginning in the Catholic Church. The bishops gathered in Rome to discuss the meaning of the Church and its role in modern society. Here is how the opening might have been reported in a school newspaper of that time.

Pope John XXIII Opens Vatican Council

October 11, 1962 • by Sandra Ruiz • Pius X High School

Today in Rome, Pope John XXIII opened the Second Vatican Council, a meeting of bishops from Africa, Asia, Europe, Australia, and the Americas. Such a gathering has not occurred since 1870.

Goals of the Council

The goals of the council are to renew the Church's liturgy; to help the Church respond to the problems of today's world, especially the need for peace and justice; to promote unity among all believers; and to find new ways to spread the gospel. Pope John has surprised everyone by asking for this meeting, which will go on for many months. The work of this council is sure to influence the Church in many ways.

© Our Sunday Visitor Curriculum Division

 What more have you heard about the Second Vatican Council?

Observers at the Council

Some people who are not bishops will come to the council as observers. These people will share ideas and help the bishops make decisions. The observers represent Orthodox churches, Protestant denominations, and various other groups. Some women have also been invited to participate.

The Wider World

The Second Vatican Council will be reported worldwide by television, radio, and newspapers. The council's opening address, "Message to Humanity," begins with these words: "We take pleasure in sending to all [people] and nations a message concerning that well-being, love, and peace which were brought into the world by Jesus Christ . . . and entrusted to the Church." The Church is confident that it has a message of good news to share. The world is watching.

Activity — Share Your Faith

Reflect: Imagine that you are a news reporter assigned to cover a new council.

Share: With a small group, decide what questions you would ask the pope, bishops, and observers.

Act: Write three questions that your group thinks are important.

_____
_____
_____

Explore

Welcome to God's Kingdom

 **Focus** In what ways do you help fulfill the mission of the Church?

Pope John XXIII died eight months after he opened the Second Vatican council.

The Second Vatican Council was a sign to the world of the Church's continuing mission to point people toward God's reign. The Church is one, holy, catholic, and apostolic. These are the marks by which all people can see God's kingdom at work in the Church. You, too, are a sign of God's kingdom when you help those in need, forgive those who have hurt you, and welcome new members into the Church. You *are* Church, and you live the faith and witness to the reign of God when you reflect Jesus' love and extend the gift of his salvation.

The Church is an assembly—a gathering of people called the **People of God**. This gathering is also called the **Body of Christ** because, through the Church, Christ is present in the world. The Church is like a building in which the Holy Spirit makes its home. The people are like the stones of the sturdy walls and floor. Jesus is the cornerstone that holds the building together.

SCRIPTURE 1 Peter 2:4–5

Built of Living Stones

Come to [Jesus], a living stone, rejected by human beings but chosen and precious in the sight of God, and, like living stones, let yourselves be built into a spiritual house to be a holy priesthood to offer spiritual sacrifices acceptable to God through Jesus Christ.

1 Peter 2:4–5

❓ **What qualities does a person need to become a sturdy part of the Church?**

© Our Sunday Visitor Curriculum Division

Signs of Unity

The first of the <mark>marks of the Church</mark> is unity—the Church is one. Just as many materials are needed to construct a single building, so are many people brought together to become one in faith. Important signs of the Church's unity are these:

- The oneness of its faith
- Its common celebration of worship, especially in the sacraments
- Its close connection to the Apostles, whose authority has been handed down to the pope and bishops through the Sacrament of Holy Orders.

Yet, throughout history and to this day, divisions in the Church have weakened it as a sign to the world. Therefore, perfect unity is a goal for which the Church must constantly pray and toward which it must work. The Holy Spirit continues to help the Church achieve this goal of oneness by bringing together all the faithful. In the gathering of people of all backgrounds and ways of life, the Church works to create one People of God.

❓ In what ways do you show unity as a member of the Church at home and in school?

Words of Faith

People of God means the Church, called by Christ to share in his mission.

The **Body of Christ** is the Church. Jesus is the head, and his followers are the members.

There are four **marks of the Church**. The Church is one, holy, catholic, and apostolic. These marks, or characteristics, are signs to the world that God's reign is already present, though incomplete.

Activity — Connect Your Faith

Praise God for Unity Working in small groups, write a slogan in praise of the Church's unity. As a group, be ready to recite your slogan for the other groups.

Our group slogan is _____

_____

_____

Explore

Visions of the Church

 **Focus** How do you think of the Church?

The Bible includes a variety of images that describe and help people understand the Church. Each of these reveals a part of the nature of the Church. Together the images give a clearer picture of the mystery of the Church.

The Church in the Bible

Body of Christ
Christ remains present in the world through his body, the Church. Just as the parts of a human body need one another to be whole, so the Church needs each of its members.

People of God
Christians are called the People of God because they are called and chosen by God and because they share in Christ's mission.

Pilgrim People
Pilgrims are people who travel together on a prayerful journey to a holy place. The Church is a pilgrim people journeying to its true home—eternal life with God.

Bride of Christ
The Church is the Bride of Christ. Christ loves and remains with the Church.

❓ Which of these images seems most important to you now?
❓ What gives you the greatest sense of belonging to the Church?

Activity Live Your Faith

Our Parish In small groups, choose one image of the Church from the opposite page and work together to find examples of how your parish resembles that image. Examples can be found in parish bulletins and newsletters and on the parish Web site or bulletin board. Record your findings below, and be prepared to share them with the class.

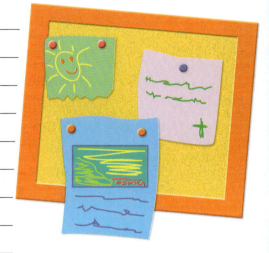

Prayer of Petition

 Let Us Pray

Gather and begin with the Sign of the Cross.

Leader: Every time the members of the Second Vatican Council gathered, they began with a prayer to the Holy Spirit. Today, we too will ask the Holy Spirit to help us be faithful witnesses to Christ and his Church.

Reader 1: We are here before you, O Holy Spirit, conscious of our sins, but united in a special way in your holy name.

All: **Come, and remain with us. Enter our hearts.**

Reader 2: Be the guide of our actions, indicate the path we should take, and show us what we must do so that with your help, our work may be in all things pleasing to you.

All: **Amen.**

Reader 3: O Holy Spirit, you who are infinite justice, never permit us to be disturbers of justice. Unite our hearts to you alone, and do it strongly, so that we may be one in you and not depart in any way from the truth.

All: **Amen.**

Adapted from "Prayer of the Council Fathers"

Leader: The Church is God's building, always being renewed. In it the Holy Spirit dwells. To celebrate our life as the Church, we will sing together now.

Sing together.

Send down the fire of your justice, Send down the rains of your love.

"Send Down the Fire", Marty Haugen, © 1989, GIA Publications, Inc.

CHAPTER 10
Review

A **Work with Words** Circle True if a statement is true, and circle False if a statement is false. Correct any false statements.

1. The People of God is another name for the Church, called by Christ to share in his mission.

   True   False   _____

2. Jesus' followers are the head of the Body of Christ.

   True   False   _____

3. One, holy, catholic, and apostolic are the theological virtues.

   True   False   _____

4. The followers of Jesus are called to be "living stones," just as Jesus himself is.

   True   False   _____

5. The Second Vatican Council was primarily concerned with the Church and its role in the United States.

   True   False   _____

B **Check Understanding** Write a brief response to each statement or question.

6. What did Pope John XXIII do to renew the Church?

   _____

7. What are the bonds of unity in the Church?

   _____

8. How is it possible for people of all backgrounds and ways of life to form one Church?

   _____

9–10. Name and explain two of the four images of the Church.

   _____
   _____
   _____

157

UNIT 4: CHAPTER 10
Family Faith

Catholics Believe

- As members of the Church, we are all united in living out the mission of Christ.
- The Church's unity is expressed in the images of the Body of Christ and the People of God.

SCRIPTURE

Read *Ephesians 6:1–4* to learn more about how families can give all members equal respect.

 www.osvcurriculum.com
For weekly scripture readings and seasonal resources

Activity
Live Your Faith

Support Your Family The family is called a domestic Church. If the Church is called to reflect unity in the world, then families are, too. Discuss opportunities you have this week to support one another. It might be by attending someone's school performance as a family, by going to Mass together, or by helping keep the house quiet when someone has a project to complete. Choose what you will do, and agree to it.

People of Faith

▲ Saint Robert Bellarmine 1542–1621

Robert Bellarmine, an Italian priest, lived in an age of controversy between Catholics and Protestants. He defended Catholic teaching at such length that people thought that a team of people must have helped him. He also contributed to an important catechism. This holy man, who devoted much of his life to protecting the truths of the Catholic faith, was gentle and gracious. He prayed daily for his enemies. Saint Robert's feast day is September 17.

Family Prayer

Saint Robert Bellarmine, pray for us as we work to be signs of God's reign in the world. Ask God to teach us wisdom as he taught you and to give us the same grace of gentleness and tolerance that was yours. Amen.

© Our Sunday Visitor Curriculum Division

In Unit 4 your child is learning about the CHURCH.
CCC *See Catechism of the Catholic Church 738, 775, 776, 813–816, 820 for further reading on chapter content.*

Chapter 11: The Teaching Church

 **Let Us Pray**

Leader: God our Father, make us obedient to your will.
"Give me insight to observe your teaching,
to keep it with all my heart."

Psalm 119:34

All: God our Father, make us obedient to your will. Amen.

Activity

● **Face a Hurdle** Ballerina Allegra Kent recalls a special moment in fifth grade. With her teacher's help, she planned her first high jump: "I looked at . . . the exact point where I would take off. . . . I would have to be in possession of my body every moment of the run and jump." She made the jump successfully. "Something inside me was thrilled. It was a transforming moment."

Think about a time when you first learned a skill or understood a particular idea. How did you feel about your teacher and about yourself?

What qualities make a teacher effective?

_____
_____

Which of these qualities do you have?

_____
_____

✏️ **Write a Paragraph** Think about all the things you know how to do. On a separate sheet of paper, write about the skills you could teach and who might like to learn them.

159

Explore

The Need to Learn

 **Focus** Who teaches you about being a follower of Jesus?

All humans have a need to learn and improve themselves. Allegra Kent was fortunate enough to have a teacher who could help her learn and succeed. The following story is about a boy who wanted very much to learn, even when no one would teach him.

BIOGRAPHY

Frederick Learns

As a slave, young Frederick Douglass had no chance to learn to read. He was going to be a field hand and work hard in the sun all day. Then, when Frederick was eight, his owner sent him to Baltimore to work for another family. He loved hearing his mistress read the Bible. "Teach me to read," Frederick asked her. With the woman's help, Frederick was soon reading short words.

One day the woman's husband discovered this, and he became angry. "Slaves must not learn to read," he said. "It will make them unhappy and disobedient." Frederick's lessons stopped.

But Frederick was convinced that learning was the road to freedom. Whenever he went on errands, he asked questions of children who attended school so that he could learn on his own.

Frederick put his learning to good use. Secretly he taught other slaves to read and write. Eventually Frederick Douglass won his freedom and became a powerful leader who helped end slavery in the United States.

❓ **What are some of the best ideas or skills you have learned?**

❓ **How might they help you learn more?**

160

Faithful to the Truth

The achievement of Frederick Douglass shows that one of God's greatest gifts to humans is the ability to learn. Teaching and learning are wonderful abilities when you use them in harmony with God's plan and in the light of God's truth. Members of your family and of your parish community help you come to know about God and trust in his love and guidance.

As your teacher, the Church faithfully passes on what God has revealed through his Son, Jesus. The Church teaches by example and by handing on its beliefs and customs to its members.

SCRIPTURE — Matthew 28:19–20

Teach All Nations

To proclaim the faith and establish God's kingdom, Jesus sent out his Apostles and their successors:

"Go, therefore, and make disciples of all nations, baptizing them in the name of the Father, and of the Son, and of the holy Spirit, teaching them to observe all that I have commanded you. And behold, I am with you always, until the end of the age."

Matthew 28:19–20

Activity — Share Your Faith

Reflect: Think about those who have taught you about the Catholic faith and what you have learned from them.

Share: With a partner, discuss some of the things you have learned from teachers.

Act: Write one thing about the Catholic faith that you would like to teach to someone else.

_____
_____
_____
_____

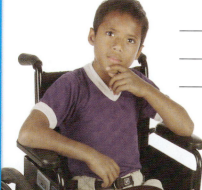

The Church on Earth

Focus Who are the teachers in the Catholic Church?

Jesus entrusted his ministry to the Apostles. From among the Apostles, Jesus chose Peter to be the leader.

SCRIPTURE
Matthew 16:15–19

Upon This Rock

Jesus asked the Apostles this question: "Who do you say that I am?"

Peter replied, "You are the Messiah, the Son of the living God." Jesus knew that only God could have shown Peter this truth.

He said to Peter, "I say to you, you are Peter, and upon this rock I will build my church." Jesus also promised Peter the keys to the kingdom of heaven.

Based on *Matthew 16:15–19*

When Jesus sent the Apostles out to spread the good news of his Father's kingdom, he also established the mission and authority of the Apostles' successors. In this way, the teaching authority of the Apostles is passed on.

The successors of the Apostles are all of the bishops, in union with the pope. They carry on the Apostles' mission, with the assistance of priests, to proclaim the good news and teach in the name of Jesus. Because the Church is built on the lasting foundation of the Apostles, the Church is apostolic.

❓ **What is your answer to Jesus' question, "Who do you say that I am?"**

The Teaching Office

Together, the pope and the bishops make up the **magisterium**, or "body of teachers." The pope is the successor of Peter, the bishop of Rome and head of the Church. Each bishop is also the leader of a particular diocese. Bishops have received the fullness of the Sacrament of Holy Orders.

With the guidance of the Holy Spirit, the magisterium protects and explains the word of God. Because the Holy Spirit guides the Church in the right direction in crucial matters, the magisterium officially declares that its most important teachings are free from error. This is called the doctrine of **infallibility**. Guided by the Holy Spirit, the Church's leaders settle certain important questions of faith and morals in order to help deepen understanding of the teachings of Jesus and the Apostles. This understanding also helps the People of God make right choices in living good moral lives.

Infallibility is connected to another important fact about the Church. The Holy Spirit guides the People of God to the truth. When the People of God—the pope, the bishops, and all the faithful—come to a common understanding about an important or central truth, they can be sure that they are correct. This is called the "sense of the faithful." The Holy Spirit works through the community of the faithful, giving the community itself a faith-filled understanding of the truth. Because of this, you can say that the Church is both human and divine.

Words of Faith

The **magisterium** is the teaching office of the Church.

Infallibility is a gift of the Holy Spirit to the Church by which the pope and the bishops together declare definitively that a matter of faith or morals is free from error and must be accepted by the faithful.

Activity — Connect Your Faith

Fill Your Toolbox With a partner, make a list of the "tools" you will need to build your lifelong journey of faith. How can the Church help you use these tools more effectively?

Explore

Church Vocabulary

 **Focus** What special language does the Church use?

The Catholic Church uses several terms and titles when it speaks about its teaching. These ways of talking about the Church allow all its members to be precise and to avoid misunderstanding. They will also be helpful to you in learning about the Church.

Words for Understanding

- Remember that a **doctrine** or **dogma** is an important teaching revealed by Christ and taught by the Church's magisterium. As a Catholic, you are required to believe these revealed truths.

- Appreciate that a **catechist** or **teacher** is someone who teaches the faith and helps people learn how to live according to the faith. Most catechists are laypeople.

- Recognize that an important ministry of the **pope** and **bishops** is to teach with the guidance of the Holy Spirit. It is their duty to interpret the Catholic faith and explain it to all people.

- Understand that **priests** and **deacons** assist the bishops in carrying out the teaching ministry. They do so by preaching, celebrating the sacraments, and guiding the people.

? What makes the Church different from other groups or organizations?
? How have you learned most about the Church?

Activity

Research In groups, research the teachings of your local bishop on a particular issue, such as world hunger or peace. Report your findings to the class. A good place to find information is the diocesan Web site. The bishop's teachings may also be available through the diocesan newspaper or from a particular diocesan office. Record your information below.

The issue we chose is: _____
_____

We looked for and found information here: _____
_____
_____
_____
_____
_____

This is what we discovered: _____
_____
_____
_____
_____
_____
_____
_____
_____
_____
_____
_____
_____
_____

Celebration of the Word

 **Let Us Pray**

Gather and begin with the Sign of the Cross.

Leader: Blessed be the name of the Lord.

All: **Now and for ever.**

Reader: Jesus is our teacher. He knows our needs and answers our longing for wisdom and truth. Listen to Jesus' teaching from the Sermon on the Mount.

Read Matthew 5:17–20.

The Gospel of the Lord.

All: **Praise to you, Lord Jesus Christ.**

Leader: Grateful for the teachings of Jesus, we turn to God in prayer.

The Sermon on the Mount, **Fra Angelico**

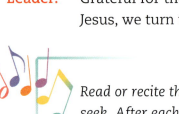 *Read or recite the prayers you seek. After each prayer, sing together.*

God ever-faithful, God ever-merciful, God of your people, hear our prayer.

"69, General Intercessions", Michael Joncas, © 1990, GIA Publications, Inc.

Leader: To conclude our prayers, lift your hands and pray the prayer that Jesus taught us.

Pray the Lord's Prayer aloud.

Leader: Go in peace.

All: **Thanks be to God.**

CHAPTER 11
Review

A **Work with Words** Write the answers to the questions in the boxes below. Unscramble the letters that appear in the circle boxes to find the answer to the last question.

1. Which Apostle did Jesus call the "rock," and to whom did Jesus give the keys to the kingdom of God?
2. What is the quality of being error-free in matters of faith and morals?
3. What is the Church's teaching office called?
4. Who guides the People of God to the truth and preserves them from error in crucial matters?
5. Whom did Christ send out to teach and baptize all nations?

1. ☐☐☐☐☐
2. ☐☐☐☐☐☐☐☐☐☐☐☐
3. ☐☐☐☐☐☐☐☐☐☐
4. ☐☐☐☐☐☐☐☐

5. _____

B **Check Understanding** Match each description in Column 1 with the correct term in Column 2.

Column 1

____ 6. learning to be like Jesus

____ 7. believed learning was the road to freedom

____ 8. successors of the Apostles

____ 9. important teaching revealed by Christ, taught by the magisterium

____ 10. teacher of the faith, most often a lay person

Column 2

a. doctrine

b. catechist

c. your lifelong task

d. Frederick Douglass

e. pope and bishops

167

UNIT 4: CHAPTER 11
Family Faith

Catholics Believe

- The Apostles proclaimed God's good news and brought the reign of God toward its fullness.
- Under the guidance of the Holy Spirit, the pope and the bishops continue the Apostles' mission to teach.

SCRIPTURE

Read *Acts* 3:1–26 to learn more about how the Apostles served God.

Activity
Live Your Faith

Research Every Christian has an obligation to grow in understanding of his or her faith. Make a choice to work as a family this week to learn more about the Church's teachings. Discuss what you find in your research and how it affects your faith. You might want to use your diocesan newspaper or one of the Church's official websites. You can find the web addresses by using an Internet search engine.

 www.osvcurriculum.com
For weekly scripture readings and seasonal resources

▲ Saint Thomas Aquinas
c. 1225–1274

People of Faith

When **Thomas Aquinas** was a young Dominican friar studying at the University of Paris in France, the other students called him the "dumb ox" because he was big, heavy, silent, and gentle. But their teacher, Albert the Great, predicted that the quiet voice of this great soul would someday be heard around the world. Albert was right. Thomas became one of the greatest teachers and theologians in the history of Christianity. He wrote a three-part study of the Catholic faith called the *Summa Theologica*. Saint Thomas's feast day is January 28. He is the patron of students.

Family Prayer

Saint Thomas, pray for us that we may share your love of Christian truth. May we always rejoice in God's love for us and take comfort in that love when the judgment of others is harsh and unkind. Amen.

© Our Sunday Visitor Curriculum Division

In Unit 4 your child is learning about the Church.
 See *Catechism of the Catholic Church* 84–86, 88, 424, 551–553, 857–863 for further reading on chapter content.

Chapter 12: Called to Holiness

Let Us Pray

Leader: Holy God, may we praise you always.
"Sing praise to the LORD, you faithful;
give thanks to God's holy name."
Psalm 30:5

All: Holy God, may we praise you always. Amen.

Activity — Let's Begin

On Being a Champion

A champion is a winner, / A hero . . .
Someone who never gives up
Even when the going gets rough,
A champion is a member of / A winning team . . .
Someone who overcomes challenges
Even when it requires creative solutions.
A champion is an optimist, / A hopeful spirit . . .
Someone who plays the game,
Even when the game is called life . . .
Especially when the game is called life.
There can be a champion in each of us,
If we live as a winner, / If we live as a member of the team,
If we live with a hopeful spirit, / For life.

Mattie Stepanek

Now think of some champions you know.

Why could saints be considered champions?

Write a Poem In the first verse, write about someone who has been a champion for God. In the second verse, write about how you can be more like that person.

169

Saints as Examples

 **Focus** Why is it important to know about the saints?

Saints are champions. They never give up. They are signs of hope for us. Saints are not too perfect to imitate. Most saints are ordinary people, gifted with God's grace at Baptism, as all of the faithful are. What makes them saints is how they live their lives. Saints let the grace of God shine through, and they become living signs of God's love.

On Being a Saint

"A saint is one who makes goodness attractive."
Laurence Housman

"The great painter boasted that he mixed all his colors with brains, and the great saint may be said to mix all his thoughts with thanks."
G. K. Chesterton

"I knew [Frances Cabrini] and didn't know she was a saint. She didn't know, either."
Adela Rogers St. Johns

"Saints are persons who make it easier for others to believe in God."
Nathan Söderblom

"From somber, serious, sullen saints, deliver us, O Lord."
Saint Teresa of Ávila

Choose one of these statements. What did this person want you to understand about saints?

Saint Teresa of Ávila

Saint Paul Miki

Saint Frances Cabrini

Saint Juan Diego

The Gift of Salvation

You cannot buy or earn salvation. Salvation is a gift from God that is yours because of the sacrifice of Jesus. Your good works show that you accept and thank God for his generosity. They are also a means by which, through God's grace and Christ's merit, you grow in holiness. Good works are a response to the prompting of the Holy Spirit's calling you to goodness.

Saints are models for you because they have listened and responded to the Holy Spirit's call. By their example of faithful living, the saints remind you that God is the source of all life and holiness.

One of the marks of the Church is that it is holy. The saints point to Jesus, who sacrificed himself to make the Church holy. The Holy Spirit, the **Sanctifier**, dwells within the Church and makes it holy. As members of the Church, all Catholics are called to personal **holiness**.

Words of Faith

The Holy Spirit, the **Sanctifier**, makes holy, or sanctifies, the Church.

Holiness is the quality of being sacred, or belonging to God.

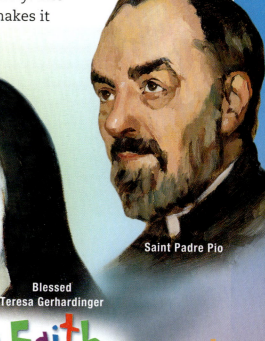

Blessed Kateri Tekakwitha

Blessed Teresa Gerhardinger

Saint Padre Pio

Activity — Share Your Faith

Reflect: Look at the images of some of the saints on these pages.

Share: Choose one of the images, and tell a partner what qualities of the saint you can see from the painting.

Act: On the lines below, write a question that you would like to ask this saint.

_____
_____
_____

Explore

Lives of Holiness

 **Focus** How can you become a saint?

The Church honors saints because of their lives of holiness. Many saints have feast days. Parishes and people are often named for saints. Saints are chosen to be patrons of persons, countries, and organizations.

Saints help you by their prayers and example. These models of Christian holiness show the obedience of faith that Mary, Queen of Saints, showed by saying "yes" to God.

SCRIPTURE
Luke 1:30–31, 38

The Handmaid of the Lord

Then the angel said to her, "Do not be afraid, Mary, for you have found favor with God. Behold, you will conceive in your womb and bear a son, and you shall name him Jesus." . . . Mary said, "Behold, I am the handmaid of the Lord. May it be done to me according to your word." Then the angel departed from her.

Luke 1:30–31, 38

From the beginning of her existence, Mary was without sin. This doctrine is called the Immaculate Conception. From the time that he was born, Jesus, the Son of God made man, was the center of Mary's life. Catholics believe in Mary's Assumption—that after her earthly life she was taken into heaven, body and soul, to be with Jesus. By honoring Mary, Catholics show their belief that all of God's faithful people will share, body and soul, in the glory of Christ's Resurrection.

 How do you say "yes" to God in your daily life?

Honor the Saints

The New Testament refers to all members of the Church as saints because they have been baptized by the power of the Holy Spirit into the Paschal mystery. The Church today can also canonize, or publicly recognize as saints, certain people of faith who have died. The community is encouraged to ask these saints for prayer and look to them as examples. Worship is reserved for God alone. But by honoring the saints and praying for their intercession, the Church also honors God.

Liturgical Year

The liturgical year celebrates what God has done for all people in Christ. On certain days, the Church also honors Mary and the saints for the role they play in God's plan of salvation. The Church officially honors a particular saint almost every day of the year. This is called the sanctoral cycle of the Church year. Here are some major feast days honoring Mary.

January 1	Mary, Mother of God
March 25	the Annunciation
August 15	the Assumption
August 22	the Queenship of Mary
December 8	the Immaculate Conception
December 12	Our Lady of Guadalupe

Words of Faith

The pope can **canonize** a person by making a solemn declaration that he or she is enjoying eternity with God and that his or her life can be a model for all Christians.

The **liturgical year** is the Church's public celebration of the whole mystery of Christ in the liturgy through the feasts and seasons of the Church calendar.

In what ways do you honor the saints?

Activity — Connect Your Faith

Honor Mary Mary showed her complete trust in God by devoting her entire life to God and to her son, Jesus. Make a banner for Mary. Create a message in words and symbols that you will use to honor her. Sketch your ideas here.

Praying the Rosary

 **Focus** How do you pray the Rosary?

The Rosary is a prayer honoring Mary. It is also a religious article with five sets of ten beads; each set is called a decade. When people pray the Rosary, they keep in mind important events in the lives of Jesus and his mother. These events are called the mysteries of the Rosary.

How to Pray the Rosary

- Hold the crucifix, and pray the Apostles' Creed.
- Then say the Our Father and three Hail Marys, followed by a Glory to the Father.
- The Rosary is divided into five decades. Each decade is made up of an Our Father, ten Hail Marys, and a Glory to the Father.
- Use the beads as you pray each of the five decades.
- During each decade, think about the mystery it represents.
- Close the Rosary by praying Hail, Holy Queen.

Hail, Holy Queen, mother of mercy, hail, our life, our sweetness, and our hope. To you we cry, the children of Eve; to you we send up our sighs, mourning and weeping in this land of exile. Turn, then, most gracious advocate, your eyes of mercy towards us; lead us home at last and show unto us the blessed fruit of your womb, Jesus: O clement, O loving, O sweet Virgin Mary.

❓ Why do you think praying the Rosary is such a popular devotion?

Activity: Live Your Faith

Research the Rosary's History In small groups, discuss and research the history of the Rosary so that you can answer the questions below. Record your results, and discuss ways, that you might incorporate the Rosary into your prayer life.

Did you learn anything about the Rosary from your family? If so, who told you about it?

_____
_____
_____

What are the origins of the Rosary?

_____
_____
_____

Which saints are particularly noted for their devotion to this prayer?

_____
_____
_____

What organizations are associated with praying the Rosary?

_____
_____
_____

Who is Our Lady of Fatima, and what did she say about the Rosary?

_____
_____
_____

Celebrate

Litany to Mary

 Let Us Pray

Gather and begin with the Sign of the Cross.

Leader: Loving God, we thank you for the gift of your saints. We ask Mary, the mother of Jesus, to pray for us so that we may be faithful, as she was.

All respond "Pray for us" after each title of Mary.

Holy Mary,	Cause of our joy,
Mother of Christ,	Help of Christians,
Virgin most faithful,	Queen of angels,
Mirror of justice,	Queen of all saints,
Seat of wisdom,	Queen of peace,

Leader: Pray for us, O holy Mother of God,

All: **That we may be worthy of the promises of Christ.**

Leader: Let us pray.

Bow your heads as the leader prays.

All: **Amen.**

Sing together.

And holy is your name through all generations!
Everlasting is your mercy to the people you have chosen,
and holy is your name.

"Holy Is Your Name", David Haas,
© 1989, GIA Publications, Inc.

CHAPTER 12
Review

A **Work with Words** Fill in the circle next to the correct response.

1. Saints can help you by their _____.
   - ○ divinity and power
   - ○ prayer and example
   - ○ example and divinity

2. Mary showed the obedience of faith by saying _____ to God.
   - ○ "I AM"
   - ○ "yes"
   - ○ "I am afraid"

3. The Church is holy because of the presence of the _____ within the Church.
   - ○ candles
   - ○ Holy Spirit
   - ○ liturgical calendar

4. Those who follow Jesus are called _____.
   - ○ disciples
   - ○ sanctifiers
   - ○ handmaids

5. During _____, the Church honors Jesus and all the saints.
   - ○ Christmas time
   - ○ wars and famine
   - ○ the liturgical year

Solve the crossword puzzle.

Across

7. Solemnly declare that a person is enjoying eternity with God
9. The Church's public celebration of the whole mystery of Christ (two words)
10. The quality of being sacred or belonging to God

Down

6. The Holy Spirit, who makes the Church holy
8. Mary's being taken into heaven, body and soul

UNIT 4: CHAPTER 12
Family Faith

Catholics Believe

- Mary and the saints provide the Church with models of holiness.
- Canonization declares that a model Christian is enjoying eternity with God.

SCRIPTURE

Read *Luke 1:46–55* to listen to Mary's prayer of praise.

www.osvcurriculum.com
For weekly scripture readings and seasonal resources

Activity
Live Your Faith

Pray the Rosary The Rosary is a repetitive and meditative prayer that reflects on the mystery of Christ as seen through the life of Mary. This week, pray the Rosary (or a decade of the Rosary) as a family. If you do not know how to pray the Rosary, you can find information about it in your parish library, at a Catholic bookstore, or on the Internet.

▲ Queenship of Mary

People of Faith

The Church has traditionally honored **Mary**, the mother of Jesus, as Queen of Heaven and Earth. This title suggests that she remains ever close to her son in heaven as she did when he lived on earth. Although all of the saints rejoice in God's presence, Mary enjoys a special place among them. The crowning of Mary by her son in heaven is a favorite subject of Catholic art. The last of the Glorious Mysteries of the Rosary celebrates Mary's coronation as Queen of Heaven and Earth. The Church celebrates the Queenship of Mary on August 22.

 Family Prayer

Mary, Queen of Heaven and Earth, pray to Christ for us that we may follow your example of holiness. Seek for us his protection from sin as we venerate your queenship with all of the angels and saints of heaven. Amen.

© Our Sunday Visitor Curriculum Division

In Unit 4 your child is learning about the CHURCH.

CCC See *Catechism of the Catholic Church* 828, 829, 1173, 2013, 2030 for further reading on chapter content.

DISCOVER

Catholic Social Teaching:

The Dignity of Work and the Rights of Workers

In this unit you learned that you are a sign of God's kingdom when you help those in need. The saints show you how to live this life of service to others. That service is often the work that people do.

The Dignity of Work

Because work is done by people created in God's image, it is holy. Work honors the skills and the talents we have from God. Your work is to study in school so that you can become a responsible member of society. Your parents work to provide for you.

Employers must respect the rights of their workers. Workers need fair pay to provide for their families. They also have the right to decent working conditions and the right to organize in order to protect themselves against unfair treatment.

People everywhere depend on farm workers for fruit and vegetables, and yet many of them are mistreated. Migrant workers earn less than the minimum wage. Many of them live with several other workers or family members in just one room, and some have no shelter at all. In the fields they are often without drinking water or toilet facilities. Many of the children cannot attend school because of moving and work. Many are immigrants and fear that they will be sent out of the country if they complain.

❓ **Why do you think employers have little regard for the rights of farm workers?**

CONNECT With the Call to Justice

A Prophet for the World's Farm Workers

Catholics must recognize the way in which farm workers are being harmed and work to change the system that allows it. Let's see how one man led the way and made an enormous difference in the lives of many.

Cesar Chavez was born into a family of farm workers in 1927. He completed elementary school in spite of the hardships and ridicule he experienced there. Instead of going to high school, he went to work in the fields, but education was always important to him. He read about heroes like Saint Francis and Mahatma Gandhi, and he learned the principles of nonviolence.

Chavez began to realize that he could help farm workers in their struggle. His first task was voter registration. In 1962 Chavez founded the National Farm Workers Association, which later became the United Farm Workers. He raised awareness of the conditions that farm workers faced. He organized nonviolent activities to force changes in the system. Chavez went on water-only fasts three times during critical talks between the growers and the workers. One of his fasts continued for 36 days. He saw these fasts as a prayer to strengthen all those who were working in the movement. Chavez died in 1993.

Cesar Chavez has been called a prophet for the world's farm workers. In 1994, one year after his death, he was awarded the Medal of Freedom for "facing formidable, often violent opposition with dignity and nonviolence." He also received the highest award the Mexican Government gives to those who are not citizens of Mexico. The UFW, the union founded by Cesar Chavez, continues its work of improving conditions for farm workers.

❓ What do you think made Cesar Chavez decide to do something to help the farm workers?

❓ Why do you think Cesar Chavez had a commitment to nonviolence?

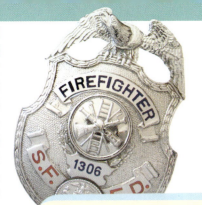

Reach Out!

SERVE Your Community

Plan an Interview

All around there are people at work. If these people suddenly stopped their work, other people might realize just how valuable and necessary workers are.

How many jobs and professions do you know about? List them below.

_____ _____ _____
_____ _____ _____
_____

Now think of the information you need in order to understand what is involved in a particular job. For instance, you probably need to know how much time a worker spends on the job and what makes the job easy or difficult. Write questions that you could ask to learn about the job. Don't write questions that can be answered with only *yes* or *no*.

_____
_____
_____
_____

Share your questions with a partner or small group.

Make a Difference

Show Appreciation With your classmates, make a list of people and jobs to support. (Don't forget to consider the people who work in your school.) Work until there are as many jobs as there are students. Organize so that each of you has a different job to support. The task will be to visit a person who does that job and show your respect and appreciation for that person's contribution to your community. As a class, brainstorm ideas for concrete ways to honor these workers.

UNIT 4 REVIEW

A **Work with Words** Find ten important terms from this unit in the word search below, and write them on the lines next to the clues.

```
E Q W T C P N I N I U Y X L F
N R Z K M T B N L B O W I Q K
O A M I Y B O F J P O T B F S
T R N Q A C D A L K U R P V U
S D U N L Q Y L C R Z C I Y T
R S A Y U M O L G T P O A O G
E Y R K R N F I G K L F E D P
N I T C J Y C B C H Y N I E X
R B P O U A H I O O W M R Z D
O Q H L L Q R L A J X A R I G
C Y U Y P E I I C T T M N N H
L R E H D N S T S A I C I O V
F A I E E L T Y O G F O S N P
R P R S Y R E I F I T C N A S
C F S V E K Q B F K A C W C G
```

1. March 25 _____
2. Jesus is the head _____
3. Make a model for Christians _____
4. Knew that learning was the road to freedom _____
5. All Catholics are called to it _____
6. Holy Spirit's gift to the Church _____
7. Promised to Peter _____
8. Celebration of the mystery of Christ _____
9. Jesus _____
10. The Holy Spirit _____

B **Check Understanding** Match each description in Column 1 with the correct term in Column 2.

Column 1

_____ 11. built on the lasting foundation of the Apostles

_____ 12. the pope and the bishops

_____ 13. studied the Church's role in modern society

_____ 14. assembly called by Christ to share in his mission

_____ 15. These show God's kingdom at work in the Church.

Column 2

a. People of God

b. one, holy, catholic, and apostolic

c. apostolic

d. Second Vatican Council

e. magisterium

C **Make Connections** Write a response to each statement.

16–20. Explain the role of individuals as members of the Pilgrim People, using the following terms:

catechist   doctrine   priest

_____
_____
_____
_____

Choose one of the other images of the Church (People of God, Body of Christ, or Bride of Christ), and explain what it means.

_____
_____

Name the image that best describes your participation in the Church, and give the reasons for your choice.

_____
_____

Unit 5
Morality

In this unit you will...

learn that evil is a result of humans turning away from God's goodness. We are redeemed from the power of evil and sin through the power of Jesus' death and Resurrection. We experience the salvation of God's grace through the sacraments. We receive God's forgiveness especially through the Sacrament of Penance and Reconciliation.

Faith in Action!

**Catholic Social Teaching Principle:
Solidarity of the Human Family**

Chapter 13: The Mystery of Evil

 **Let Us Pray**

Leader: God of mercy, deliver us from evil.
"Turn from evil and do good,
that you may inhabit the land forever."
Psalm 37:27

All: God of mercy, deliver us from evil. Amen.

Activity — Let's Begin

● **A Path of Destruction** Even if the only tornado you've ever seen is the one that sweeps Dorothy and Toto away in *The Wizard of Oz,* you know that a tornado is one of the most destructive of all weather-related events. A tornado can cut a path of destruction up to one mile wide and 400 miles long! If you live in an area that experiences many tornadoes, radio and television channels will give you regular updates to help you be safe during dangerous weather.

Why do you think a destructive force such as a tornado exists in the world of goodness that God created?

What are some natural disasters that your community has had to face?

_____
_____
_____

Make a List Think of all the ways people can help one another in times of crisis. List them on a separate sheet of paper.

The Source of Sorrow

 **Focus** How did evil enter the world?

Some bad things that happen, like tornadoes, are beyond human control. But others are the result of sinful decisions and actions. As you recall this familiar story, think about why the characters make their choices.

A TALE

Hansel and Gretel

Two children lived with their father, who was a poor woodcutter, and their stepmother. One day the woman said a terrible thing to her husband. "We do not have enough food, and soon we will starve. Take Hansel and Gretel out in the woods and leave them—then the two of us will be able to eat." The man objected at first but later agreed to the plan.

The starving children wandered for days. At last they came upon—of all things—a house made of sweets. They were eating pieces of the roof when an old woman came to the door and invited them in. Once inside, they were trapped. The old woman was a witch, and she meant to kill and eat them.

❓ Which characters do the evil things in this story?

❓ What do you think makes them want to do such bad things?

Sin Enters the World

Hansel and Gretel never gave up hope. They used their cleverness and imagination to free themselves from the evil witch. Eventually, they returned home with food and jewels that they found, and their family was never hungry again.

God is good and desires only good for people. Yet sin and evil are found in human life. The Book of Genesis teaches that the first humans' choice to disobey God ended the original justice and holiness that God created. The disobedience of the first humans, and its effects on all humans, is known as **original sin**. With original sin, the harmony between humans and God, between humans and nature, and among all people was destroyed. Death entered the world, and people became subject to the inclination to sin. All humans have been affected by the first humans' decision. All share in the human condition of original sin.

God did not abandon humans to the power of sin and evil. He sent his Son to be their Redeemer. And, says Saint Paul, the gift is much greater than the sin.

Words of Faith

Original sin is the sin of the first humans, which led to the sinful condition of the human race from its beginning.

SCRIPTURE — Romans 5:19

New Life in Christ

For just as through the disobedience of one person the many were made sinners, so through the obedience of one the many will be made righteous.

Romans 5:19

Activity — Share Your Faith

Reflect: Read the story of the Fall as told in *Genesis 3:1–6*.

Share: Write one thing you have learned about sin and one thing you have learned about God from the reading. Share your response with a partner.

About Sin	About God
_____	_____
_____	_____

Act: With your partner, act out the story of the Fall.

Explore

Personal Sin

 **Focus** What are mortal sin and venial sin?

The presence of evil and of innocent suffering in the world are two of the hardest things for humans to face. Why evil exists is the hardest question to answer. Only faith can provide an adequate explanation.

Christians know that evil can be overcome and that God's kingdom will triumph. They base their hope on Jesus Christ. By his death on the cross, Jesus saved all people from the power of sin and everlasting death.

Mortal Sin

Personal sin is a deliberate choice to think, say, or do something that goes against your relationship with God or contradicts God's law. Sin harms or destroys your relationship with God, with others, and even with yourself.

Mortal sin is the most serious form of personal sin. Someone who commits mortal sin turns completely away from God. Mortal sin involves complete selfishness. For a sin to be mortal, it must be a serious matter, done with a person's full knowledge and complete consent. Examples of such serious matters are murder and extreme forms of injury and discrimination against others. Even in these cases, the other two conditions of full knowledge and consent must be met before a sin is mortal. A person who has tried to live in friendship with God does not easily choose to sin so seriously.

To restore friendship with God after committing mortal sin, the sinner must repent and seek forgiveness. God's grace helps the sinner do this.

 How can a person avoid mortal sin?

Venial Sin

Venial sin weakens a person's relationship with God. A sin is venial when it involves disobeying God's law in a less serious matter than one associated with mortal sin. For example, someone who makes fun of another because of gender, physical or mental abilities, or appearance causes harm to that person's dignity and worth. This lack of respect for another can be a venial sin.

Venial sin may sometimes lead to mortal sin. A person who lies about or steals small things may be establishing a pattern of behavior that can lead to more serious sins. Small acts of discrimination can lead to extreme forms that could be mortally sinful if a person eventually chooses to show only hate rather than love. Mortal sin occurs when selfishness wins out completely.

Words of Faith

Personal sin is the deliberate choice to think, say, or do something that goes against your relationship with God or goes against God's law.

Mortal sin is the most serious form of personal sin, through which a person turns completely away from God.

Venial sin is a less serious personal sin that weakens, but does not destroy, a person's relationship with God.

The Forgiveness of Sins

Even in cases of serious sin, God always forgives sinners when they are truly sorry and wish to turn their hearts to him again. Through the grace of the Sacrament of Reconciliation, people can have their sins forgiven and rebuild a loving relationship with God.

Activity: Connect Your Faith

Reflect on Choices Imagine that you have been recruited to produce a television program based on a choice you have made between good and evil. What approach would you take? Would it be a factual program, a game show, or a drama? Describe your plan for the show.

_____
_____
_____
_____

Explore

Prayer in Difficult Times

 **Focus** How do you express pain and sorrow?

From the Bible you learn that in the face of tragedy, God's people bring their feelings of sorrow and anger to God. Such prayers of sorrow and anger are called *lamentations*. They express the need for God's presence in times of difficulty. Psalm 55 is an example of a prayer of lamentation. Use it to understand how you can pray in this way.

Prayer of Lamentation

You can follow these steps in order to tell God about your feelings of anger and sorrow.

Express your feelings honestly. Describe the feeling you wish to pray about.

- Tell God how you really feel.
- Remember that he already knows and wants to help you, but you must find the words to express clearly what you need.

Name the painful situation clearly. In Psalm 55, the psalmist has been betrayed by a friend. The violent city is also mentioned.

- In your prayer, include every aspect of the situation you wish to pray about.
- What is the event? Who or what caused it? What would you like to do about it?

Express your hope and trust in God. In this part of the prayer, it is important to express your trust in God's power and goodness.

- Like the psalmist who said, "God will give me freedom and peace" *(Psalm 55:19)*, you will find strength when you affirm your faith in him.
  - What do you believe he has already done for you? What do you believe he is doing right now? What do you believe he will do?

❓ Why is it so important to trust God when you are hurting?

❓ What makes it hard to express feelings honestly?

© Our Sunday Visitor Curriculum Division

Activity

Write Prayers As a group, brainstorm situations in today's world that are a cause for sorrow or anger. In small groups, choose two situations. For each situation, write a prayer of lamentation in three parts, using the steps explained on the opposite page.

Situation: _____

Our feelings

What's wrong

We believe that God will...

Situation: _____

Our feelings

What's wrong

We believe that God will...

191

Litany of Repentance

 Let Us Pray

Gather and begin with the Sign of the Cross.

Leader: God our loving Father, you are always ready to forgive us. Let us reflect on how we have sinned.

After each prayer verse, sing together the refrain.

Hold us in your mercy. Hold us in your mercy.

You who shared the sinner's table . . .

You who cleansed the leper's flesh . . .

You who shared our life and labor . . .

You who silenced raging demons . . .

You who chose to walk our roads . . .

You who bear our cross with us . . .

"Hold Us in Your Mercy: Penitential Litany"
Rory Cooney, © 1993, GIA Publications, Inc.

Leader: All pray the Act of Contrition together. It is found in the Catholic Source Book.

Let us pray.

Bow your heads as the leader prays.

All: Amen.

CHAPTER 13
Review

A **Work with Words** Match each description in Column 1 with the correct term in Column 2.

Column 1

_____ 1. the sin of the first humans and the sinful human condition

_____ 2. disobedience to God's law in a serious matter with complete knowledge and full consent

_____ 3. any sin deliberately chosen by an individual

_____ 4. prayer of sorrow and anger

_____ 5. disobedience to God's law in a matter that is not deeply serious

Column 2

a. mortal sin
b. lamentation
c. venial sin
d. personal sin
e. original sin

B **Check Understanding** Fill in the circle next to the correct response.

6. Saint Paul says that the gift of _____ is much greater than original sin.
   ○ faith   ○ the Redeemer   ○ prophecy

7. Only _____ can provide a sufficient answer to the question of evil.
   ○ faith   ○ the Church   ○ wisdom

8. To restore friendship with God after committing mortal sin, the sinner must _____.
   ○ repent and receive Penance   ○ receive Communion   ○ write a psalm

9. Venial sin may sometimes lead to _____.
   ○ mortal sin   ○ repentance   ○ eternal life

10. The Book of Genesis teaches that the first humans' choice to disobey God ended the original _____ and holiness that he created.
    ○ free will   ○ justice   ○ shame

UNIT 5: CHAPTER 13

Family Faith

Catholics Believe

- Evil is the result of humans' turning away from God's goodness.
- God sent his Son to redeem people from the power of sin and evil.

SCRIPTURE

Read *Matthew 18:21–35* to find a parable about forgiveness.

Activity
Live Your Faith

Apologize and Forgive   Because sin is a deliberate choice, it is important to learn to say "I'm sorry" and to ask forgiveness of God and of one another. Set aside a time for prayer in which family members can ask for, give, and receive forgiveness for the ways in which they may have hurt one another during the week. Conclude with a sign of peace.

www.osvcurriculum.com
For weekly scripture readings and seasonal resources

People of Faith

▲ Michael the Archangel

According to Scripture, archangels are the second of nine choirs of angels. The Book of Daniel describes **Michael** as a prince and as a guardian angel for the Jewish people. The writer of the Book of Revelation discusses a vision in which Michael appears as the military leader of the good angels. Michael and his army of angels defeat Satan and the other evil angels and drive them out of heaven. In Christian art Michael has been pictured wearing armor and carrying a sword. The Church remembers Michael the Archangel on September 29.

Family Prayer

Michael the Archangel, pray for us that we may have courage in the face of evil and, with God's help, may overcome it. Be our defender and our shield against the power of darkness as we seek to follow the light. Amen.

In Unit 5 your child is learning about MORALITY.
See *Catechism of the Catholic Church* 309, 311, 312, 397, 1855 for further reading on chapter content.

© Our Sunday Visitor Curriculum Division

Chapter 14
Reborn in Christ

 **Let Us Pray**

Leader: Loving Father, hear our prayer.
"Show us, Lord, your love;
grant us your salvation."
Psalm 85:8

All: Loving Father, hear our prayer. Amen.

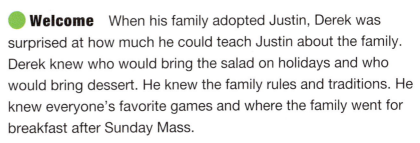

● **Welcome** When his family adopted Justin, Derek was surprised at how much he could teach Justin about the family. Derek knew who would bring the salad on holidays and who would bring dessert. He knew the family rules and traditions. He knew everyone's favorite games and where the family went for breakfast after Sunday Mass.

What could you tell a new family member to help him or her feel at home?

You are part of God's family and the Catholic Church. What is your favorite Catholic symbol?

_____

_____

What are some things you could share with someone who wants to join your family of faith?

_____

_____

✏️ **Write a Letter** On a separate sheet of paper, explain to a pen pal in another country how and why your family celebrates Easter.

Explore

One Step at a Time

 **Focus** How are the Sacraments of Initiation celebrated for adults?

Just as it takes time to become part of a family, so it takes time to prepare to be baptized and to be initiated into the Church. The Church welcomes new adult members through a step-by-step process called the Rite of Christian Initiation of Adults, or the Order of Christian Initiation.

A STORY

United to Christ and to the Church

Although Jenny was twenty-three years old, she could feel butterflies in her stomach when she rang the doorbell of Saint Benedict's. As soon as Father Paul sat down with her, Jenny blurted out, "I'd like to become a Catholic. What tests do I have to take?" The priest smiled warmly and said, "Let's take this one step at a time. The process of becoming a member of the Church, which we call *initiation*, takes time." He invited Jenny to a gathering where she would meet people who were on a similar faith journey.

After a few months, Jenny decided that she wanted to prepare for Baptism, and she became a catechumen. During this time, the lives of those committed to the faith were an example to her. Jenny also had support from her sponsor, Ellen. Ellen came to sharing sessions at the church with Jenny. She prayed with Jenny and told her what being Catholic was like. Jenny came to know and love the Christian way of life and the Catholic Church.

Many months later, on the First Sunday of Lent, Jenny became one of the elect. This meant that she would celebrate the Sacraments of Initiation at the Easter Vigil on Holy Saturday.

A Night to Remember

Finally, Holy Saturday arrived. At the baptismal pool, Father Paul asked Jenny to declare her faith in God the Father, Son, and Holy Spirit. As Father Paul immersed her in the water three times, he said, "I baptize you in the name of the Father, and of the Son, and of the Holy Spirit." Jenny was given new life in Christ.

After a prayer to the Holy Spirit, Father Paul placed his hands on Jenny's head and confirmed her with the oil of chrism, saying, "Jenny, be sealed with the Gift of the Holy Spirit."

At last the moment came to receive the Eucharist. Jenny stood before Father Paul to receive Communion. "The Body of Christ, the Blood of Christ" echoed in her mind and heart as she returned to her place after receiving Holy Communion for the first time. Now, Jenny felt truly united to Christ and to the Church.

❓ **Have you ever wanted to join a group? Why?**

❓ **How did you go about joining?**

The **Rite of Christian Initiation of Adults**, or RCIA, is the process by which adults and some children become members of the Catholic Church through the Sacraments of Initiation.

A **catechumen**, or "learner," is a person preparing to celebrate the Sacraments of Initiation.

A **sponsor** is a representative of the Christian community who supports an older child or adult celebrating the Sacraments of Initiation.

Activity: Share Your Faith

Reflect: Think about the steps Jenny took in the process of initiation.

Share: With a partner, create a time line of Jenny's faith journey. Use these words in your outline: *immersed, catechumen, inquiry, chrism, elect.*

Act: Write one way in which you can support someone going through the process of the Rite of Christian Initiation of Adults in your parish.

_____
_____

197

Explore

Sacraments of Initiation

 **Focus** What new life is given in Baptism?

At Baptism you first received grace and began a new way of life. The Sacraments of Confirmation and Eucharist complete your initiation as a member of the Catholic Church, but they do not mark the end of your journey of faith. They are the beginning of this journey. With these three sacraments, you are initiated into a relationship with Christ and his Church. Through the sacraments, Jesus shares with you his ministry as priest, prophet, and king.

Priest
- praise God
- offer your life to God
- pray with and for others

Prophet
- know the Church's teachings on morality and justice
- stand up for what is right
- speak God's word

King
- be responsible
- be a leader
- act with justice, mercy, and love

Paul compares the new life of Baptism with the Resurrection of Jesus. When a person is baptized, he or she is said to have "died" to sin. Paul points out that the baptized person then "rises" to new life in Christ in the community of the Church.

SCRIPTURE   Romans 6:10–11

Living for God

As to his death, [Jesus] died to sin once and for all; as to his life, he lives for God. Consequently, you too must think of yourselves as [being] dead to sin and living for God in Christ Jesus.

Romans 6:10–11

 What do you think it means to live for God?

The New Life of Grace

Jenny was an adult when she chose to be baptized as a Catholic. Most Christians are baptized as infants, which is the customary practice of the Catholic Church. At Baptism, a person is reborn in Christ and freed from both original sin and personal sin. Through the Church, the grace of the sacraments is given to sustain this new life.

❓ **How does the Catholic Church help you become closer to Christ?**

Grace and Conversion

Through the sacraments of the Church, God shares his divine life with you. The grace given in the sacraments is not earned—it is a gift from God. You respond to God's gift of grace by turning away from sin and living according to the law of love that Jesus taught. The movement away from sin and into the mystery of God's love is called *conversion*. It begins with God's call and is sustained through life by your cooperation with God's grace.

Activity — Connect Your Faith

Continue the Journey Write a thank-you note to your godparents or to someone in your parish community who has helped you on your journey of faith. Be sure to say how the person or persons have helped you.

_____
_____
_____
_____
_____

Help Along the Way

 **Focus** What can deepen your faith as you grow as a Christian?

The Sacraments of Initiation bring you to new life as a Catholic Christian and prepare you to continue your journey of faith. There are some practices that can help you along.

The Tools

Focus on Your Faith	• Base your decisions on the Ten Commandments and the teachings of Jesus. • Count on the guidance of the Holy Spirit. • Pray to God, who is always ready to listen.
Participate at Mass	• Active participation at Mass strengthens your bond with Jesus and with your parish. • In the Eucharist, God gives you his grace to sustain you on your journey.
Rely on Your Faith Community	• Church members can help you on your way. These people may include your family, your pastor, or your religion teacher. • Talk to them or others whom you know and trust about questions or problems.
Set an Example	• "Learn by doing." • Participate in the life of the Church, and make a habit of service to others. This strengthens your love and commitment to the Church and gives witness to the truth of your faith.

❓ What part of your faith life would you like to improve?

❓ What might help you be stronger in faith?

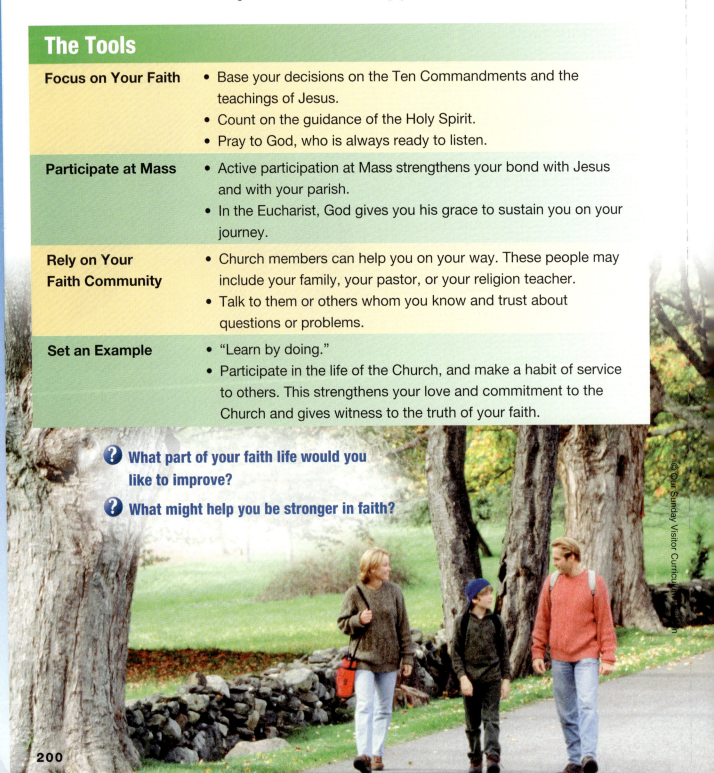

Activity: Live Your Faith

Report Your Findings Working in small groups, brainstorm ways that you can be an example of Catholic living. Consider the activities (such as festivals), organizations (such as youth groups), and individual efforts of people in your parish (such as sponsoring an exchange student). Be sure that your suggestions are specific and practical. Collaborate on writing a report of your findings to share with other groups.

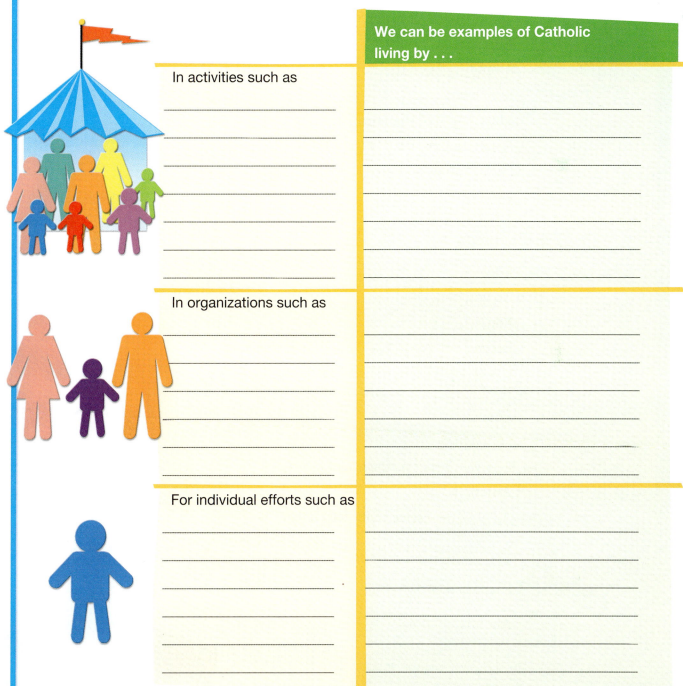

	We can be examples of Catholic living by . . .
In activities such as	
In organizations such as	
For individual efforts such as	

Celebration of the Word

 **Let Us Pray**

Gather and begin with the Sign of the Cross.

Leader: Let us pray. Loving God, we sing your praise, for you have given us new life through the grace of Baptism. Enfold us within your Church, through Christ our Lord.

All: **Amen.**

Reader: A reading from the holy Gospel according to John.

Read John 3:1–21.

The Gospel of the Lord.

All: **Praise to you, Lord Jesus Christ.**

Leader: Let us renew the promises of our Baptism.

Leader: Do you reject Satan, all his works, and all his empty promises?

All: **I do.**

Leader: Do you believe in God, the Father almighty?

All: **I do.**

Leader: Do you believe in Jesus Christ, his only Son?

All: **I do.**

Leader: Do you believe in the Holy Spirit, the holy catholic Church, the communion of saints, the forgiveness of sins, and life everlasting?

All: **I do.**

Leader: Let us pray.

Bow your heads as the leader prays.

All: **Amen.**

All bless themselves with holy water.

Sing together the refrain.

Alleluia, alleluia.

"Alleluia" *Lectionary for Mass,*
© 1969, 1981, and 1997, ICEL.

Chapter 14 Review

Check Understanding Circle True if a statement is true, and circle False if a statement is false. Correct any false statements.

1. A catechumen is a person who acts as a sponsor for someone who wishes to become a Catholic.

    True   False   _____

2. Focusing on faith, participating at Mass, relying on the faith community, and setting an example are all ways to welcome a new family member.

    True   False   _____

3. Baptism frees a person from original sin and personal sin.

    True   False   _____

4. The grace of the sacraments must be earned.

    True   False   _____

5. The sacraments call for a response.

    True   False   _____

Using the words in the Word Bank, describe the Rite of Christian Initiation of Adults.

6–10. _____

WORD BANK

conversion
Easter Vigil
catechumen
Sacraments of Initiation
sponsor

UNIT 5: CHAPTER 14
Family Faith

Catholics Believe

- The process of becoming a Catholic is called the Rite of Christian Initiation of Adults.
- The Sacraments of Initiation are Baptism, Confirmation, and Eucharist.

SCRIPTURE

Read *Matthew 3:13–17* to learn about Jesus' baptism.

GO online www.osvcurriculum.com
For weekly scripture readings and seasonal resources

Activity
Live Your Faith

Share Memories Baptism is a priceless gift that families share with their children. Research the dates of each family member's celebration of this sacrament, and make note of these dates. Revisit baptismal celebrations of various members of your family, using photographs, stories, and mementos. If possible, invite godparents to join you and share memories of the celebration of Baptism. Light a candle and pray that God will continue to bless your family's journey of faith.

People of Faith

▲ Saint Cyril of Jerusalem
315–386

Cyril was a great teacher of the early Church. The bishop of Jerusalem asked him to prepare catechumens for Baptism. Cyril explained the beliefs of the Church to the catechumens. His lectures are the best records of the instruction that catechumens received in the early Church. Later, as bishop of Jerusalem himself, Cyril continued to give these lectures because he considered the work so important. Saint Cyril was named a Doctor of the Church in 1882. His feast day is March 18.

Family Prayer

Saint Cyril, pray for us that we may cherish the gift of Baptism. Intercede for all those who are preparing for initiation into the Church, that they may receive the fullness of the Holy Spirit. Amen.

In Unit 5 your child is learning about MORALITY.
See *Catechism of the Catholic Church* 1212, 1213, 1229–1233, 1316, 1391 for further reading on chapter content.

© Our Sunday Visitor Curriculum Division

Chapter 15: Forgiveness and Healing

Let Us Pray

Leader: We praise you for your mercy, O Lord.
"May God be gracious to us and bless us;
may God's face shine upon us."

Psalm 67:2

All: We praise you for your mercy, O Lord. Amen.

Activity — Let's Begin

A Poison Tree

I was angry with my friend:
I told my wrath, my wrath did end.
I was angry with my foe:
I told it not, my wrath did grow.

A selection from the poem by William Blake

Now think about how you react when you are angry or when your feelings are hurt.

What could you hear from a person who has hurt you to make it easier for you to forgive?

_____
_____
_____

- **Picture It** Design DVD covers for films about friends making up after fights and disagreements and for films about sick and injured people being cured.

Explore

Reconciliation and Forgiveness

 **Focus** How can you bring forgiveness and reconciliation into your relationships?

Jesus understood that anger can have a negative effect on even close relationships. In this story of forgiveness and reconciliation, Jesus taught his followers a lesson that he also lived.

SCRIPTURE Luke 15:11–32

The Two Sons

Jesus told a story about a man with two sons. The younger son said, "Father, give me the share of your estate that should come to me." The father did so, and the son went far away. He wasted his money and was soon starving. Desperate, he decided to return to his father's house. He went home, where his forgiving parent greeted him with joy and love. The father told his servants to prepare a feast to celebrate his son's return. When the older son heard about this, he was angry and complained to his father. But the father, who loved his sons equally, replied, "My son, you are here with me always; everything I have is yours. But now we must celebrate . . . because your brother was dead and has come to life again; he was lost and has been found."

Based on *Luke 15:11–32*

❓ Why is the older son so angry?

❓ What does he learn by expressing his anger to his father?

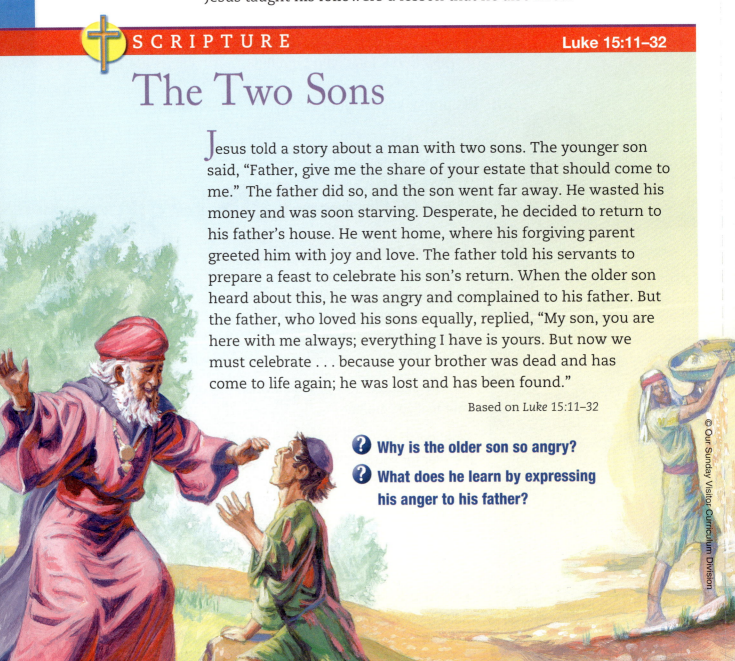

A Generous Father

Like the father in the story that Jesus told, God always wants you to come home to his love. No one is ever far from God's mercy. Christ continues to share God's forgiving love through the Church in the Sacrament of Reconciliation.

Catholics who commit serious sin are required to celebrate the Sacrament of Reconciliation, but the Church encourages all to celebrate it. Sin wounds or destroys relationships with God, the Church, and others. Reconciliation heals these relationships. After you confess your sins to the priest, he gives you a penance, which not only reminds you to be sorry for your sins but also helps you turn away from sin in the future.

After you have confessed your sins, the priest will ask you to pray the Act of Contrition. This prayer helps you express **contrition**, or sorrow, for your sins and your intention to do better. It reminds you that the God who always hears your prayers is forgiving, just, and merciful. Your confession of sins and the **absolution**, or pardon, given by the priest bring you God's peace and grace.

Words of Faith

Contrition is sincere sorrow for having sinned.

Absolution is the forgiveness of sins in God's name through the Sacrament of Reconciliation.

SACRAMENT OF RECONCILIATION

Parts	• Contrition • Confession • Penance • Absolution
Signs	• Confession • Words of absolution • Extension of priest's hand
Effects	• Forgiveness of sins • Reconciliation with God and the Church • Peace and spiritual strength

Activity — Share Your Faith

Reflect: Think of an idea for a modern-day parable of forgiveness. Begin by thinking of current situations in which people find it hard to forgive.

Share: With a partner, decide whether you would tell your story as a play, a poem, or a short story.

Act: Write the form you would use and three to five sentences telling what the situation would be or what your parable would be.

_____
_____
_____
_____

The Sacrament That Heals

 **Focus** Why is the Anointing of the Sick called a Sacrament of Healing?

Faith Fact
The symbol for the Sacrament of the Anointing of the Sick is an olive branch.

In the Hawaiian Islands of the late 1800s, no healing was available for those stricken with Hansen's disease, or leprosy. All victims were exiled to Molokai, one of the Hawaiian Islands.

BIOGRAPHY

Father Damien and the Lepers

Belgian missionary priest Damien de Veuster volunteered to serve on Molokai. When he arrived, conditions in the settlement were horrible. Disorder and despair were everywhere.

Father Damien cared for the outcasts and taught them to help one another. He built homes for orphans. He baptized people and brought them the other sacraments. Because of his great faith, he was inspired to love these very sick people and to stay with them to the end. This compassionate priest eventually contracted leprosy himself and thereafter referred to himself and his flock as "we lepers."

❓ **What do you think it meant to the people that Father Damien said "we lepers"?**

COMPASSION FOR THOSE WHO ARE SICK

Father Damien could not cure illness, but he could ease pain, help restore dignity, and bring hope to those he served. Through the sacraments, Father Damien brought people God's healing and forgiveness. Although Molokai's exiles had been separated from family and friends, they learned from this good priest the truth that they could never be separated from the love of God in Jesus Christ.

During his life on earth, Jesus showed compassion for those who were sick and often healed them. Through the Sacrament of the Anointing of the Sick, the Church continues in the name of Christ to touch and heal those who suffer illness. Anyone who is seriously ill, at an advanced age, or facing surgery can receive this sacrament. It should also be celebrated when someone is thought to be near death.

SACRAMENT OF THE ANOINTING OF THE SICK	
Signs	Laying on of hands, prayer, anointing of the forehead and hands
Effects	Union with the sufferings of Christ, peace, courage, the strength to bear illness, the forgiveness of sins, preparation for eternal life, and sometimes physical healing

Activity — Connect Your Faith

Share Healing Love Share the healing love of Christ with others. In the space below, design a card or write a get-well note to someone who is sick. If possible, re-create the card or note on stationery and deliver it to the person.

Explore

Examine Your Conscience

 **Focus** How do you prepare yourself to receive forgiveness?

God's love and goodness help you see your need for forgiveness and healing. Examining your conscience regularly helps you recognize your sin as well as bad habits that can lead to sin. It prepares you to receive the Sacrament of Penance.

Steps to Take

Take time to think about each question. You do not share your responses or thoughts. So be very honest with yourself and with God.

1 Pray to the Holy Spirit for help in recalling your sins. Ask the Spirit to guide you in acknowledging your sins and expressing sorrow.

Do you understand how your actions can hurt? What things are hard for you to feel sorry for?

2 Reflect on your life. Have you neglected your relationship with God or with others? How have you misused what you have been given? Have you forgiven those who have hurt you?

3 Think about the Ten Commandments, the Beatitudes, the teachings of the Church, and the command to love. Cheating, spreading rumors, disobeying, and stealing are against the commandments.

How have you failed to live by the Beatitudes? Have you not thought of others' needs or done little to avoid fights? Have you not been helpful or cooperative at home? Have you failed to stand up for what is right or neglected treating others with respect and consideration?

4 Ask for help. Ask God to give you the grace to live a life that mirrors his love and goodness. Ask for humility.

5 Make a decision to do better. Do something positive to make up for your sins.

6 Thank God. Praise God for loving you even when you fail to love him or others as you should.

7 Pray an Act of Contrition. Ask God for forgiveness.

© Our Sunday Visitor Curriculum Division

Activity: Live Your Faith

Ways To Undo Wrongs As a class, find examples of ways to make amends for wrongs such as those suggested below. Write down the suggestions so that you will be able to remember them when you need them.

generous

When I have been careless and made work for my parents and others:
_____

When I have said mean things to others out of anger or jealousy:
_____

When I have neglected my chores or schoolwork:
_____

loyal

When I have bullied those who have no power to protect themselves:
_____

When I have repeated gossip or spread rumors about others:
_____

When I have been disloyal to my friends out of fear of not being accepted:
_____

kind

When I have made jokes at another's expense:
_____

When I have lied in order to avoid the consequences of a bad choice:
_____

When I have been greedy or selfish with my possessions:
_____

When I have been disrespectful of others:
_____

selfless *trusting* *helpful*

Celebrate

Prayer of Peace

 Let Us Pray

Gather and begin with the Sign of the Cross.

Sing together.

1. Peace before us, peace behind us, peace under our feet.
   Peace within us, peace over us, let all around us be peace.

2. Love before us, love behind us, love under our feet.
   Love within us, love over us, let all around us be love.

3. Light before us, light behind us, light under our feet.
   Light within us, light over us, let all around us be light.

Leader: A reading from the holy Gospel according to John.

Read John 14:27.

The Gospel of the Lord.

All: **Praise to you, Lord Jesus Christ.**

4. Christ before us, Christ behind us, Christ under our feet.
   Christ within us, Christ over us, let all around us be Christ.

5. Alleluia, alleluia, alleluia, Alleluia, alleluia, alleluia.

6. Peace before us, peace behind us, peace under our feet.
   Peace within us, peace over us, let all around us be peace.

"Prayer of Peace", David Haas © 1987, GIA Publications, Inc.

All exchange a sign of peace at the conclusion of the hymn.

CHAPTER 15 Review

A **Work with Words** Complete each sentence with the correct term from the Word Bank.

WORD BANK

contrition
Reconciliation
feast
the Anointing of the Sick
absolution
prayer
service

1. _____ is the forgiveness of sins in God's name through the Sacrament of Reconciliation.

2. The father in the parable celebrated the return of his son with a _____.

3. _____ is sincere sorrow for having sinned.

4. Absolution is part of the Sacrament of _____.

5. The strength to bear illness is an effect of _____.

B **Check Understanding** Cross out any incorrect answers you find in the items below.

6. The signs of the Sacrament of the Anointing of the Sick are (laying on of hands, anointing with oil, doing penance).

7. The basic elements of the Sacrament of Reconciliation are (contrition, confession, penance, Communion, absolution).

8. Some steps to take in examining your conscience are (to reflect, to think about the commandments, to sing hymns, to decide to do better).

9. Contrition for sins (is unnecessary, must be sincere, helps restore damaged relationships with God and the Church).

10. Father Damien is a heroic example of reconciliation and healing because he (found a cure for Hansen's disease; devoted himself to the care of those exiled on Molokai; brought comfort, dignity, and hope to those in his care).

UNIT 5: CHAPTER 15
Family Faith

Catholics Believe

- The Church receives God's forgiveness through the Sacraments of Healing.
- The Sacrament of Reconciliation includes contrition, confession, penance, and absolution.

✝ SCRIPTURE

Read *2 Kings 20:1–21* to learn more about God's forgiveness and healing of the faithful.

GO online www.osvcurriculum.com
For weekly scripture readings and seasonal resources

Activity
Live Your Faith

Imagine Your Reaction Forgiveness and healing are a lifelong calling. However many times the stories of Jesus are told, they can always spark a new response. Read the story of the Lost Son. (See *Luke 15:11–32*.) Ask each family member to share what he or she, as one of the characters in the parable, would have thought or felt.

People of Faith

▲ Saint John Vianney
1786–1859

John Vianney found schoolwork, especially Latin, difficult. For this reason his superiors were reluctant to see him ordained. They allowed him to be ordained because he was a model of goodness. In 1818 he was appointed pastor of the only church in a village called Ars. By the 1830s, thousands of people were traveling there every year to hear his powerful sermons and to confess their sins to him. John Vianney often spent sixteen hours a day hearing confessions and counseling people on how to be closer to God. His feast day is August 4.

Family Prayer

Saint John Vianney, pray for us that we may always seek God's forgiveness and healing. May we face challenging and difficult tasks with the same humility and acceptance you showed during your life on earth. Amen.

In Unit 5 your child is learning about MORALITY.
CCC See *Catechism of the Catholic Church* 1421, 1491, 1527, 1531 for further reading on chapter content.

© Our Sunday Visitor Curriculum Division

DISCOVER

Catholic Social Teaching:

The Solidarity of the Human Family

Faith in Action!
CATHOLIC SOCIAL TEACHING

In this unit you learned that human beings suffer because of their sinful nature. God has provided the means to heal that suffering through his Church and the sacraments. God wants all people to live in friendship, and, like the father in the parable of the Two Sons, he is eager to welcome back those who lose their way.

Solidarity

The Church teaches that as children of God, all people are united in the spirit of solidarity, or dedication to the good of all. However, the people of God have a special responsibility in justice to ensure that all humans can live in freedom and dignity. Those who live in richer countries must work to help those who live in poorer countries. People have more wealth than ever before, yet many of the world's people still suffer hunger, poverty, and lack of education. Christians must work to change this.

Many organizations within the Catholic Church reach out to people in need. It is the work of everyone who follows Jesus to help care for the whole human family.

❓ Why do Catholics in America have a special responsibility to help others throughout the world?

❓ What are some ways in which your parish works to help those in need in other countries?

215

CONNECT With the Call to Justice

A Maryknoll Family

Paul and his family are Maryknoll lay missioners. Martha Benson, Glenn Rabut, their 11-year-old son, Paul, and Paul's sister, Ana, live in one of the barrios (neighborhoods) of Venezuela. Volunteers like Paul's family travel to all parts of the globe to live and work with people in need. As missioners, they give up a comfortable and convenient life in the United States for the poverty and simplicity of another country.

For Paul, moving to a new country was very difficult. He had to give up many of the things he took for granted. He missed his friends and the things that they had done together. In Venezuela, everything was different: his home, the food, the climate, the schools, and the language that was spoken. Paul was shocked by the poverty that he saw. In the three years Paul lived there, he developed a strong sense of solidarity. He now knows what it is like to be poor and to do without. His values have changed, and he thinks of others before himself. He has even come to feel that he is at home in the barrio.

More than one hundred children have gone with their parents to missions since Maryknoll began sending out lay missioners in 1974. Families work in Africa, Asia, South and Central America, or wherever they are needed. Their commitment to work for others serves as a model for everyone.

The Gospel challenges Christians to live for others. Some do this through prayer and money. Others send food and clothes. Others leave home and work as missionaries or missioners.

Paul, his sister, and their parents share a moment in their Venezuelan home.

❓ **What motivates people to become missionaries?**

❓ **How do their children benefit from the experience?**

© Our Sunday Visitor Curriculum Division

Reach out!

SERVE Your Community

Imagine Being a Missioner

You may not be able to travel around the world, but there are many ways in which you can be a part of the work of the missions today.

Take yourself on an imaginary mission. Choose a familiar country. Describe the conditions there.

_____
_____

What would be scary about going there?

_____

What would be interesting or exciting?

_____

How would the members of your family act in and adjust to this new place?

_____
_____
_____
_____

Describe what work you would do and how you would adapt to your new surroundings.

_____
_____
_____
_____

Make a Difference

Find Ways to Help Conduct a class discussion to find ways to support the missions. These are things others are doing:

- "Adopting" a child in another country.
- Gathering and sending needed supplies to missionaries.
- Inviting missionaries to the school to share their experiences.
- Writing to the children of missionaries throughout the world.

Plan how your goal will be accomplished.

Let others know what you are doing. Invite their participation.

UNIT 5 REVIEW

A **Work with Words** Complete each sentence with the correct term(s) from the Word Bank.

WORD BANK
catechumen
contrition
consent
original
absolution
witness

1. A _____, or "learner," is a person preparing to celebrate the Sacraments of Initiation.

2. For a sin to be mortal, it must be a serious matter, done with full knowledge and complete _____.

3. _____ sin is the sin of the first humans, which led to the sinful condition of the human race from its beginning.

4. _____ is sincere sorrow for having sinned.

5. _____ is the forgiveness of sins in God's name through the Sacrament of Reconciliation.

B **Check Understanding** Circle the letter of the choice that best completes each sentence.

6. We should always remain confident and hopeful, even though sin and evil are in the world, because _____.

   a. of Baptism
   b. all Christians go to heaven
   c. a, d, and e
   d. of Reconciliation
   e. of God's power over sin

7. Baptism is like the Resurrection because _____.

   a. Jesus had both
   b. both are sacraments
   c. new life begins
   d. both need water
   e. both heal

8. The Sacraments of Reconciliation and the Anointing of the Sick both use _____ to show God's grace.

   a. oil of chrism
   b. repentance
   c. signs
   d. a pall
   e. a and d

9. The Church celebrates the Sacraments of Baptism, Confirmation, and Eucharist all together _____.

   a. on Pentecost
   b. never
   c. every Sunday
   d. only in Constantinople
   e. during the Easter Vigil

10. Venial sin _____ but does not _____ a person's relationship with God.

    a. weakens / destroy
    b. improves / deny
    c. changes / weaken
    d. reverses / change
    e. strengthens / start

C Make Connections Write a response to each statement or question.

Name three of the steps in an examination of conscience.

11. _____

12. _____

13. _____

Describe three ways that as a member of the Body of Christ, you can get help to deepen your faith.

14. _____

15. _____

16. _____

17. What is the purpose of a prayer of lamentation?
_____

18. What will solve the problem you express in a lamentation?
_____

19. When you are faced with the problem of evil, what helps you?
_____

20. How are sins forgiven?
_____
_____
_____
_____

Unit 6
Sacraments

In this unit you will...

learn that in the liturgical assembly the Holy Spirit strengthens the whole community and forms us as an assembly. In worship and daily living, the community shows that through the Eucharist Christ lives in us, and we live in Christ. The Eucharist closely unites Christ's followers to him and to one another.

Faith in Action!

Catholic Social Teaching Principle:
Call to Family, Community, and Participation

Chapter 16: Gathered for Mass

Let Us Pray

Leader: Loving God, bring us together as a community.

"When I went in procession with the crowd,
I went with them to the house of God."
Psalm 42:5

All: Loving God, bring us together as a community. Amen.

Activity

Let's Begin

● **Do Your Part** An elephant met a hummingbird lying on its back with its feet straight up in the air. "What are you doing?" the elephant asked. The hummingbird replied, "I have heard that the sky is going to fall and I am trying to hold it up." The amazed elephant said, "How can one hummingbird keep the sky from falling?" The hummingbird answered, "We all must do our part."

Think about what part you play in your family, in your group of friends, and in the Church.

Why is it important for everyone to do his or her part?

_____
_____

What tasks can best be accomplished by people working together as a group?

_____
_____

● **Describe Your Role** Tell a partner about a time when you did your part to make something great happen.

221

Explore

United in Christ's Body

Focus What is the liturgical assembly?

At Sunday Mass, Sally sees Billy Yuan with his grandfather, Mr. Jones, who is in his wheelchair. There's Father Burke, talking with Deacon Tom; and Sister Teresita is with the Dixon family. Sally says hello to DJ and waves to Zoe, who always comes early to pray the Rosary. Happy or sad, people come. All are welcome.

The Assembly of Believers

The worshipers at Sally's church have come from different places to assemble as one community of faith. When the opening hymn begins and all raise their voices in song and prayer, they become something more than just a group of assorted individuals. They become a **liturgical assembly**, doing the most important thing that Catholics can do—celebrating the Eucharist.

When a parish community comes together to celebrate the Eucharist, you can see that all kinds of people make up the Body of Christ. Rich and poor, old and young, hearty and frail, people come together from all nations and cultures to share in the Mass, the celebration of their salvation through Christ. Together they become an assembly of the People of God. Christ is truly present in the people assembled.

? Who are the people you see at Mass on Sunday?

? What sights and sounds make you feel welcome?

The Real Presence

The Eucharist is central to Catholic life because it unites Christ's followers more closely to him and to one another. In the liturgy, Catholics celebrate the special presence of Christ. During the Eucharist, Christ is present in the assembly, in the priest, in the word of God, and in the Eucharist. Most important, Christ is present in the sacred Bread and Wine, which truly become his Body and Blood. This unique, true presence of Christ in the Eucharist under the appearance of bread and wine is called the Real Presence.

In the liturgy the people remember with thanksgiving the Paschal mystery of the Lord through prayer, song, sacrament, listening, active participation, and reception of Holy Communion. All gathered are united to the sacrifice of Christ through which new life comes.

The **liturgical assembly** is the community of believers who come together for public worship, especially in the Eucharist.

The **Real Presence** is the true presence of Christ in the Eucharist under the appearance of bread and wine.

Activity — Share Your Faith

Reflect: Think about all of the people who are included in the Sunday assembly.

Share: With a partner, discuss each person or group mentioned in the web below.

Act: Beneath the reference to each group or person, write a sentence stating how each one shows the belief that Jesus is present.

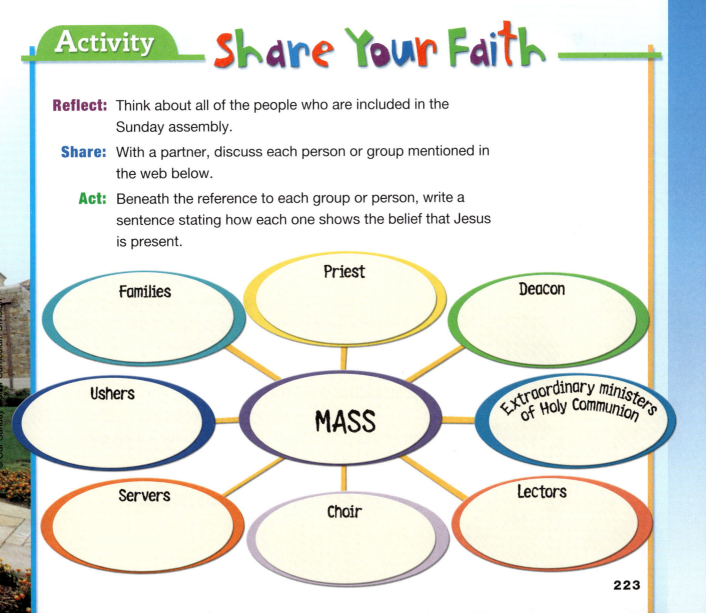

Explore

Participation in the Community

 **Focus** Why do Christians celebrate the Lord's day?

When Sally joins the parish community for Mass on Sunday, she may not be aware that she is stepping into a living tradition many centuries old. In the time of the early Christians, Sunday was the Lord's day, the day on which the community celebrated the Resurrection of Jesus. The Church continues this practice today.

The Eucharist is the high point of a life of faith shared by a community. The Christian community must be built day by day, as Saint Paul advised an early Church community.

SCRIPTURE

"We urge you, brothers, admonish the idle, cheer the fainthearted, support the weak, be patient with all. See that no one returns evil for evil; rather, always seek what is good [both] for each other and for all. Rejoice always. Pray without ceasing. In all circumstances give thanks, for this is the will of God for you in Christ Jesus."

1 Thessalonians 5:14–18

Sunday Observance

According to Jewish custom, the Sabbath began on Friday evening. The early Jewish Christians adopted this custom. Similarly, the Church begins its observance of Sunday on Saturday evening. Because of this, Saturday evening Mass is considered part of the Sunday observance.

Participation in the Sunday Eucharist is a privilege and a duty. It offers the opportunity to meet God in a dialogue through Christ and the Holy Spirit. To deliberately stay away from Mass on Sunday regularly without a very good reason is a serious matter.

 How does your parish observe Sunday?

Liturgical Ministries

Within the community, certain members of the Church are called to special service as ordained ministers—bishops, priests, and deacons. By the power of the Holy Spirit, bishops and priests *preside,* or act as leaders of the Eucharistic assembly. Deacons assist them.

Other members called by the community also have distinct roles in the liturgy. They are greeters, choir members, cantors, musicians, readers, altar servers, and extraordinary ministers of Holy Communion. All of these people help the assembly worship as one community.

❓ **If you could choose to serve in any of these liturgical roles, which would you choose? Explain your choice.**

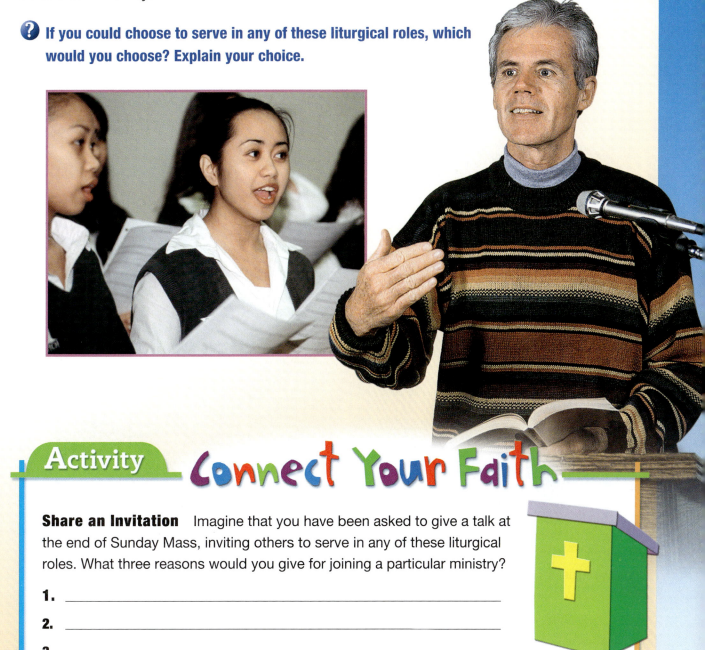

Activity — Connect Your Faith

Share an Invitation Imagine that you have been asked to give a talk at the end of Sunday Mass, inviting others to serve in any of these liturgical roles. What three reasons would you give for joining a particular ministry?

1. _____
2. _____
3. _____

225

Forms of Service

Focus What are the specific responsibilities of liturgical ministers?

All members of the parish are invited to participate in the Eucharist. Some members are called to serve the assembly in special ways. Think about the skills and qualities required for each one.

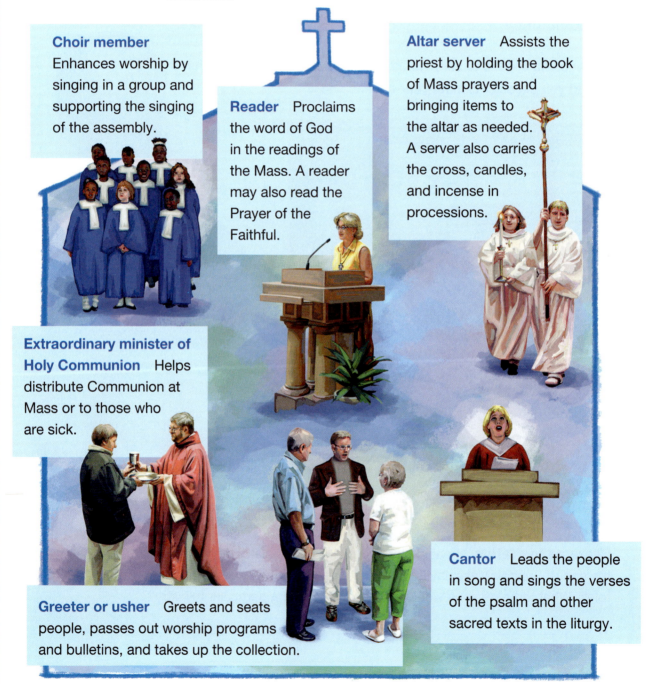

Choir member Enhances worship by singing in a group and supporting the singing of the assembly.

Reader Proclaims the word of God in the readings of the Mass. A reader may also read the Prayer of the Faithful.

Altar server Assists the priest by holding the book of Mass prayers and bringing items to the altar as needed. A server also carries the cross, candles, and incense in processions.

Extraordinary minister of Holy Communion Helps distribute Communion at Mass or to those who are sick.

Greeter or usher Greets and seats people, passes out worship programs and bulletins, and takes up the collection.

Cantor Leads the people in song and sings the verses of the psalm and other sacred texts in the liturgy.

? What skills or abilities do you have that would make you good at one of these ministries?

Activity: Live Your Faith

Job Descriptions On the chart below, add the names of those you know in your parish who perform these services. Get help from other students, and consult the parish bulletin or Web site. Then write a note to thank the people for their service to the parish. Use the space below to plan your note. Then write it on a separate sheet of paper and mail it.

Greeters/Ushers	
Servers	
Choir Members	
Readers	
Extraordinary Ministers of Holy Communion	

Celebration of the Word

 Let Us Pray

Gather and begin with the Sign of the Cross.

Leader: God has gathered us as a community of faith. We bring our joys and sorrows, our faith, and our love for one another.

Reader: A reading from the holy Gospel according to Matthew.

Read Matthew 5:23–24.

The Gospel of the Lord.

All: **Praise to you, Lord Jesus Christ.**

Reflect quietly on the reading.

Leader: Taught by our Savior's command, and formed by the word of God, we dare to say:

All pray the Lord's Prayer.

Leader: Let us pray.

Bow your heads as the leader prays.

All: **Amen.**

Leader: The peace of the Lord be with you always.

All: **And with your spirit.**

Leader: Let us share with one another a sign of Christ's peace.

Share a sign of peace.

Sing together.

Gather us in—the lost and forsaken,
Gather us in—the blind and the lame;
Call to us now, and we shall awaken,
We shall arise at the sound of our name.

"Gather Us In", Marty Haugen,
© 1982, GIA Publications, Inc.

CHAPTER 16 Review

A **Work with Words** Match each description in Column 1 with the correct term in Column 2.

Column 1

_____ 1. ordained ministers who assist bishops and priests

_____ 2. called together by God to celebrate the liturgy

_____ 3. presides at the Eucharist

_____ 4. community built up by daily faithful living

_____ 5. has a role in the Eucharistic celebration

Column 2

a. bishop or priest

b. liturgical assembly

c. Body of Christ

d. each individual

e. deacons

B **Check Understanding** Fill in the circle next to the correct response.

6. The true presence of Christ in the Eucharist under the appearance of bread and wine is called the _____.
    - ○ Paschal mystery
    - ○ Eucharistic miracle
    - ○ Real Presence
    - ○ Holy Communion
    - ○ Incarnation

7. The Body of Christ is made up of _____.
    - ○ spirit and flesh
    - ○ humanity and divinity
    - ○ Father and Holy Spirit
    - ○ all kinds of people
    - ○ saints

8. During Mass, Christ is present in all of these except _____.
    - ○ the assembly
    - ○ the bells and incense
    - ○ the priest
    - ○ the word of God
    - ○ the Eucharist

9. Participation in the Sunday Eucharist is _____.
    - ○ a privilege and an option
    - ○ merely a duty
    - ○ a privilege and a duty
    - ○ merely an option
    - ○ the same as praying at home

10. All these are particular roles in the liturgy except _____.
    - ○ cantor
    - ○ reader
    - ○ server
    - ○ greeter
    - ○ catechumen

UNIT 6: CHAPTER 16
Family Faith

Catholics Believe

- The wheat bread and grape wine become the Body and Blood of Jesus in the Sacrament of the Eucharist.
- In the liturgical assembly, the Holy Spirit's grace of faith strengthens the community.

SCRIPTURE

Read *1 Peter 3:8–12* to learn more about how members of a faith community are to behave toward one another.

www.osvcurriculum.com
For weekly scripture readings and seasonal resources

Activity
Live Your Faith

Introduce Yourself Part of belonging to the liturgical assembly is getting to know others. This week:

- plan to attend Mass as a family.
- arrive early for Mass or stay after Mass.
- introduce yourself to several parishioners and liturgical ministers.
- write down names so that you will remember them.
- reflect on the experience. What did you learn by doing this?

People of Faith

▲ Saint Catherine of Siena 1347–1380

Catherine's father owned a small cloth-dyeing business in the Italian republic of Siena, but her family was not influential. From her earliest years, Catherine was drawn to a life of prayer and self-denial. Through her relationship with God, she acquired such force of personality that she became an important spiritual counselor to many people. Before reaching the age of thirty, she was a valued adviser to two popes. Saint Catherine's feast day is April 29. She was declared a Doctor of the Church in 1977.

Family Prayer

Saint Catherine, pray for us that we may share your learning and your great love for God. May we strive to be a force for healing and wisdom in the world, as you were. Amen.

In Unit 6 your child is learning about SACRAMENTS.

 *See Catechism of the Catholic Church 1141, 1373–1381 for further reading on chapter content.*

Chapter 17: Liturgy of the Word

Let Us Pray

Leader: Gracious God, help us trust you in all things.
"For the LORD's word is true;
all his works are trustworthy."
Psalm 33:4

All: Gracious God, help us trust you in all things. Amen.

Activity — Let's Begin

● **Family Story** The family huddled around the computer screen. "Look! There's the ship!" exclaimed one of the kids. "And there's Great-Grandma Julia's name on the passenger list!" They were visiting the Ellis Island Web site to find records of their family's immigration to the United States. The blurry photograph and the old-fashioned handwriting revealed a moment in history that had influenced many of the circumstances of their lives.

What are some important and happy events in your family's life? How did these events affect your family?

_____
_____
_____
_____
_____

● **Tell Family Stories** Share with a partner a family story.

231

The Dead Sea Scrolls

 **Focus** Why are the Dead Sea Scrolls important?

Faith Fact

Bedouin comes from the Arabic word *bedu,* which means "inhabitant of the desert."

Family records, photographs, and books help you learn from the past about your family. Similarly, ancient documents help modern scholars understand biblical times. In 1947 some ancient documents called the Dead Sea Scrolls were found in caves near the Dead Sea. Here is the story of their discovery.

BIOGRAPHY

Voices from the Past

One day in 1947, three shepherds of the Ta'amireh tribe of bedouin people were herding their goats on a rocky cliff along the northwest shore of the Dead Sea in Palestine. One shepherd, Jum'a Muhammed, saw the goats climbing too high, and he climbed the cliff to bring them back.

The shepherd noticed a cave—but the opening was too small for him to enter. Could there be a treasure inside? He called his cousins, Khalil Musa and Muhammed Ahmed el-Hamed. They climbed up to see, but it was getting dark.

Two days later, Muhammed Ahmed el-Hamed got up at dawn. He left his two cousins asleep and climbed the cliff. The slender youth squeezed through the narrow opening and lowered himself into the cave. Tall, narrow jars lined the walls.

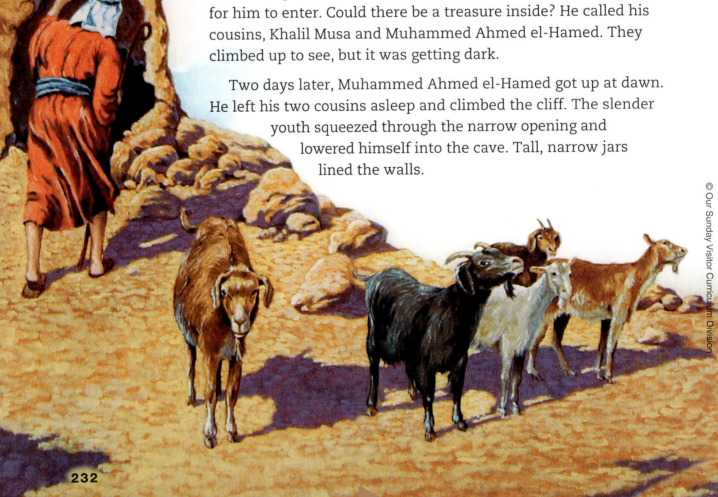

Muhammed Finds a Treasure

Muhammed reached into one jar after another. Eight of them were empty. The ninth was filled with dirt. Exploring further, he finally felt three bundles, two wrapped in cloth and one in leather. Muhammed pulled them out and rushed back to his cousins, eager to show them what he had found.

The others were disappointed. What kind of treasure was this? A pile of old scrolls! The shepherds had no idea that they held in their hands the greatest archaeological discovery of the century. The Dead Sea Scrolls, as they became known, contain the earliest complete text of the Book of Isaiah, as well as other fragments of Scripture. The scrolls, which have been carefully preserved, probably date from the first century before Christ.

❓ **What would you have done if you had found such objects in a cave in Palestine? Why?**

Activity — Share Your Faith

Reflect: Read *Isaiah 66:1–2*. Reflect silently on its meaning.

Share: With a partner, take turns telling what the passage means to each of you.

Act: Write three sentences that summarize your understanding of the passage.

_____

_____

_____

God Speaks to Us

 **Focus** Why is the Liturgy of the Word important?

Every time you open the Bible, you discover a treasure—the word of God. Even though the Bible was written long ago, it still reveals a message from God to you today.

God's word in **Scripture** is not something you can interpret on your own. The Church's understanding of the message of Jesus comes to you from the Apostles and from the life of the Church and its teachers. That understanding, handed on to and further understood by each new generation of Christians, is called **Tradition**. Scripture and Tradition have one common source: the Word of God conveyed through God's revelation.

✝ SCRIPTURE

"Let the word of Christ dwell in you richly, as in all wisdom you teach and admonish one another, singing psalms, hymns, and spiritual songs with gratitude in your hearts to God."

Colossians 3:16

❓ How do you express your gratitude to God during the Liturgy of the Word?

Honoring God's Word

Ritual actions let the assembly know the importance of the word of God. The readings are proclaimed from the ambo, the podium-like structure situated to the side of the altar. A lighted candle is usually placed near the ambo. After the first and second readings, the reader pauses and then says, "The word of the Lord," and you reply, "Thanks be to God."

Sometimes, incense is used to reverence the Book of the Gospels. After the priest or deacon reads the Gospel, he raises the book and then kisses it to show honor and love of God's word.

Proclaimed and Preached

The Liturgy of the Word is the first of the two main parts of the Mass. In readings from the Old and New Testaments, God speaks to the heart of each person. Jesus is truly present in the word as it is proclaimed and preached in the liturgy, just as he is truly present in the consecrated Bread and Wine.

The Liturgy of the Word

First Reading	The first reading is from the Old Testament or from the Acts of the Apostles.
Responsorial Psalm	The assembly usually sings a response taken from the psalm, and the choir sings the verses.
Second Reading	The second reading is from one of the New Testament Letters or from the Book of Revelation.
Gospel Acclamation	An alleluia is sung, except during Lent, to express the assembly's anticipation of the Gospel.
Gospel Dialogue/ Gospel Reading	Each person traces a cross on forehead, lips, and heart before the Gospel is proclaimed.
Homily	The priest or deacon explains God's word.
Creed	Usually, the Nicene Creed is professed.
Prayer of the Faithful	The assembly prays for the needs of Church leaders, the faithful, and the world.

Scripture is the holy writings of the Old and New Testaments, the written word of God.

Tradition is the living process of handing on the message of Jesus through the Church, especially through its teachers.

Activity — Connect Your Faith

Respond to God Write a psalm prayer in response to the gift of God's word in Scripture. Use this form:

- Write words of praise and thanks.

  _____

- Describe what God has given or taught you through his word.

  _____

- Tell what you will do in response.

  _____

Explore

Breaking Open the Word

 **Focus** How do you live God's word?

The word of God nourishes the Christian community in the liturgy. By reflecting on the Sunday readings either before or after Mass, you allow God's word to become a real part of your life. When that happens, you live God's word.

Reflect on the Word

Use these steps to reflect on the Sunday readings:

- Begin with a prayer asking the Holy Spirit to open your heart to hear God's word.
- Read the Gospel or one of the other readings aloud.

Ask yourself the following questions:

- **What** words in the reading are important to me?
- **If** I were going to tell someone the message of this reading, what would I say?
- **How** does this message apply to my life today?
- **What** action can I take today that will make the message of God's word come alive in the world in which I live?

❓ What kind of help do you need in order to hear God's word better?

236

Activity: Live Your Faith

Read with Understanding With a small group, use a selection from next Sunday's liturgy and read it according to the instructions on the previous page.

Compose a prayer to the Holy Spirit.

_____
_____
_____
_____

Read the passage aloud as a proclamation of God's word.

What words in the reading are important to you?

_____
_____
_____
_____

What is the message of the reading?

_____
_____
_____

How does it apply to you right now?

_____
_____
_____

What can you do to bring this message to the world in which we live?

_____
_____
_____

Celebration of the Word

 Let Us Pray

Gather and begin with the Sign of the Cross.

Leader: God our Father, open our hearts to see the wisdom of your word.

All: **Amen.**

Reader 1: A reading from the Book of Isaiah.

Read Isaiah 40:28–31.

Reader 1: The word of the Lord.

All: **Thanks be to God.**

Sing together.

My shepherd is the Lord, nothing indeed shall I want.

"Psalm 23" © 1963, The Grail, GIA Publications, Inc., Agent

Reader 2: A reading from the Letter of Saint Paul to the Ephesians.

Read Ephesians 1:3–6.

Reader 2: The word of the Lord.

All: **Thanks be to God.**

Reader 3: Sing Alleluia!

All: **Alleluia, Alleluia, Alleluia**

Reader 4: A reading from the holy Gospel according to John.

Read John 10:1–11.

Reader 4: The Gospel of the Lord.

All: **Praise to you, Lord Jesus Christ.**

Leader: Let us pray.

Bow your heads as the leader prays.

All: **Amen.**

CHAPTER 17
Review

A. Work with Words
Complete each sentence with the correct term from the Word Bank.

WORD BANK
Acclamation
Scripture
Tradition
Nicene Creed
candle
ambo
homily

1. The Bible is also called _____.
2. The living process of understanding the message of Jesus that is handed on to each new generation of Christians comes from _____.
3. The _____ explains the reading in the Liturgy of the Word.
4. Readings are proclaimed from the _____ near the altar.
5. The homily is usually followed by the _____.

B. Check Understanding
Circle the letter of the choice that best completes the sentence or answers the question.

6. The Responsorial Psalm is said or sung after the _____.
   - a. first reading
   - b. Gospel
   - c. Creed
   - d. second reading
   - e. homily

7. Jesus is present in the _____.
   - a. Eucharist alone
   - b. Word alone
   - c. Tradition alone
   - d. Scripture alone
   - e. Word and Eucharist

8. Participation in the Liturgy of the Word includes all of these except _____.
   - a. listening
   - b. fasting
   - c. reflecting
   - d. reading
   - e. responding

9. Scripture and Tradition have one _____ source.
   - a. historical
   - b. biblical
   - c. common
   - d. written
   - e. human

10. The complete text of the Book of _____ was discovered among the Dead Sea Scrolls.
    - a. Job
    - b. Ruth
    - c. Jeremiah
    - d. Isaiah
    - e. Psalms

UNIT 6: CHAPTER 17

Family Faith

Catholics Believe

- The Word of God is conveyed through Scripture and Tradition.
- Jesus is truly present in the word as it is proclaimed and preached in the liturgy.

SCRIPTURE

Read *Matthew 26:1–30* to learn more about the events surrounding the Last Supper.

GO online www.osvcurriculum.com
For weekly scripture readings and seasonal resources

Activity

Live Your Faith

Drive Home You can prepare to meet Christ in the word by reading the Scripture readings before going to Sunday Mass. Find the readings for the next Sunday in the parish bulletin or worship aid. Choose one reading to read aloud at home. Name something you noticed in the reading. On your way home after Mass, practice "driving the word home." Discuss the main message you heard in the readings.

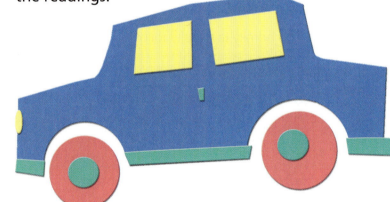

People of Faith

Jerome was a Christian, but he loved the Latin literature written before the Romans accepted the Christian faith. One night in a dream, God accused Jerome of preferring this literature to the Bible. Jerome awoke from his dream a changed person. He spent the rest of his life studying the Bible. Jerome's knowledge of Hebrew and Greek enabled him to produce a Latin translation of the Bible, called the *Vulgate*, which the Church used for the next 1,500 years. Saint Jerome's feast day is September 30. He is the patron saint of biblical scholars.

▲ Saint Jerome
c. 341–420

Family Prayer

Saint Jerome, pray for us that we may love the word of God as you did. We praise God for your brilliance and thank him for all the benefits that have flowed from your work and continue to enlighten our minds and hearts. Amen.

© Our Sunday Visitor Curriculum Division

In Unit 6 your child is learning about SACRAMENTS.

CCC See Catechism of the Catholic Church 84, 108, 1088, 1100 for further reading on chapter content.

Chapter 18 Liturgy of the Eucharist

 **Let Us Pray**

Leader: God our Father, feed us with heavenly food.
"You bring bread from the earth,
and wine to gladden our hearts,"
Psalm 104:14–15

All: God our Father, feed us with heavenly food. Amen.

Activity

● **Food Facts**

- Every day 800 million people in the world go hungry.

- In the United States 12 million children have to skip meals or eat less than they want so that their families can make ends meet.

- Each year 6 million children die from causes related to hunger.

- The basic health needs of the world's poorest people could be met for less money than what animal lovers in the United States and Europe spend on pet food each year.

Statistics from Bread for the World

Now think about how those who are hungry depend on others. Would you be willing to sacrifice so that others could eat?

How could you reduce waste in your home and school?

_____

_____

 Write a Paragraph Think about all the ways that food is part of your family activities and celebrations. On a separate sheet of paper, describe some special food that your family has on a certain holiday or special occasion.

Explore

Feed the Hungry

 **Focus** What hunger does the Eucharist satisfy?

This story, adapted from Russian writer Yevgeny Yevtushenko's life story, shows how sacrifice and generosity can lead to renewed hope and life.

BIOGRAPHY

Yevgeny's Story

One day during World War II, I was standing with my mother in Red Square in the center of Moscow. We saw a huge crowd of Russian women with angry faces gazing with hatred at the group of 20,000 German prisoners of war being marched into the square. All of the women were mourning family members who had been killed by the Germans. The Russian women shouted at the German generals and threatened them. But then, as the German soldiers came into view, the mood of the crowd changed. The soldiers were thin, hungry, dirty, and wounded. The square became still. All I could hear was the sound of the marchers' plodding feet.

Suddenly a poor old woman pushed her way past the police. She walked up to one tired soldier, unwrapped a small piece of brown bread, and put it in the soldier's pocket. Other women began to do the same. From every side women were running toward the soldiers to give them bread.

❓ What did the actions of the Russian women show?

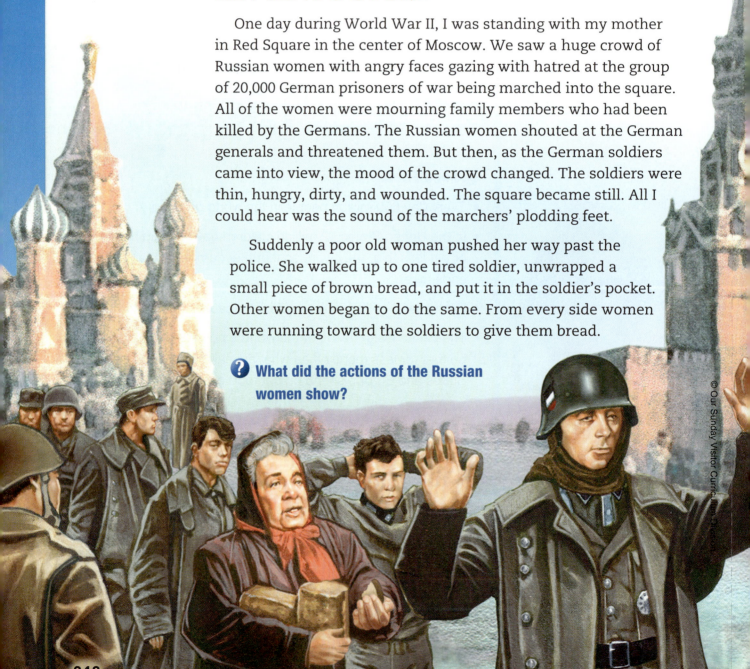

Eucharist

The story you have just read illustrates both the necessity of food and the way that food and hunger can create a bond among people.

No matter what the cause, the hunger that people suffer is real. But those who hunger for bread also hunger for spiritual food. This hunger is as real as physical hunger. It is the hunger for happiness and love. Only God can feed this hunger, for God alone is the source of true happiness. God gave people a taste of true happiness in Jesus, the Savior.

In the Sacrament of the Eucharist, you share the Bread of Life and the Cup of Salvation. You taste the happiness you will one day experience fully with God in heaven. The bread you eat at meals and the Bread of Life in the Eucharist are similar in that both offer nourishment. The Bread of the Eucharist, however, offers lasting spiritual nourishment and the promise of eternal life.

Activity — Share Your Faith

Reflect: Imagine that you are producing a movie called *Bread of the World*.

Share: With a partner, discuss ways in which the Eucharist is food for others.

Act: Draw one scene for your movie. Describe your idea to the class.

The Eucharistic Mystery

 **Focus** Why is the Eucharist a sacrifice?

At the Last Supper, Jesus' words and actions changed the traditional Passover meal into something new. It became a living memorial of the sacrifice that Jesus was about to make by his death.

SCRIPTURE — Matthew 26:26–28

The Last Supper

While they were eating, Jesus took bread, said the blessing, broke it, and giving it to his disciples said, "Take and eat; this is my body." Then he took a cup, gave thanks, and gave it to them, saying, "Drink from it, all of you, for this is my blood of the covenant, which will be shed on behalf of many for the forgiveness of sins."

Matthew 26:26–28

❓ **In what part of the Mass do you hear the words of this Scripture passage?**

In order to give himself to his followers as the Bread of Life, Jesus died on the cross. His death was a perfect sacrifice of love. It brought salvation and the abundance of God's grace to the world. In the Eucharist, Christ unites his followers to his own sacrifice so that they can experience salvation.

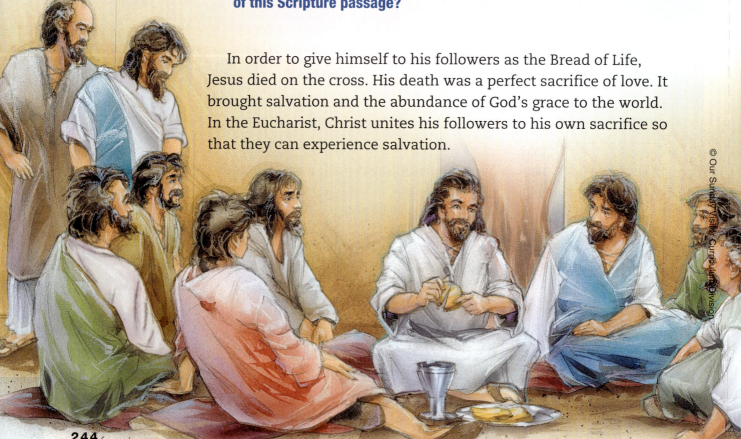

Through the Holy Spirit

Every time you participate in the Eucharist, you share both in the meal and in the sacrifice of Jesus. Throughout the Mass, the assembly is gathered and led by God's Spirit. In the Eucharistic Prayer, the people, led by the priest, ask the Father to send the Spirit. This great prayer is at the heart of the second half of the Mass—the Liturgy of the Eucharist.

The priest calls on the Holy Spirit to make holy the assembly and the gifts of bread and wine. In the part of the prayer called the **consecration**, the priest uses Jesus' own words from the Last Supper to consecrate the bread and wine. By the words of the priest and the power of the Holy Spirit, the wheat bread and grape wine are transformed into something sacred. They become the Body and Blood of Jesus. The Church refers to this mystery as **transubstantiation**. Through the action of the priest, Christ himself offers the sacrifice. Prayers for the whole Church follow. The Eucharistic Prayer ends with praise for the Trinity, and the assembly responds with the Great Amen.

When you truly believe and respond in faith, you can be transformed by the Body and Blood of Jesus. Through the Eucharist you live in Christ, and Christ lives in you.

Words of Faith

The **consecration** is that part of the Eucharistic Prayer in which the words of Jesus are prayed over the bread and wine, and these elements become the Body and Blood of Christ.

Transubstantiation is the process by which the power of the Holy Spirit and the words of the priest transform the bread and wine into the Body and Blood of Jesus.

Activity: Connect Your Faith

Talk About Symbols Why do you think that Jesus chose bread and wine to symbolize his Body and Blood? In the two figures, write all the things that bread and wine can signify that make them good symbols for Jesus' sacrifice.

Bread

Wine

Explore

Live the Eucharist

 **Focus** What does it mean to live the Eucharist?

Having received Christ in the Eucharist, the assembly is sent forth to live the Eucharist. There are ways to be more active in living the Eucharist in your daily life.

Share the Gift of Love

As you perform these actions, remember that you are acting in Jesus' name. You are following his example of love and service.

Give thanks
Every day, think about the gifts that you and your friends and family have been given and thank God for them.

Communicate
When you are with a friend or family member, listen to what that person is saying. When it is your turn, share your thoughts and feelings.

Sacrifice
Once each day, do something to help someone else, but do not tell anyone about it.

Remember
Set aside some special time to read the stories of Jesus in the New Testament. Think about what they are saying about your own life.

Go forth
Observe your school and neighborhood. Identify people who need help or situations that you could improve, and take some action.

? How is the Eucharist a gift?

? What responsibility does the Eucharist impose on us?

Activity — Live Your Faith

Draw a Comic Strip In the frames provided, design and draw a comic strip that shows people your age living out the Eucharist. Show as many of the ways explained on the opposite page as you can.

Litany of the Eucharist

 Let Us Pray

Gather and begin with the Sign of the Cross.

Leader: Brothers and sisters, in the Eucharist Jesus continues to give us his life and his love. Let us praise and thank him for his goodness.

Reader 1: Praise to you Lord Jesus, Bread of Life;

All: **You share your life with us in the Eucharist.**

Reader 2: Praise to you Lord Jesus, Cup of Salvation;

All: **The life you give us knows no end.**

Reader 3: Praise to you Lord Jesus, Food of Pilgrims;

All: **You strengthen us on the journey of faith.**

Reader 4: Praise to you Lord Jesus, Wine of Compassion;

All: **You sustain us in times of sorrow and pain.**

Reader 5: Praise to you Lord Jesus, Nourishment of our Spirits;

All: **All who accept you will be satisfied and filled.**

Reader 6: Praise to you Lord Jesus, Chalice of Blessing;

All: **May we know the joy of your presence forever.**

Leader: Let us pray.

Bow your heads as the leader prays.

All: **Amen.**

 Sing together the refrain.

Eat this bread, drink this cup, come to him and never be hungry. Eat this bread, drink this cup, trust in him and you will not thirst.

"Eat This Bread" © 1984, Les Presses de Taige, GIA Publications, Inc., agent

CHAPTER 18
Review

A **Work with Words** Circle the choice that best completes the sentence.

1. The Eucharist is both a _____ and a _____. (sacrament/commandment, sacrifice/sacred meal, sacrifice/tabernacle)

2. Living the Eucharist means having gratitude for God's gifts and showing it through _____. (meditation, sacrificing for others, doing penance)

3. The changing of bread and wine into the Body and Blood of Jesus is called _____. (redemption, celebration, transubstantiation)

4. In the Eucharistic Prayer, the words and activities of the priest and the power of the Holy Spirit bring about the _____ of the bread and wine. (consecration, sacrifice, celebration)

5. Jesus gave himself _____. (to change the Third Commandment, as a perfect sacrifice of love, to consecrate a tabernacle)

B **Check Understanding** In the boxes provided, write the words that complete the sentences. If your other answers are correct, the answer to number 10 will appear in the shaded boxes.

6. The Russian women gave bread to the _____.

7. The Bread of the Eucharist offers lasting spiritual _____.

8. When you truly believe and respond in faith, you can be _____ by the Body and Blood of Jesus.

9. "This is my blood of the _____, which will be shed on behalf of many for the forgiveness of sins."

10. In the Sacrament of the Eucharist, you share the Bread of _____ and the Cup of Salvation.

Family Faith

UNIT 6: CHAPTER 18

Catholics Believe

- In Sunday worship and daily living, the community shows that the Eucharist is the source and the summit of the Catholic Church.

- The Eucharist closely унites Christ's followers to him and to one another.

SCRIPTURE

Read *1 Corinthians 11:23–34* to learn more about the Lord's Supper.

www.osvcurriculum.com
For weekly scripture readings and seasonal resources

Activity

Live Your Faith

Improve Meals Discuss the experience of mealtimes in your home. Are they enjoyable, hectic, or a little of both? Recall the best meals you have shared as a family. Did they nourish your spirit as well as your body? Decide on three simple choices you can make to improve your family mealtimes. Now put your ideas into practice!

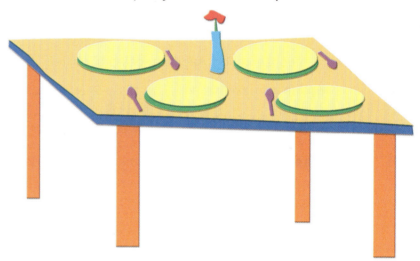

People of Faith

▲ Saint Clare of Assisi 1194–1253

Clare grew up in Assisi with Francis, who also later became a saint, and she was one of his first disciples. She led a group of women who wished to lead a life of poverty and prayer. Clare asked the pope to allow her sisters to live entirely by begging! Despite her poverty, Clare lived happily. The townspeople loved her. Twice, when enemies threatened Assisi, the people brought Clare, holding in her hands the Blessed Sacrament, to the city walls. Both times the enemies fled. Saint Clare's feast day is August 11. She is the patron saint of television.

Family Prayer

Saint Clare, pray for us that we may share your joy in poverty and your love of peace. May we learn from you to remain faithful to the prompting of the Spirit and always keep our hearts fixed on the will of God. Amen.

© Our Sunday Visitor Curriculum Division

In Unit 6 your child is learning about SACRAMENTS.

CCC See *Catechism of the Catholic Church* 1324, 1372, 1398 for further reading on chapter content.

DISCOVER

Catholic Social Teaching:

Call to Family, Community, and Participation

In this unit you learned that the liturgical assembly is made up of people of all different ages and sizes who become one in the Eucharist. Just as each member of your family has different responsibilities, so each member of God's faith family can participate in the liturgy in different ways.

Call to Community

The Church teaches that the family is the fundamental community in society. God created families in which you can grow as the person he wants you to be. Your role in the family helps you understand your role in society. As you grow and become a member of other communities, you have responsibilities to them as well. You care for those who are young, old, handicapped, or poor. Jesus spoke clearly about your responsibility to reach out. The Corporal Works of Mercy describe your responsibility.

You have many opportunities. Some neighborhoods have people living in poverty, most have elderly citizens, and some may have people who need homes or jobs. You know the discomfort of unfamiliar surroundings. Immigrants face problems that you can help them manage. Members of Catholic Social Services live the Corporal Works of Mercy each day as they help others.

❓ **To what communities do you belong? What responsibilities do you have as a member of those communities?**

CONNECT With the Call to Justice

North Carolina Welcomes New Neighbors

Many people travel to the United States to find a better life. It is sometimes hard for them to buy food, to find housing, and to learn about their new home. Let's see how people in North Carolina help.

Ana Morrison traveled to North Carolina from California. She had come to California from El Salvador and experienced difficulties in adjusting to life in the United States. She gradually learned to speak English and eventually began to feel that she belonged in her new land.

Ana decided to do something for other immigrants so that they would have an easier time than she did. Her "English as a Second Language" classes helped immigrants adjust to life in America. These classes helped them read signs and newspapers and made it easier for them to converse with workers, shopkeepers, and others whom they met. They became able to understand and respond. Ana Morrison said, "We must try to educate ourselves if we are going to be effective."

Catholic Social Services also helps immigrants in North Carolina. Through a program called Casa Guadalupe, this organization works for Hispanic and Latino newcomers. For example, Casa Guadalupe workers help the newly arrived immigrants find work, find doctors and housing, understand their rights, and do their banking. Casa Guadalupe also provides food and clothes to those who need them. These services are offered free of charge.

- Why is it hard for people to be accepted into a new community?
- What could be done to help people feel at home in their new community?

© Our Sunday Visitor Curriculum Division

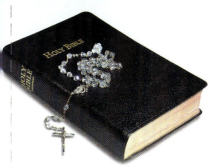

Reach Out!

SERVE Your Community

Plan a Prayer Service

Jesus calls his followers to help those who are closest to them but also to help others in this world. You can look for opportunities to carry out the Corporal Works of Mercy each day.

Take some time to think of needs you know about in your neighborhood, city, or town. You may have learned of special needs from the news or heard about them from other people. You may also know some needs from firsthand experience. Make your list as complete as you can.

_____
_____
_____
_____

Now write three petitions for a prayer service that will ask for God's help in meeting the needs on your list.

_____
_____
_____

There will be three committees: one to choose Scripture, another to choose music, and a third to write the prayers. Enter the name of the committee on which you work, and write notes about your decisions.

Committee: _____

Notes: _____
_____
_____
_____

Make a Difference

Pray for Your Family and Community

With the help of your teacher, conduct the prayer service you have planned. Offer the petitions you have written at the appropriate time. At the end of the prayer service, during several minutes of silence, decide on something that you can do to help meet one of the needs you mentioned in a petition. Choose something that you are willing to do, and commit yourself to it. Write it on a separate sheet of paper. When you have fulfilled your promise, give it to your teacher to post in the room.

I PLEDGE

I Pledge to visit my grandmother in the hospital.

Signature: *Steve Kibler*

UNIT 6 REVIEW

A **Work with Words**   Match each description in Column 1 with the correct term in Column 2.

Column 1

_____ 1. words that are prayed over the bread and wine so that they become Christ's Body and Blood

_____ 2. community of believers who come together for public worship

_____ 3. living process of handing on the message of Jesus through the Church

_____ 4. the heart of the second half of the Mass

_____ 5. the true presence of Christ in the Eucharist

Column 2

a. Tradition

b. Eucharistic Prayer

c. Real Presence

d. the consecration

e. liturgical assembly

Complete each statement.

6. The bread you eat at meals and the Bread of Life in the _____ are similar in that both offer nourishment.

7. By the power of the Holy Spirit, bishops and priests, _____ ministers, preside or act as leaders of the Eucharistic assembly.

8. The Dead Sea Scrolls, which have been carefully preserved, probably date from the _____ before Christ.

9. At the _____, Jesus' words and actions changed the traditional Passover meal into a living memorial of the sacrifice he was about to make by his death on the cross.

10. The _____ are the holy writings of the Old and New Testaments, the written word of God.

B **Check Understanding** Complete each sentence with the correct term.

11. Through the _____, you live in Christ, and Christ lives in you.

12. Jesus is truly present in the _____ as it is proclaimed and preached in the liturgy.

13. All the _____ help the assembly worship as one community.

14. In the liturgy the people remember with thanksgiving the _____ mystery of the Lord through prayer, song, sacrament, listening, active participation, and reception of Communion.

15. Rich and poor, old and young, hearty and frail, people come together from all nations and cultures to share in the _____, the celebration of their salvation through Christ.

C **Make Connections** Write a response to each of the statements.

16–20. Explain the best way for you to participate in the Liturgy of the Word, using the following terms:

   reader   reflection   God's word
   _____
   _____
   _____
   _____
   _____

   Use the following terms to explain what living the Eucharist means:

   give   thanks   sacrifice
   _____
   _____
   _____

Unit 7
Kingdom of God

In this unit you will...

learn that answering God's call through the Sacraments at the Service of Communion helps to build the kingdom of God on earth. Faith in the Resurrection is the basis of our hope in eternal life and for happiness with God in heaven. As we wait for Christ's second coming, we pray and work for justice.

Chapter 19

Chapter 20

Chapter 21

Faith in Action!

Catholic Social Teaching Principle: Option for the Poor and Vulnerable

Chapter 19
Answering God's Call

 **Let Us Pray**

Leader: God our Father, help us keep our promises.

"Offer praise as your sacrifice to God;
fulfill your vows to the Most High."
Psalm 50:14

All: God our Father, help us keep our promises. Amen.

 Activity 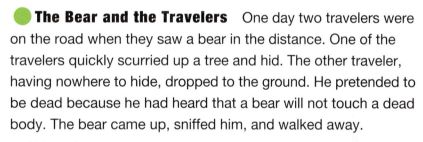 Let's Begin

● **The Bear and the Travelers** One day two travelers were on the road when they saw a bear in the distance. One of the travelers quickly scurried up a tree and hid. The other traveler, having nowhere to hide, dropped to the ground. He pretended to be dead because he had heard that a bear will not touch a dead body. The bear came up, sniffed him, and walked away.

When the bear had left, the other traveler jumped down from the tree and said, "That was certainly a close call! What did that bear say to you when he sniffed around your ear?"

The first traveler said, "He told me to beware of fair-weather friends who desert you at the first sign of danger!"

From a fable by Aesop

Now think about when you have failed to help someone.

What was the cause of your failure?

_____

What should you have done instead?

_____

✏️ **Write a Note** On a separate sheet of paper, thank all the people who have helped you, especially those you don't know.

257

Our Duty to God

 **Focus** What are vocations that serve God and others?

Here is a true story about selfless sacrifice for the good of others.

BIOGRAPHY

Saints Isidore and Maria

Near the end of the eleventh century, a humble farm laborer named Isidore lived in Spain with his wife, Maria. Their only son died young, and thereafter the couple lived a life of complete devotion to God. Although Isidore and Maria remained poor, they were good people who worked hard and prayed often. They became known as champions of those who were poor and sick.

It is said that Isidore shared his meals with others so generously that often he had only scraps left for himself. Another story relates that some fellow workers complained to the master that Isidore was always late to work in the fields because he went to Mass in the morning. But Isidore explained that he had no choice but to report first to a higher Master.

❓ Isidore and Maria offered their daily work to God. What everyday activities do you offer to God?

❓ How does making these offerings help you?

A Vocation to Serve

Isidore and Maria served God as a married couple. Marriage is one of the particular ways to answer God's call, or vocation. Isidore and Maria lived a simple life of work and daily prayer. They dedicated themselves to each other, just as Christ dedicated himself to the Church and to the service of God and his kingdom.

The mission of the Church is to be catholic, or universal, and to welcome every person who wishes to be a disciple of Jesus. Through Baptism, all Christians are called to spread the gospel and build up the Body of Christ. In the Church, this is accomplished with God's grace through the efforts of both **ordained ministers** and the **laity**, also known as laypeople.

Lay men and women have a special responsibility to bring the good news of Jesus to the world around them through work, public service, and family life. Other men and women are called to **religious life**. They take vows, or make sacred promises, to dedicate their lives in service to God. Some deacons, priests, and bishops belong to religious communities.

Some men are called to the ordained ministry of teaching, guiding, and leading the assembly in worship. These ordained men, as well as lay people and men and women religious, are given charisms, special gifts or graces, to live out the Christian life and to serve the common good in building up the Church.

Words of Faith

Ordained ministers, through the Sacrament of Holy Orders, serve God and the Church as bishops, priests, and deacons.

Laity is the name for members of the Church who are not priests or consecrated sisters or brothers.

Religious life refers to the lives of men and women in religious communities who make vows of poverty, chastity, and obedience as religious priests, sisters, brothers, monks, or friars.

Activity: Share Your Faith

Reflect: Think of a lay person or an ordained minister whom you particularly admire because of his or her service to others.

Share: With a partner, discuss the qualities you both admire in such persons.

Act: Write on a separate sheet of paper the qualities that you and your partner have chosen. From these, choose one quality that each of you will practice this week. At the end of the week, report to your partner on your progress.

Our Duty to Others

**Focus** How do people live the Sacraments of Service?

All Christian vocations flow from the grace received in Baptism. Every man and woman has the responsibility to answer his or her call from God and to choose a vocation that continues the work of the reign of God.

Any vocation to which you are called by God involves work. Your work is a reflection of your goodness and good acts. Through honest and useful work, you participate in the work of creation and God's reign.

When Jesus saw the needs of the people around him, he wanted to help them. Through his disciples, Jesus reached out to people everywhere.

SCRIPTURE

Matthew 9:35–38

Laborers for the Harvest

Jesus went around to all the towns and villages, teaching in their synagogues, proclaiming the gospel of the kingdom, and curing every disease and illness. At the sight of the crowds, his heart was moved with pity because they were troubled and abandoned, like sheep without a shepherd. Then he said to his disciples, "The harvest is abundant but the laborers are few; so ask the master of the harvest to send out laborers for his harvest."

Matthew 9:35–38

- What is the harvest that Jesus sees in this crowd of people?
- What does this tell you about the mission of all baptized followers of Jesus?

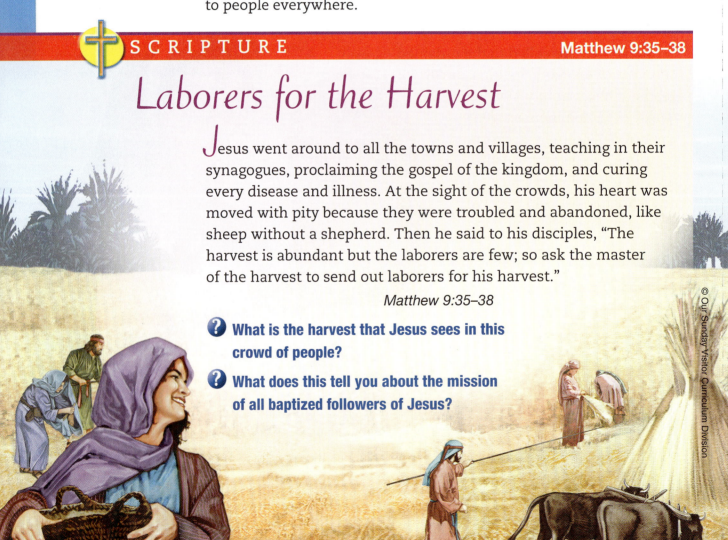

Sacraments of Service

The Church celebrates two sacraments that particularly help Christians answer the call to service. These Sacraments of Service are Matrimony and Holy Orders.

In Matrimony a man and a woman promise to love and be faithful to each other throughout their lives. They receive grace that will help them lead lives of love that reflect Christ's love for his Church. They commit to sharing married love only with each other. The man and woman also promise to be open at all times to the possibility of having children and to love, care for, and educate any children they may have. The Sacrament of Matrimony is celebrated publicly before a priest or deacon, witnesses, and the gathered assembly. In Holy Orders, bishops, priests, and deacons promise to serve the Church faithfully. Priests and deacons promise to obey the bishop, and bishops promise to exercise their authority in accordance with other bishops and the pope.

SACRAMENTS OF SERVICE	Minister of the sacrament	Signs
HOLY ORDERS	The bishop	The laying on of hands and the prayer of consecration
MATRIMONY	The couple (in Eastern Rite Churches, the priest)	The exchange of promises

Activity — Connect Your Faith

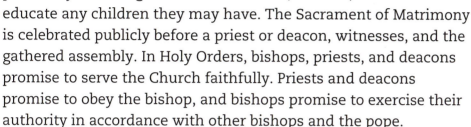

Answer the Call Design an advertisement that encourages people to live out their vocations as single people, married persons, ordained ministers, or men and women religious. Think about the vocation to which God may be calling you.

Explore

Explore the Religious Life

 **Focus** What does a religious vocation require?

Religious communities dedicate themselves to lives of service. Those who are called to a religious vocation can join one of a large number of communities. Each community has its own gift, or charism, that determines the kind of service to which the members of the community give their lives.

Many Ways to Serve

A variety of features distinguish one religious community from another. You can learn about the communities by looking at these aspects.

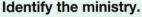

Trace the history.
- Who founded the community? Some were founded by great and famous saints like Benedict and Francis. Others have been founded by groups or little-known individuals.
- Why? Some communities were started in order to meet certain needs. Monastic communities began when many Christians felt called to leave the busy life of the world and live a life of contemplation. Other groups came into being to serve a very specific need in the world or in the Church. Ignatius Loyola founded the Jesuits to defend the Church against attacks from certain reformers.
- How has the community developed over time? Many communities change their purpose as needs or social conditions change.

Identify the ministry.
Often a community is identified with its ministry. Some communities are devoted entirely to prayer. Others are known for teaching, health care, or missionary work.

Understand the commitment.
Many religious take vows of poverty, chastity, and obedience. Others take additional vows.

Examine the lifestyle.
Like the early Christians, religious communities often share a simple life and have developed special ways of praying, working, and living together. They may follow a common, unifying rule of life.

? Why is the word *community* used to describe these groups?

262

Activity

Research Communities In groups, gather literature from some religious communities and use the information on the previous page to assemble a description of one or more of these communities. Share results among the groups. Discuss each group member's reaction to what he or she has learned. You may wish to start your search with Web sites given to you by your teacher.

Name of the community _____

Founded by _____

Original purpose _____
_____

Current mission _____
_____

Special characteristics _____
_____
_____

Ministry _____

Commitment _____

Lifestyle _____
_____
_____

Explain how or why you would or would not be a suitable member of this community.

_____
_____
_____
_____
_____

Celebration of the Word

 **Let Us Pray**

Gather and begin with the Sign of the Cross.

Leader: God our Father, you call us in Baptism to continue the work of your Son. Help us hear your word to us today.

Reader: A reading from the First Book of Samuel.

Read 1 Samuel 3:1–10.

The word of the Lord.

All: **Thanks be to God.**

Sing together.

Here I am, Lord. Is it I, Lord? I have heard you calling in the night. I will go, Lord, if you lead me. I will hold your people in my heart.

"Here I Am, Lord" © 1981, Daniel L. Shulte and New Dawn Music. Published by OCP Publications.

Leader: Let us pray.

Bow your heads as the leader prays.

All: **Amen.**

Chapter 19 Review

A **Work with Words**   Match each description in Column 1 with the correct term in Column 2.

Column 1

_____ 1. vocation

_____ 2. dedicated to God and a community by vows

_____ 3. ordination of bishops, priests, and deacons

_____ 4. members of the Church who are not ordained

_____ 5. sacrament joining a man and a woman

Column 2

a. Matrimony

b. Holy Orders

c. men and women religious

d. God's call

e. laypeople

B **Check Understanding**   Circle True if a statement is true, and circle False if a statement is false. Correct any false statements.

6. Religious life refers to the lives of men and women in religious communities who make vows of fidelity, hopefulness, and love.

   True   False   _____

7. Ordained ministers serve God and the Church through the Sacrament of Matrimony.

   True   False   _____

8. Rather than being bitter about the loss of their son, Isidore and Maria devoted their lives to God.

   True   False   _____

9. Charisms are graces that forgive sins.

   True   False   _____

10. The minister of Holy Orders is the bishop.

    True   False   _____

UNIT 7: CHAPTER 19

Family Faith

Catholics Believe

- The vocations of ordained and married people build the reign of God and serve others.
- The Sacraments of Service are Holy Orders and Matrimony.

Read *Matthew 4:18–22* to find out about the call of the first disciples.

GO online www.osvcurriculum.com
For weekly scripture readings and seasonal resources

Activity
Live Your Faith

Discuss Lives of Service Discuss the call to service of such professionals as firefighters, nurses, doctors, social workers, and teachers. What inspires people to enter these professions? If you have family members who are in the religious life or the ordained ministry, discuss how their vocations have affected or influenced your family.

People of Faith

▲ Saint Francis Xavier 1506–1552

Francis Xavier was one of the original companions of Ignatius Loyola, the founder of the Jesuit order. In 1541 Ignatius sent Francis to Asia as a missionary. For nine years Francis preached in the Portuguese colonies in the East Indies. He organized church communities and baptized many new members into the Church. Travelers' stories about Japan inspired Francis to take the gospel to the Japanese people. In the two years preceding his death, Francis planted the seeds of Christianity in Japan. His feast day is December 3.

 Family Prayer

Saint Francis Xavier, pray for us that we may find our vocation and be faithful to it. May we see the beauty of God's love in all cultures, as you did, and celebrate the glory of the diversity of creation. Amen.

© Our Sunday Visitor Curriculum Division

In Unit 7 your child is learning about the KINGDOM OF GOD.
CCC See Catechism of the Catholic Church 1534, 1570, 1653 for further reading on chapter content.

Chapter 20: The Last Things

Let Us Pray

Leader: Almighty God, we thank you and we praise you.
"For my soul has been freed from death, my eyes from tears, my feet from stumbling."

Psalm 116:8

All: Almighty God, we thank you and we praise you. Amen.

Activity

All Creatures of Our God and King
And you, most kind and gentle death,
Waiting to hush our final breath,
O praise him! Alleluia!
You lead to heav'n the child of God,
Where Christ our Lord the way has trod. . . .

A selection from the poem by Saint Francis of Assisi

Now think about what gives Francis comfort in the face of his death.

How can death be kind and gentle?

_____
_____
_____

Write a Poem On a separate sheet of paper, write your own poem about death and heaven.

267

Final Destinations

 **Focus** How do you picture life after death?

Dante Alighieri was born in Florence, Italy, in 1265. He is the author of a famous poem called *The Divine Comedy*, which tells of an imaginary voyage during which Dante travels through hell, purgatory, and paradise—the three realms where the souls of the dead wait for the last judgment.

Faith Fact

Jesus taught that whenever you care for the needs of people who suffer, you are caring for Jesus himself.

A STORY

A Poet's Voyage

Dante describes hell as a huge, noisy, funnel-shaped cave beneath the earth. At each stage of his descent, Dante meets a new group of sinners who are receiving their punishment. At the bottom of hell, frozen in an icy lake, are the devil and the worst human sinners.

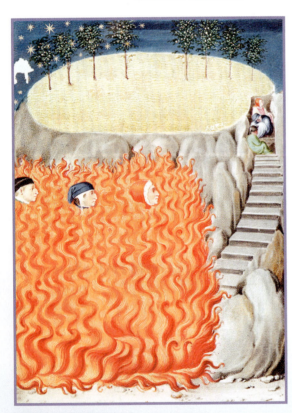

Inferno, Purgatory, and Paradise 14th Century Illustration

Purgatory is described as a gigantic mountain rising from the sea, far above the highest clouds. Here, too, souls of the dead endure punishment, but the punishment is temporary because these people were sorry for their sins before death. The souls in purgatory are joyful because their punishment will end, and they will enter paradise.

Journey to Paradise

At the end of his journey, Dante passes through nine heavens, where he meets and talks with the saints, who shine like many-colored stars. At last, Dante arrives at the highest heaven, where he is given a brief glimpse of the glory of God.

Dante expects his readers to understand that the details of his story are imaginary. The main point Dante makes in his poem is that what happens to people after death is the result of choices they freely make in life.

? **What are your images of heaven, hell, and purgatory?**

The Real Difference

Like Dante, you probably wonder what heaven and hell are like. While no one can provide an exact explanation, Christians know that Jesus promised his followers <mark>eternal life</mark>. Christians prepare for eternal life by serving God and loving one another right now. They know from Jesus that their happiness will depend on the quality of service they give to one another in this life.

The choice between heaven and hell is freely made. Those who choose not to show love will suffer eternal separation from God. Only those who choose love can enter into the life of the Holy Trinity, for the Trinity is love itself.

Eternal life is life forever with God for all who die in friendship with God.

SCRIPTURE — Matthew 25:31–40

The Judgment of the Nations

When the Son of Man comes again, those who have loved will be separated from those who have not.

Then the king will say to those on his right, "Come, you who are blessed by my Father. Inherit the kingdom prepared for you from the foundation of the world. For I was hungry and you gave me food, I was thirsty and you gave me drink, a stranger and you welcomed me, naked and you clothed me, ill and you cared for me, in prison and you visited me." Then the righteous will ask when they did any of these things. And the king will say to them, "Amen, I say to you, whatever you did for one of these least brothers of mine, you did for me."

Based on *Matthew 25:31–40*

Activity — Share Your Faith

Reflect: Think of some ways that you can build the reign of God.

Share: With a partner, brainstorm some of the ways you can make small, loving choices day by day.

Act: On each block, write a daily choice that you can make.

Eternal Life

 **Focus** What happens at the end of your mortal life?

Catholics believe that death as it is experienced by humans was not part of the Creator's original loving plan. Humans suffer bodily death because of original sin. But the death and Resurrection of Jesus establish hope for a happy death and for eternal life with God.

Some early Christians in the city of Corinth began to declare that those who had died would not be raised. News of this view reached the Apostle Paul. He did not hesitate to tell the Corinthians that they were completely wrong!

✝ SCRIPTURE

"If for this life only we have hoped in Christ, we are the most pitiable people of all. . . . But thanks be to God who gives us the victory through our Lord Jesus Christ."

1 Corinthians 15:19, 57

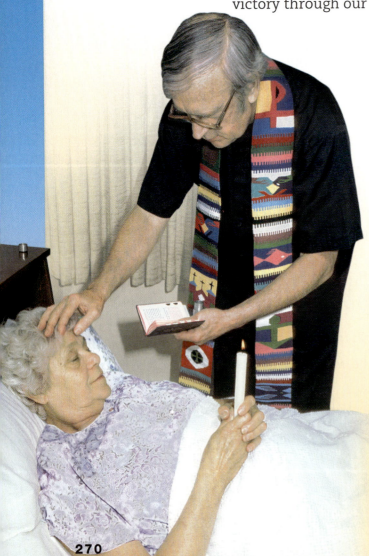

Care for the Dying

The Church helps people prepare for death through prayer and rites. These rites include the Anointing of the Sick, the final Eucharist, called **viaticum**, or "food for the journey" and sometimes the Sacrament of Reconciliation. The Rite of Christian Funerals reflects the community's belief and hope that those who die in faith will enter eternal life with the Trinity. In the Eucharist the Church continues to pray for those who have died. Every Mass is offered not only for the souls of the living but also for the souls of those who have died.

❓ **Why do the last rites sometimes include the Sacrament of Reconciliation?**

The Journey Home

After a person has died, the Church celebrates a Mass of Christian Burial. The Church community gathers to proclaim the message of eternal life and to pray that the one who has died will experience its joy. The coffin containing the body or the urn containing the cremated remains of the person who has died is met by the presider at the church entrance. The presider blesses the coffin or urn with holy water. The lighted Easter candle reminds those gathered of the person's dying and rising in Christ. The pall, a white cloth like the garment received in Baptism, is draped over the coffin.

The Scripture readings at a funeral Mass focus on God's mercy and forgiveness. The homily offers words of consolation, or comfort, based on the Paschal mystery. During the Liturgy of the Eucharist, the assembly remembers the sacrifice of Jesus' death and the glory of his Resurrection.

In the final farewell before burial, the Church commends, or gives, to God the person who has died. Then the Church calls upon choirs of angels to welcome the person into the paradise of God's heavenly kingdom. There all the faithful will be together in Christ.

Viaticum is the Eucharist given to a person who is near death to sustain him or her on the journey to eternity.

Activity: Connect Your Faith

Prepare for Eternity If you knew that you had only one month left to live, what would you do during that time to prepare to meet God? Write one idea for each week.

1. _____
2. _____
3. _____
4. _____

Explore

The Journey Through Grief

 **Focus** How do you comfort the sorrowful?

To bury the dead is one of the Corporal Works of Mercy, and to comfort the sorrowful is one of the Spiritual Works of Mercy. As members of Christ's Body, Church members must support those who have lost loved ones. But it is often difficult to know what to do.

The Role of the Comforter

Understand that grieving is a process that takes time.

When someone dies, those who mourn will experience many different feelings. There is no quick or easy way to get through the process of grieving and no set period of time in which grieving should be finished.

Gather with the community of faith to pray.

The most common occasions for communal prayer are the wake or prayer service, the funeral, and the graveside service.

Support those who mourn.

If you go to a wake or a funeral, tell the grieving family that you are sorry for their loss, or share something with them about the one who died. It helps those who have lost someone they love to know that they are not alone in missing the person. Offer your prayers, sympathy, and understanding throughout the year.

On the feast of All Saints, November 1, and on All Souls Day, November 2, the Church encourages members to remember those who have died and to pray for them.

? **What words or actions have comforted you when you have felt sorrow or loss?**

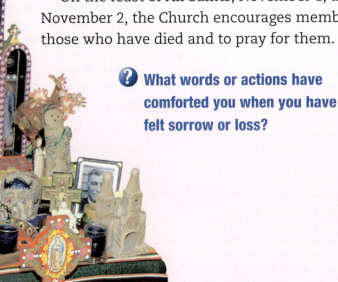

Activity

Live Your Faith

Make a Card Complete each sentence by unscrambling the words below. Then use the letters in the circled boxes to answer the question at the end.

1–2. As a _____ and as a follower of Jesus, you should support those who _____.

3. _____ is a good way for the Church to support those who have lost a loved one.

4. You can find ways to express your _____ to those who are grieving.

5. Friends and relatives often gather to give comfort and to pray at a _____.

6–8. The _____ Mass is the main liturgical _____ for a member who has _____.

9. The presider blesses both the coffin and the grave with _____.

10. These are all ways to perform which Corporal and Spiritual Works of Mercy?

You're In Our Prayers

1. NEFRID
2. ROMUN
3. CUALOMNM RAREPY
4. PATYMSYH
5. WEAK
6. RUFLAEN
7. NAETIEROBCL
8. DIDE
9. HYOL WEART

10. _____

Decide as a class how you can comfort the sorrowful in your parish and school.

Design a sympathy card for your class to send to those in the community who have suffered the loss of a loved one, or volunteer as a group to assist your parish bereavement committee in providing hospitality after a funeral liturgy.

273

Celebration of the Word

 Let Us Pray

Gather and begin with the Sign of the Cross.

Leader: God our Father, we remember today that you are our beginning and our end.

Reader: A reading from the Second Letter to the Corinthians.

Read 2 Corinthians 5:6–10.

The word of the Lord.

All: **Thanks be to God.**

Leader: Let us pray for those who have died, that they might experience fully the love of Christ. Trusting in God, let us pray for them and for anyone who will die today.

Pray silently for a few moments.

Leader: Let us conclude by praying together the following words from the funeral liturgy.

All: **May the angels lead them into paradise; may the martyrs come to welcome them.**

From the Mass of Christian Burial

Sing together the refrain.

And I will raise you up, and I will raise you up, and I will raise you up on the last day.
Yo le resucitaré, Yo le resucitaré,
Yo le resucitaré el dia de El.

"I Am the Bread of Life Yo Soy el Pan de Vida", Suzanne Toolan, © 1966, 1970, 1986, 1993, GIA Publications, Inc.

CHAPTER 20 Review

A **Work with Words** Match the description in Column 1 with the correct term in Column 2.

Column 1

_____ 1. separation from God forever

_____ 2. life forever with God for all who die in friendship with him

_____ 3. happiness in God's presence forever

_____ 4. cause of bodily death

_____ 5. rituals near the time of death

Column 2

a. heaven

b. care for the dying

c. hell

d. eternal life

e. original sin

B **Check Understanding** Write a brief response to each question.

6. How did Dante reach heaven in his poem, *The Divine Comedy*?

7. What are the needs of a person who is grieving?

8. Why is the Easter candle lit during a funeral?

9. What will happen at the Judgment of Nations?

10. What is viaticum?

UNIT 7: CHAPTER 20

Family Faith

Catholics Believe

- Faith in the Resurrection is the source of hope in eternal life and happiness with God in heaven.
- The Church cares for the dying through prayer and celebration of last Eucharist, known as viaticum.

SCRIPTURE

Read *Matthew 27:57—28:10* to find out about Jesus' burial and Resurrection.

GO online www.osvcurriculum.com
For weekly scripture readings and seasonal resources

Activity

Live Your Faith

In Memoriam The Church encourages prayer for those who have died, especially on the feast of All Saints, November 1, and on All Souls Day, November 2. You may wish to adopt the Mexican custom of the Day of the Dead. You might visit the cemetery to honor friends or relatives who have died or light a candle and pray for family members who have gone before you to eternal life.

People of Faith

Stephen was the first Christian martyr. He was a deacon chosen to distribute food to the Greek-speaking Christian community in Jerusalem. Stephen was a great preacher whose views worried Jewish leaders. For example, Stephen told Christians that they need not worship at the Temple in Jerusalem. The Jewish leaders put Stephen on trial. Found guilty of blasphemy, Stephen was stoned to death. As he died, Stephen, like Jesus, forgave his persecutors. Saint Stephen's feast day is December 26.

▲ Saint Stephen martyred c. A.D. 36

Family Prayer

Saint Stephen, pray for us that we may face death with courage and faith. May we receive from God the strength to hold to our faith as you did in the face of criticism and abuse. Amen.

© Our Sunday Visitor Curriculum Division

 In Unit 7 your child is learning about the KINGDOM OF GOD. *See Catechism of the Catholic Church 989, 1012, 1024, 1523–1525 for further reading on chapter content.*

Chapter 21 Come, Lord Jesus

 **Let Us Pray**

Leader: Generous God, we thank you for our dwelling place.
"The earth is the LORD's and all it holds,
the world and those who live there."
Psalm 24:1

All: Generous God, we thank you for our dwelling place. Amen.

Activity  Let's Begin

● **Where You've Been** Look at maps or a globe, and find some places that you have visited or in which you have lived. Perhaps you can share a story about someone you met or something you discovered in those places.

Now think about some places you would like to see, far or near.

If you could invite Jesus to go with you, what do you think he might show you?

_____
_____
_____

What message of Jesus do you want everyone in the world to hear?

_____
_____
_____

✏️ **Write a Paragraph** On a separate sheet of paper, explain how people in other countries or places are different from you. Then tell how you are all alike.

Explore

To Bring the Good News

 **Focus** What are the qualities of a missionary?

The Church has a mission to bring the good news of Jesus Christ to all people everywhere. Blessed Charles de Foucauld accepted that mission fully.

BIOGRAPHY

Apostle of the Sahara

As a young man in France, Charles de Foucauld rejected the Catholic faith in which he had been raised. He found and embraced his faith again at age twenty-eight, when he went into the desert and lived with Muslims among slaves and those who were poor. He learned their language and became their friend.

"I have lost my heart to this Jesus of Nazareth," wrote de Foucauld, "and I spend my life trying to imitate him. When people see me, they must be able to say, 'Because this man is good, his religion must be good.'"

Charles de Foucauld believed that many people are called to spread the gospel of Jesus all over the world in quiet ways. He said, "Every Christian should be an apostle. . . . Every Christian should see every human being as a beloved brother . . . and have for all human beings the feelings of the Heart of Jesus." This was the loving way that Charles de Foucauld himself chose to live so that with God's grace he could hasten the coming of God's kingdom. He was a **missionary** of love, continuing Christ's work in the world.

❓ What did Charles de Foucauld's goodness invite people to discover?

Faith Fact

A *synagogue* is a place of worship and religious instruction for people of the Jewish faith. The name comes from a Greek word meaning "assembly."

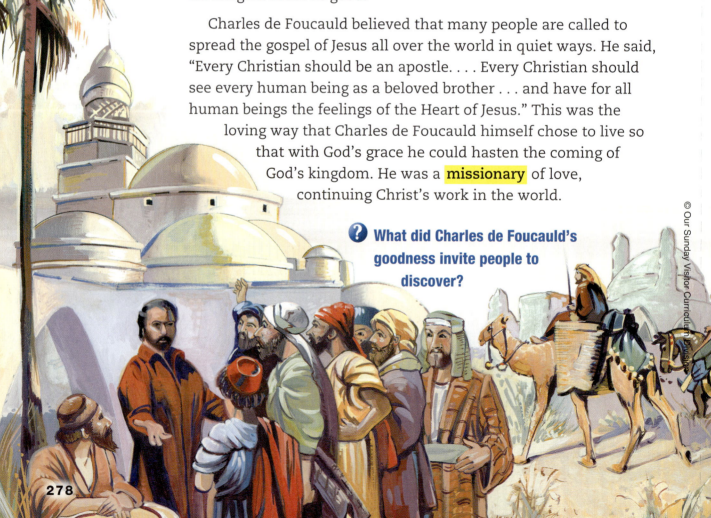

Move Toward the Kingdom

Charles de Foucauld saw every person as his brother, just as Jesus did. He wanted to bring the good news of Jesus to the desert peoples, for he knew that they, too, were children of the same Creator.

The message of Jesus is greater than any one person who proclaims it today. It takes holy people to proclaim it well, but the source of their holiness is the Holy Spirit dwelling in them through Baptism. The Holy Spirit gives you the courage to do Christ's work. The Holy Spirit empowered Jesus, too.

A **missionary** is a person who answers a call from God to devote a period of his or her life to bringing Christ's message to people who do not know it.

SCRIPTURE
Luke 4:16–21

Fulfilled in Your Hearing

He [Jesus] came to Nazareth, where he had grown up, and went into the synagogue on the sabbath day. He stood up to read and was handed a scroll of the prophet Isaiah . . .

"The Spirit of the Lord is upon me,
  because he has anointed me
    to bring glad tidings to the poor.

He has sent me to proclaim liberty to captives
  and recovery of sight to the blind,
    to let the oppressed go free,

and to proclaim a year acceptable to the Lord."

Rolling up the scroll, . . . he sat down. . . . The eyes of all in the synagogue looked intently at him. He said to them, "Today this scripture passage is fulfilled in your hearing."

Based on *Luke 4:16–21*

❓ What did Jesus mean when he said that the Scripture passage had been fulfilled?

Activity — Share Your Faith

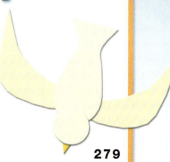

Reflect: Recall that through the power of the Holy Spirit, you can have the courage to continue Jesus' work.

Share: Proclaim to a partner what Jesus read from the prophet Isaiah.

Act: Tell one way in which you are trying to live this passage in your life. Listen while your partner does the same.

In Word and Action

 **Focus** How can you be a part of the mission of the Church?

The celebration of each sacrament is a reminder that the reign of God is among us in Jesus Christ. God's kingdom is embraced when people celebrate the Baptism of new birth in the Church and become brothers and sisters in Christ. In the celebration of Christ's sacraments, especially the Eucharist, people are blessed and nourished so that they can be blessings for others.

Even when those who have been reborn and nourished in Christ do not become missionaries, they are called to be disciples. They share the good news of Jesus by word and example. This sharing, or **evangelization**, has its origins in the first Pentecost, when the Holy Spirit came upon the followers of Jesus and strengthened them to take the good news to every nation. When you live as a disciple of Jesus, you become a sign of God's kingdom, wherever you are.

❓ **What is the relationship between the Eucharist and the work of evangelization?**

Celebration of God's Reign

Missionaries fill the needs of others in Jesus' name. To feed the hungry, to give drink to the thirsty, to clothe the naked, to shelter the homeless, to visit the sick and the imprisoned—these are the Corporal Works of Mercy of those who have lost their hearts to Christ as Charles de Foucauld did. You might become a missionary one day. But you can begin now to do the work of a disciple—right in your own neighborhood. Christ will return on the last day, and there will be no more suffering and death. Until that day, all Christians have a responsibility to be Jesus' hands and heart on earth.

Equal Before God

The works of mercy are to be offered to all who are in need, without exception. All people are equal in God's eyes because he has created them in his own image and likeness.

Your works of mercy can be acts of charity, or they can be works of justice. When you perform an act of charity, you show Christ's love to another by helping lessen the suffering of body or spirit. When you bring justice, you give others what is their due. You bring social justice when you work to provide the framework that will protect the rights of those who are poor or cast out by society. All people have a right to food, shelter, health, and dignity. When you act with charity and justice, you bring peace, and the reign of God grows.

Words of Faith

Evangelization is sharing the good news of Jesus in a way that invites people to accept the gospel.

Corporal Works of Mercy are actions that show justice, love, and peace, as Jesus did when caring for the physical needs of people.

Social justice involves the respect, rights, and conditions that societies must provide.

Activity: Connect Your Faith

Bring Justice What is the worst injustice you see in your local community? With a small group, brainstorm ways to correct it. Report the results of your discussion to the other groups. As a class, choose one concrete step that you can take to improve the situation.

_____

_____

_____

Practice Social Justice

 **Focus** How do you contribute to social justice?

The bishops of the United States named seven themes of Catholic social teaching that embrace the Gospel message. As Christians we may find it easier to live the Gospel message of social justice among people who are familiar to us. Social justice demands that we extend the same respect and love to those whom we don't know directly and who have a culture and outlook different from ours.

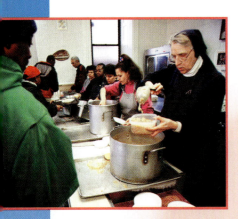

Themes of Catholic Social Teaching

Applying these themes will help you act justly.

1. Respect the **life and dignity of every person.** All policies and personal decisions must show a value for human life and dignity.

2. Value **family, community, and participation.** The well-being of individuals depends on community and family. All people have a right and a duty to participate in society.

3. Uphold **rights and responsibilities.** Human rights must be protected, and responsibilities to others must be met.

4. Evaluate actions in terms of how they affect **those who are most vulnerable.** Because the world often favors those who are rich, a basic moral test is to ask whether an act will help those who are poor.

5. Honor **the dignity of work and the rights of workers.** Workers deserve a just wage and the right to form unions, to hold private property, and to act independently of outside influence or control.

6. Practice **solidarity** with others. Be committed to the common good globally as well as locally.

7. **Care for God's creation.** To practice social justice, take care of the earth's natural resources.

? Which of these principles do you feel called to help with?

Activity: Live Your Faith

Class Quilting Bee Make a square for a "class quilt" on the space below. Choose one of the themes of Catholic social teaching from the opposite page, and make a drawing that shows your understanding of it and your willingness to support it in your own life.

The Lord's Prayer

 Let Us Pray

Gather and begin with the Sign of the Cross.

Leader: Let us reflect on part of the prayer that Jesus taught his disciples as our guide to social justice.

Reader 1: When we say "Our Father, who art in heaven,"

All: **we mean that we are ready to accept all people as our brothers and sisters on earth.**

Reader 2: When we say "Hallowed be thy name,"

All: **we mean that the name of God is our strength and our song as we work for the human dignity of all.**

Reader 3: When we say "Thy kingdom come,"

All: **we mean that we are ready to put God first, ahead of loyalties to state, nation, family, or race.**

Reader 4: When we say "Thy will be done on earth as it is in heaven,"

All: **we mean that we are filled with zeal for God's kingdom of peace and justice in our world.**

Sing together the refrain.

Healer of our every ill,
light of each tomorrow,
give us peace beyond our fear,
and hope beyond our sorrow.

"Healer of Our Every Ill",
Marty Haugen, © 1987,
GIA Publications, Inc.

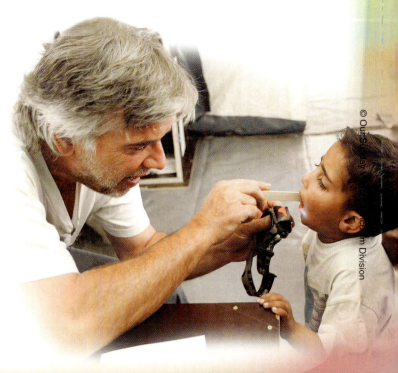

CHAPTER 21
Review

Check Understanding Circle True if a statement is true, and circle False if a statement is false. Correct any false statements.

1. You are a disciple when you follow the example of Jesus.

    True   False   _____

2. The sharing of the good news of Jesus by word and example is called *evangelization*.

    True   False   _____

3. The mission of the Church is to bring the gospel of Jesus only to those who are good.

    True   False   _____

4. Social justice requires a society to respect the dignity of its members.

    True   False   _____

5. Those who are baptized have completed their mission of evangelization.

    True   False   _____

Fill in the circle next to the correct response.

6. Corporal Works of Mercy can be works of _____.

    ○ art   ○ justice only   ○ charity only
    ○ selfishness   ○ both justice and charity

7. A _____ answers a call from God to devote a period of his or her life to bringing Christ's message to people who do not know it.

    ○ priest   ○ Christian   ○ missionary
    ○ social worker   ○ martyr

8. Charles de Foucauld lived and worked among _____.

    ○ Native Americans   ○ Muslims   ○ Koreans
    ○ children   ○ the French

9. All of the following are Corporal Works of Mercy except _____.

    ○ pray for the dead ○ feed the hungry   ○ shelter the homeless
    ○ clothe the naked   ○ visit the sick

10. When you live as a disciple of Jesus and follow in his footsteps, you become a _____ of God's kingdom.

    ○ door   ○ member   ○ saint
    ○ sign   ○ song

285

UNIT 7: CHAPTER 21
Family Faith

Catholics Believe

- The Church's mission is to bring the good news to all people everywhere.
- Every baptized person has the responsibility of sharing the good news.

SCRIPTURE

Read *Matthew 10:1–25* to learn more about how Jesus prepared the Apostles to complete their mission of service.

GO online www.osvcurriculum.com
For weekly scripture readings and seasonal resources

Activity
Live Your Faith

State Your Goal A mission statement is a document that explains the purposes and goals of a group. Write a family mission statement. Post the statement on the refrigerator door or in another prominent place where it will remind you of how your family shares the mission of spreading the good news of Jesus.

People of Faith

▲ Dorothy Day
1897–1980

Dorothy Day was a writer and social activist. In 1933 she founded the *Catholic Worker* newspaper. The paper called on Catholics to take up the cause of those who were poor. It also promoted world peace. Dorothy Day and her staff lived in a house in a run-down New York City neighborhood. They gave food, clothing, and shelter to those who were poor. In time, other groups established similar houses, called Catholic Worker Houses. Dorothy Day inspired thousands of Catholics to express their faith by working for social justice.

 Family Prayer

Dear God, give us the strength to work for social justice and peace as Dorothy Day did. Free us from all selfishness and open us to the needs of all, regardless of circumstance. Amen.

In Unit 7 your child is learning about the KINGDOM OF GOD.
CCC See *Catechism of the Catholic Church* 849, 851, 2820 for further reading on chapter content.

© Our Sunday Visitor Curriculum Division

DISCOVER

Catholic Social Teaching: Option for the Poor and Vulnerable

Faith in Action!
CATHOLIC SOCIAL TEACHING

In this unit you learned about the future—your own as well as that of others. The mission of the Church—your mission—is to bring Christ to all people. Those next door or on the other side of the world, rich and powerful or poor and weak—all are his children.

Option for the Poor

Scripture calls Christians to help those in need because every person is made in God's image. All people have a right to life and a right to secure the basic necessities of life. Catholics must protect these rights and share their own resources to ensure that everyone has enough material goods to live in dignity.

Divisions between those who are rich and those who are poor are growing. Catholics must work for the good of those who are poor because the Eucharist makes all members one body. Pope John Paul II points out that Christians are called

- to see a neighbor as an "other self."
- to pray for all who are poor.
- to look for signs of poverty and work for change.

Christians offer help not only because they are called to be charitable, but because they are called to be just. The Society of St. Vincent de Paul is an organization that gives lay people a way to make a significant contribution to this mission of the Church.

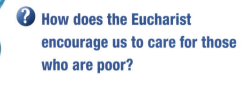 **How does the Eucharist encourage us to care for those who are poor?**

CONNECT With the Call to Justice

The Society of St. Vincent de Paul

"Come now, let us engage ourselves with renewed love to serve the poor, and let us even seek out the poorest and most abandoned of all." Let's see how these words of Vincent de Paul inspired Frederick Ozanam.

From the very beginning of the Society of St. Vincent de Paul in 1833, Frederick Ozanam sought to have the organization "wrap up the whole world in a network of charity." Today the Society has 875,000 members from all walks of life working to help end poverty throughout the world. Their mission is best expressed in these words of Blessed Frederick:

> There are many people who have too much, and who want still more. There are very many people who have nothing. . . . On one side is the power of gold; on the other is the power of despair.

These words could have been written about the world today. The Society labors to bring about changes that would erase the inequality between the "haves" and the "have nots."

The people of the Society work with governments to ensure that basic human rights are met and to change systems that oppress those who are needy. In northern California, a team of Seabees volunteers time and materials to build cabins for a camp for underprivileged children and at-risk teens. Volunteers from San Mateo, California, send health professionals, food, school materials, and other aid to San Ramon, Nicaragua. In Michigan, teens organize a service day to help seniors and those who are hungry. Society members run thrift shops, soup kitchens, and food pantries. Deeds such as these have a positive impact on poverty.

❓ Why are lay volunteers so important to the Society's success?

Reach Out!

SERVE Your Community

Generosity Inventory

Members of the Society of St. Vincent de Paul have lives full of family commitments, work or school, social activities, and fun. Yet, they find the time to help others.

On the lines below, write your favorite activities and the amount of time that you spend doing them each week.

Activity **Time Spent**

_____ _____

_____ _____

_____ _____

_____ _____

Which activities involve helping others?
_____

Which are for your own enjoyment?
_____

List some of your possessions. Put those that are true necessities in the "need" column and all others in the "want" column.

Need **Want**

_____ _____

_____ _____

_____ _____

What would you be willing to change to give more of your time to help those who are underprivileged?
_____

Write a commitment that you are willing to make.
_____

Make a Difference

Plan a Generous Summer Be accountable for your commitment. With a partner, make cards, letters, or notes that you can send to each other during the summer as reminders of your commitment to work for others.

289

UNIT 7 REVIEW

A **Check Understanding** Do the word search to find the boldface words that appear in the phrases below the box. Then fill the spaces provided with the remaining letters, in order, and you will reveal the secret message.

```
R T H T E I S
E I S S T W H
S Y T I E H E
U M A R R S S
R O F A N C G
R H R H A I O
E S T C L I D
C A N U L B S
T U R E I I M
I A L I F S E
O A C E E L R
N E B R A T C
I O N O X S Y
C O M F O R T
```

1–2. A homily offers words of **COMFORT**, liturgy proclaims the message of **ETERNAL LIFE**,

3–4. Scripture readings tell of **GOD'S MERCY**, and the **EUCHARIST** reminds us that

5. we can all share the glory of Jesus' **RESURRECTION**.

___ ___ ___ ___   ___ ___   ___ ___ ___   ___ ___ ___

___ ___ ___ ___   ___ ___   ___ ___ ___ ___ ___ ___ ___ ___ ___

___ ___ ___ ___ ___ ___ ___   ___ ___   ___ ___ ___ ___ ___ ___ ___ ___ ___ ___ .

Name three reasons that Catholics should work for social justice.

6. _____

7. _____

8. _____

Name two ways to answer the call of God.

9. _____

10. _____

Match each description in Column 1 with the correct term in Column 2.

Column 1

_____ **11.** a man and woman celebrating the Sacrament of Matrimony

_____ **12.** commitment, common life, a rule, ministries

_____ **13.** helpful effect on those who are poor

_____ **14.** the coming of the Holy Spirit upon the first disciples of Jesus

_____ **15.** prayer, Reconciliation, Anointing of the Sick, and viaticum

Column 2

a. preparation for death

b. basic test of social justice

c. ministers of the sacrament

d. communities of religious

e. Pentecost

B Make Connections Write a response to each question or statement.

16–18. Use the three terms below to explain how you would help a friend who is going through the grieving process.

understand   pray   support

_____
_____
_____
_____

19. How can you follow the example of Saints Isidore and Maria?

_____
_____

20. Explain one way in which you perform the Corporal Works of Mercy in your everyday life.

_____
_____

Catholic Source Book

Scripture

Faith Fact

INRI

The letters INRI stand for the Latin words *Iesus Nazarenus, Rex Iudaeorum,* meaning "Jesus of Nazareth, King of the Jews." Pontius Pilate ordered the words to be placed on Jesus' cross.

Gospel Formation

The Gospels according to Matthew, Mark, Luke, and John announce the good news of Jesus to Christians today. These books were formed in three stages.

1. **The life and teaching of Jesus**—Jesus' whole life and teaching proclaimed the good news.
2. **Oral tradition**—After the Resurrection, the Apostles preached the good news. Then the early Christians passed on what Jesus preached. They told and retold the teachings of Jesus and the story of his life, death, and Resurrection.
3. **The written Gospels**—The stories, teachings, and sayings of Jesus were collected and written in the Gospels according to Matthew, Mark, Luke (the synoptic, or similar Gospels), and John.

Canon

The canon of Scripture is the list of books of the Bible accepted by the Church as the inspired word of God. The word *canon* comes from an ancient Sumerian word for a straight reed used for measuring. The word *canon* can also mean a collection or a list. The Catholic Church accepts a biblical canon of 73 books—46 in the Old Testament and 27 in the New Testament.

Scripture and Tradition

Tradition is the message of the gospel as it was lived and presented to the Apostles and passed on from them to the Church through the ages. Tradition and Scripture together are the one source of God's revelation.

There are also traditions with which you might be more familiar. The more familiar tradition refers to customs and practices that are not universal. Different countries and ethnic groups have different traditions. And these are to be respected and even incorporated into liturgical celebrations. Examples include certain devotions to Mary and liturgies in honor of regional saints.

How Scripture Is Used in Liturgy

Bible readings are important in all liturgies. Words from Scripture are also found in many of the prayers in the liturgy. Songs and hymns often contain phrases and images from the Bible. Such Bible readings express the faith of the people. They remind all people of God's mighty deeds.

Because Christ is truly present in the word, the Church gives special honor to the Bible. Either the Book of the Gospels or the lectionary is carried in procession at Mass. The Book of the Gospels is placed on the altar until the gospel reading. Readers proclaim the word clearly. After reading the gospel, the priest or deacon kisses the book out of respect.

The Liturgy of the Word

Every celebration of the sacraments begins with a Liturgy of the Word. Even if the sacrament is celebrated for only one person, such as in the Anointing of the Sick, the priest begins with a Scripture passage. The Church encourages the use of God's word at all gatherings of the faithful.

The Lectionary contains the Scripture readings for every Sunday, feast day, and special occasion. These readings were chosen to suit the feasts and seasons of the liturgical year.

The lectionary readings for Sunday Mass uses a three-year cycle.

- **Year A** uses the Gospel according to Matthew.
- **Year B** presents the Gospel according to Mark.
- **Year C** highlights the Gospel according to Luke.

The Gospel according to John appears at special times in each of the three years. The passages from John are read for special celebrations, such as Christmas, Holy Thursday, and Good Friday.

Scripture

Faith Fact

ex cathedra

The Latin words *ex cathedra* mean "from the chair." The pope speaks *ex cathedra* in matters of faith and morals. These teachings are considered infallible, without error.

The Readings

- The **first reading** at Sunday Mass is from the Old Testament, except during the Easter Season. At that time the first reading comes from the Acts of the Apostles.
- The **responsorial psalm** is from the Book of Psalms. The psalm is called *responsorial* because the assembly sings a response after each verse.
- The **second reading** is from one of the New Testament letters or from the Book of Revelation.
- The **gospel reading** is from Matthew, Mark, Luke, or John.

The weekday lectionary is also arranged according to the seasons of the liturgical year. However, the weekday readings follow a two-year cycle: Year I and Year II. On weekdays only one reading and a psalm are spoken before the gospel.

Sacramental Symbols

Sacramental symbols are found throughout Bible.

- **Water** and **light** are central symbols that reflect the power of God the Creator, who gives life to all. In Baptism light and water are used to show God's gift of new life. The words and the symbols of water and light recall creation, the flood, and the crossing of the Red Sea. These prayers also recall Jesus' baptism in the Jordan River and the water that flowed from his side as he hung on the cross. The newly baptized hold lighted candles to show that they will "keep the flame of faith alive" in their hearts. They will be ready to meet Christ when he returns.
  - **Oil** was used to anoint great leaders. It was also used for healing. Oil is used in the Sacraments of Baptism, Confirmation, Holy Orders, and the Anointing of the Sick.
  - Unleavened **bread** and **wine** are the symbols used in the celebration of the Eucharist. These fruits of the earth were and are used in the Seder or Passover meal. Jesus gave new meaning to these symbols when he blessed them and gave them to his friends at the Last Supper—now his Body and Blood.

Creed

I Believe

Both the Apostles' Creed and the Nicene Creed are Trinitarian in structure and flow from the baptismal formula: Father, Son, and Holy Spirit.

- The Apostles' Creed received its name because it is a summary of the Apostles' faith. However, the earliest reference to this creed appears in fourth-century writings, and the earliest text dates from the eighth century.
- The Nicene Creed appeared after the Council of Nicaea in 325 and the Council of Constantinople in 381. These councils discussed the divine nature of Christ. The creed became part of the liturgy of the Church in Rome in 1014 and remains part of the liturgy today.

Faith Fact

It is generally believed that all the Apostles were martyred except John and Judas (who denied Jesus and then hung himself in remorse).

The Holy Trinity

God is a communion of Persons: Father, Son, and Holy Spirit. God the Father is the creator and source of all things. God the Son, Jesus, is the Savior of all people. God the Holy Spirit guides and makes holy all people and the Church.

The Holy Trinity is honored in the Sign of the Cross and the Doxology, and particularly in the liturgy of the Church. Christians are baptized "In the name of the Father, and of the Son, and of the Holy Spirit." In the opening and final blessing and in the Eucharistic Prayer, prayers are directed to God the Father, through the Son, in the Holy Spirit.

God the Father

The first Person of the Blessed Trinity, God the Father, is Creator of all that is. He is all-powerful and all-knowing. He is the one who journeys with you, as he did with Abraham. He is the faithful and compassionate God who freed his chosen people from slavery. He is as revealed to Moses, "I am who am." God is gracious and merciful and steadfast in his love.

He is a God whom you can call Father, as Jesus taught in the Lord's Prayer. And, as he also taught, God is love.

Creed

Faith Fact

The crucifix is a cross on which Jesus may be shown either in his suffering or as Risen Lord. A crucifix must always be placed over, on, or near the altar where Mass is celebrated. The cross is carried in the entrance procession at Mass.

God the Son

Through the power of the Holy Spirit, the second Person of the Trinity took on human nature and was born of the Virgin Mary. This is known as the **Incarnation** and is celebrated at Advent and Christmas. Jesus is both true God and true man.

The **Paschal mystery** includes Jesus' suffering, death, Resurrection, and Ascension. By the Paschal mystery Jesus completed the work of salvation and won for all people the promise of eternal life. The Paschal mystery is celebrated in each of the sacraments, particularly the Mass, and in the Seasons of Lent, the Triduum, and Easter. Jesus' whole life can be said to be a **sacrament,** a sign of God, a sign of God's salvation and love. At the Last Supper Jesus said, "Whoever has seen me has seen the Father. . . . Believe me that I am in the Father and the Father is in me. . ." *(John 14:9, 11)*.

Priest, Prophet, and King
- In each sacrament Jesus is **priest.** For example, in the Eucharist Jesus brings the people's prayers to God and offers himself as a sacrifice.
- Jesus is **prophet** because he speaks for God. Jesus announced the good news of God's mercy and forgiveness. He calls people to love God and one another, to be sorry for their sins, and to live justly.
- Jesus is **king,** the judge of everything in heaven and on earth. His judgments are merciful and just.

God the Holy Spirit

The third Person of the Trinity, the Holy Spirit, is the guide who opens the minds and hearts of people to know God as he is revealed in his word, Scripture, and the living Word, Jesus. It is through the power of the Spirit that you come to know the Father and the Son.

It is the Spirit who makes the Paschal mystery real and present in the sacraments and the Mass. At Mass it is the Spirit who is called on to transform the bread and wine into the Body and Blood of Jesus. Finally, in the sharing of the Eucharist, the Holy Spirit unites the faithful with one another and with God in Christ. The Spirit brings joy, peace, and reconciliation into the lives of the faithful.

The Church

The church is a building in which God's people come together to worship. But the Church is the community of people. It was the plan of God the Father to call together those who believe in Christ. The Church is a gift from God, brought into being by the Holy Spirit to serve the mission of Jesus. The Church, in Christ, can be called a sacrament, a sign of the communion of the Trinity, the union of all people with God, and the unity among people that will reach completion in the fullness of the kingdom of God.

The Catholic Church is united in its faith, leadership structure, and seven sacraments. It is made up of Eastern Rite Catholics (Middle East and Eastern Europe) and Latin Rite Catholics (Rome and Western Europe).

The Catholic Church is governed by the pope and bishops. Through the Sacrament of Holy Orders, bishops, priests, and deacons are ordained to serve the Church.

- A **diocesan**, or **secular**, **priest** may own private property. He promises to obey the bishop of his diocese. Celibacy has been required of Latin Rite priests since the thirteenth century; exceptions are made for married men who have been ministers or priests in some other Christian Churches and seek ordination after becoming Catholic. Eastern Rite Catholic priests may marry unless they live in countries where celibacy is the rule (such as the United States).
- **Religious order priests** belong to religious communities and make vows of poverty, chastity, and obedience. They obey a superior and do not own private property.

Mary

Mary is honored above all other saints. She is the Mother of God because she is the mother of the Son of God who became a human being. When the angel Gabriel told Mary that she would be the mother of the Son of God, Mary believed and accepted God's plan. Her *yes* sets the example for all believers. Throughout the liturgical year, the Church celebrates Mary's place in Christian history. Among different cultures and traditions, devotion to Mary takes many forms.

Faith Fact

Between fifteen and twenty days after the death of a pope, the cardinals who are under the age of 80 meet in the Sistine Chapel in Rome to vote for a new pope. Each cardinal writes on a sheet of paper the name of the man (usually one of the cardinals) he wishes to elect. If a candidate does not receive a majority of votes, the papers are burned with straw to produce black smoke. If a new pope has been chosen, the papers alone are burned, producing white smoke.

Creed

- In 1858 in Lourdes, France, a young girl, Bernadette Soubirous, had several visions of a beautiful lady. The lady said, "I am the Immaculate Conception." A spring bubbled up in the area, and many people were cured.
- In 1879 in Knock, Ireland, Mary appeared to fifteen people. Saint Joseph appeared on her right and Saint John on her left.
- In 1917, a time of war, Mary appeared several times to three children in Fatima, Portugal. She told them to pray the Rosary daily for peace.

The Saints

The saints are holy people who are now in the presence of God. Catholics honor the saints and try to imitate them. They also ask that the saints join with them in praying to God for special blessings. Saints are remembered in the Eucharistic Prayer and in the Litany of the Saints at Baptisms. Statues and images of the saints on medals and holy cards are reminders that these "friends of God" can help believers grow in their friendship with God.

Everlasting Life

The greatest hope of Christians is that after death they will live in eternal happiness with God. In the Bible heaven is pictured as a house with many rooms, a city shining with light, and a joy-filled place where everyone praises God. A familiar scriptural image of heaven is the banquet, or feast. Christ is the host and his people are the guests. When the Church celebrates the Eucharistic meal, it glimpses the banquet feast of heaven.

When a person is near death, special prayers are offered. The person receives the Sacrament of the Anointing of the Sick and is given Communion for the last time. This Eucharist is called *viaticum* (Latin for "food for the journey"). After a death, the Church honors the person and ministers to the family and friends through a series of rites. They are found in the *Order of Christian Funerals*.

- prayers when the family first views the body
- Liturgy of the Word at the wake or prayer service
- prayers for a procession taking the body to church
- the funeral liturgy (which may be a Mass)
- a graveside service

Sacraments

Jesus is sometimes called the sacrament of God because his life, death, and Resurrection make him the sign of God's love in the world. The seven sacraments—Baptism, Confirmation, Eucharist, Reconciliation, Anointing of the Sick, Matrimony, and Holy Orders—have their origins in the life and teachings of Jesus. The sacraments are signs of the new covenant between God and humans.

Signs and symbols of the sacraments can be understood through human senses. They point to the invisible qualities of God. The *matter* of a sacrament consists of its material elements, such as the water of Baptism. The *form* of a sacrament consists of its words. Correct matter and form must be present for the sacrament to be real and true.

The Sacraments of Initiation

The Sacraments of Initiation are Baptism, Confirmation, and Eucharist.

- Through the words and waters of **Baptism,** God forgives all sin and gives new life in Christ.
- **Confirmation** completes the baptismal grace and strengthens a person to be a witness to the faith through the power of the Spirit.
- **Eucharist** completes the Sacraments of Initiation, nourishing the baptized with Christ's own Body and Blood and uniting the new Christians with God and one another in Jesus.

The Sacraments of Healing

The Sacraments of Healing are Reconciliation and the Anointing of the Sick.

- In **Reconciliation,** through the words of absolution, personal sins are forgiven and relationships with God and the Church are healed.
- In the **Anointing of the Sick,** one who is sick or dying is anointed with oil and with the laying on of hands. The person unites his or her suffering with that of Jesus. The sacrament gives spiritual strength and God's grace. Physical healing also may take place.

Liturgy

Faith Fact

In emergencies and other times of necessity, anyone can baptize another person. The person baptizing must intend to do what the Church does in this sacrament. He or she needs to pour water over the head of the person being baptized while saying, "I baptize you in the name of the Father, and of the Son, and of the Holy Spirit."

Faith Fact

Catholics in different dioceses in the United States receive the sacrament of Confirmation at different ages. In the Roman, or Latin, Rite candidates for Confirmation must meet certain criteria. They must believe in the faith of the Church, be in a state of grace, and want to receive the sacrament. Candidates must be prepared and willing to be a witness to Christ in their daily lives and take an active part in the life of the Church.

Liturgy

Faith Fact

In the Middle Ages Christians who could not read or write admired the monks and nuns who learned and prayed all of the 150 psalms as part of the Liturgy of the Hours. These Christians believed that they could become more holy by praying the Hail Mary 150 times each day and meditating on Jesus. As a result, the Rosary came to be made up of fifteen decades, or sets of ten, with each set containing ten Hail Marys. The total of 150 Hail Marys is the same as the number of psalms.

The Sacraments of Service

The Sacraments of Service are Matrimony and Holy Orders.

- In **Matrimony** a man and a woman, through their words of consent, make a covenant with God and one another. Marriage is for the sake of their love and any children God blesses them with.
- In **Holy Orders** the bishop lays hands on a man and anoints him with chrism. The man is empowered to serve the Church as deacon, priest, or bishop.

Liturgical Year

The liturgical year celebrates Jesus' life and work for the salvation of the world. During Advent and Christmas the Church celebrates the Incarnation. The Seasons of Lent, Triduum, and Easter explore the Paschal mystery. Easter is the high point of the liturgical year because it is the greatest celebration of the Resurrection. The life and ministry of Jesus are the focus of Ordinary Time. Mary and the saints are also remembered throughout the year in what is known as the sanctoral cycle.

The Liturgy of the Hours

The Liturgy of the Hours is the Church's public prayer to make each day holy. This liturgy is offered at set times throughout the day and night. In monasteries monks and nuns gather as many as ten times each day and night to pray the Liturgy of the Hours. Parishes that celebrate the Liturgy of the Hours do so less frequently, perhaps once or twice each day. The most common celebrations of the Liturgy of the Hours are Morning Prayer and Evening Prayer.

Music in the Liturgy

Music is an important part of worship. Saint Augustine once said, "He who sings prays twice." The people usually sing responses and songs, led by a cantor or choir. The priest and deacon may sing their parts in the liturgy as well. Although the organ is the traditional choice, almost any musical instrument may be used in the liturgy.

Order of Mass

The Mass follows a pattern, with some differences according to the feast or season of the liturgical year. The main parts of the Mass are the Liturgy of the Word and the Liturgy of the Eucharist. Here is an outline of the order of Mass:

Introductory Rites
- Entrance Chant
- Greeting
- Rite for the Blessing and Sprinkling of Water
- Penitential Act
- *Kyrie*
- *Gloria*
- Collect

Liturgy of the Word
- First Reading (usually from the Old Testament)
- Responsorial Psalm
- Second Reading (from New Testament Letters)
- Gospel Acclamation
- Dialogue at the Gospel
- Gospel Reading
- Homily
- Profession of Faith (Creed)
- Prayer of the Faithful

Liturgy of the Eucharist
- Preparation of the Gifts
- Invitation to Prayer
- Prayer over the Offerings
- Eucharistic Prayer
  Preface Dialogue
  Preface
  Preface Acclamation
  Consecration
  Mystery of Faith
  Concluding Doxology
- Communion Rite
  The Lord's Prayer
  Sign of Peace
  Lamb of God
  Invitation to Communion
  Communion
  Prayer After Communion

Concluding Rite
- Greeting
- Blessing
- Dismissal

Faith Fact

The Eucharist is known by several different names. These include the Blessed Sacrament, Holy Communion, the Bread of Heaven, Breaking of Bread, the Lord's Supper, Holy Sacrifice, Holy Mass, and the Body of Christ.

Liturgy

Liturgical Vestments

Some ministers of the liturgy wear special clothing to mark their roles in the celebration. The **alb,** symbolizing baptism, is a long white garment with sleeves. Both ordained and lay ministers may wear the alb. A **cincture** is a cloth belt or cord tied at the waist around the alb. The **stole** is a long, narrow piece of fabric that signifies ordination. A priest wears the stole over his alb, draping it from his shoulders so that both ends hang down in front. A deacon wears a stole diagonally across his chest, over his left shoulder.

At Mass the priest wears a **chasuble,** a long, poncho-like garment. The chasuble is worn over the alb and the stole. When a priest leads an outdoor procession or presides at a solemn liturgy that is not a Mass, he may wear a **cope,** a long cape that fastens at the collar, over his alb and stole. A bishop wears a hat called a **miter.** A bishop may also carry a staff, or **crosier,** modeled on a shepherd's crook. The stole, chasuble, cope, and miter are made from fabric whose color represents the liturgical season. The color for Advent and Lent is violet. For Christmas and Easter the color is white or gold. Green is worn during Ordinary Time. On Palm Sunday, Good Friday, Pentecost, and the feasts of martyrs, red is worn.

Holy Days of Obligation

Catholics must attend Mass on Sunday unless a serious reason prevents their doing so. They must also go to Mass on certain holy days. United States holy days of obligation are:

- Mary, Mother of God (January 1)
- Ascension (forty days after Easter or the Sunday nearest the end of the forty-day period)
- Assumption (August 15)
- All Saints' Day (November 1)
- Immaculate Conception (December 8)
- Christmas (December 25)

Faith Fact

November 2 is All Souls' Day. Tradition says that in the Middle Ages, beggars promised to pray for the souls of the dead in exchange for food given them on this special day. The "soul cakes" distributed on November 2 were doughnut-shaped, with a hole cut from the center. The empty circle in each cake represented eternity, which has no beginning and no end.

Rev. Peter Klein,
The Catholic Source Book.

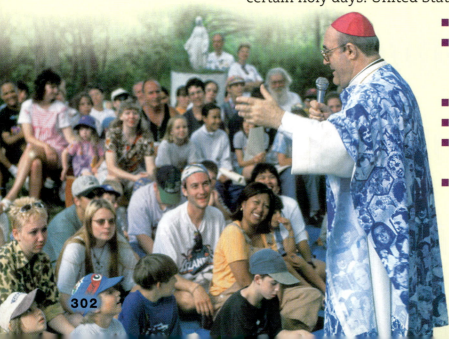

Fasting and Abstinence

To help prepare spiritually for the Eucharist, Catholics fast for one hour before Communion. They take no food or drink except water. (Exceptions can be made for those who are sick and for those of advanced age.)

To fast means to eat only one full meal and two smaller meals during the course of a day. All Catholics, from their eighteenth birthday until their fifty-ninth birthday, are required to fast on Ash Wednesday and Good Friday unless a serious reason prevents them from doing so. Another discipline of self-denial is abstinence. Catholics who are fourteen years of age or older are expected to abstain from eating meat on Ash Wednesday, Good Friday, and, in the United States, on all of the Fridays in Lent.

Liturgical Environment

Each part of the church has a name.
- **narthex** or vestibule—the lobby of a church
- **nave**—the main body of the church
- **baptistry**—the place for Baptism
- **ambry**—the place where holy oils are kept
- **sanctuary**—the area around the altar where the priest and ministers perform their functions
- **reconciliation chapel**—may be used for celebrating the Sacrament of Penance
- **Eucharistic chapel**—used for prayer and adoration of the Eucharist
- **sacristy**—room where priests put on their vestments and materials and vessels for the liturgy are prepared

Each item of furniture in a church also has a name.
- **altar**—the table of the Eucharist
- **font**—the pool or basin of water for Baptism
- **ambo**—the reading stand where Scripture is proclaimed
- **presider's chair**—the chair from which the presider leads prayer
- **tabernacle**—the box in which the consecrated bread of the Eucharist is kept
- **sanctuary lamp**—light kept lit near the reserved Eucharistic Bread in the tabernacle

Faith Fact

Often there are statues and sacred images in a church. You may notice people lighting candles or kneeling in prayer before them. People are not worshiping the image by engaging in such ritual actions; they are showing respect for the person the image represents.

Morality

Faith Fact

The phrase "doubting Thomas" comes from the Gospel according to John when Jesus appeared to the Apostles after his Resurrection. Thomas, one of the Twelve, was not present at the time, and when the others told him they had seen Jesus, Thomas said he wouldn't believe unless he could put his finger in Jesus' wounds.

Law

Divine law is the eternal law of God. It includes:
- physical law. The law of gravity is an example of physical law.
- moral law. A moral law is one that humans understand through reasoning (stealing is wrong) and through divine revelation (keep holy the Lord's day).

Natural moral law is present in every heart. It includes the principles that all humans accept as right. For example, people everywhere understand that no person may kill another unjustly. Everyone must obey natural moral law because everyone is created by God. God's commandments are based on natural moral law.

The Ten Commandments

1. I am the Lord your God. You shall not have strange gods before me.
2. You shall not take the name of the Lord your God in vain.
3. Remember to keep holy the Lord's day.
4. Honor your father and your mother.
5. You shall not kill.
6. You shall not commit adultery.
7. You shall not steal.
8. You shall not bear false witness against your neighbor.
9. You shall not covet your neighbor's wife.
10. You shall not covet your neighbor's goods.

The Great Commandment

"You shall love the Lord your God with all your heart, with all your soul, with all your strength, with all your mind; and your neighbor as yourself." *Luke 10:27*

Precepts of the Church

1. Take part in the Mass on Sundays and holy days. Keep these days holy and avoid unnecessary work.
2. Celebrate the Sacrament of Reconciliation at least once a year if there is serious sin.
3. Receive Holy Communion at least once a year during the Easter Season.
4. Fast and/or abstain on days of penance.
5. Give your time, gifts, and money to support the Church.

The Beatitudes

Blessed are the poor in spirit,
　for theirs is the kingdom of heaven.
Blessed are they who mourn,
　for they will be comforted.
Blessed are the meek,
　for they will inherit the land.
Blessed are they who hunger and thirst for righteousness,
　for they will be satisfied.
Blessed are the merciful,
　for they will be shown mercy.
Blessed are the clean of heart,
　for they will see God.
Blessed are the peacemakers,
　for they will be called children of God.
Blessed are they who are persecuted for the sake of righteousness
　for theirs is the kingdom of heaven.

Faith Fact

A Distinctive Pope

Pope Benedict XVI at age 78 is the oldest man to become pope since 1730. He is the first German pope since 1523. In addition to being a distinguished theologian, he is multilingual, plays the piano, and loves cats.

Works of Mercy

Corporal (for the body)
Feed the hungry.
Give drink to the thirsty.
Clothe the naked.
Shelter the homeless.
Visit the sick.
Visit the imprisoned.
Bury the dead.

Spiritual (for the spirit)
Warn the sinner.
Teach the ignorant.
Counsel the doubtful.
Comfort the sorrowful.
Bear wrongs patiently.
Forgive injuries.
Pray for the living and the dead.

Gifts and Fruits of the Holy Spirit

Wisdom
Right judgment (*Counsel*)
Knowledge
Wonder and awe (*Fear of the Lord*)

Understanding
Courage (*Fortitude*)
Reverence (*Piety*)

Charity
Joy
Peace
Patience

Kindness
Goodness
Generosity
Gentleness

Faithfulness
Modesty
Self-control
Chastity

Morality

Human Dignity

God created humans in his image and likeness. Because of this you have dignity and therefore need to respect your dignity and that of others.

Grace

- **Sanctifying grace** allows you to share in God's own life. It is a permanent gift that builds your friendship with God and assures you of eternal life.
- **Actual grace** is a temporary gift that helps you think or act according to God's will for you in a particular situation. Actual grace helps you understand what is right and strengthens you to turn away from sin.
- **Sacramental grace** is the gift that comes from the sacraments. Each sacrament gives its own particular grace.

Sin

- **Original sin** is the sin that the first humans committed by choosing to disobey God. This sin describes the fallen state that caused the human condition of weakness and tendency toward sin. Baptism restores the relationship of loving grace in which all people were created by God.
- **Personal sin** is any thought, word, act, or failure to act that goes against God's law. Sin is a choice, not a mistake.
- **Mortal sin** separates you from God. For a sin to be mortal, it must be a serious matter done with full knowledge and complete consent.
- **Venial sin** weakens or wounds your relationship with God. Continual venial sin can lead to mortal sin.
- **Social sin** results from the effect that personal sin has on a community. People who have been sinned against may sin in return. Violence, injustice, and other wrongs may develop within the community.

Asking forgiveness, accepting punishment, and resolving not to sin again helps a person develop as a Christian. However, one who habitually sins neglects Christian development, sets a poor example, and harms others. When individuals disobey God's law and just civil laws, the entire community suffers.

Conscience

Conscience is God's gift of an inner voice that helps you tell right from wrong and choose what is right. Having an **informed conscience** is a lifelong task. Some steps that will help you in this task are:

- pray for the guidance of the Spirit
- educate and develop it through constant use and examination
- know the Church's teachings
- seek advice from good moral people.

Examination of Conscience

Examining your conscience should be done daily and in preparation for the Sacrament of Reconciliation.

1. Pray to the Holy Spirit to help you examine your conscience.
2. Look at your life in light of the Beatitudes, the Ten Commandments, the Great Commandment, and the precepts of the Church.
3. Ask yourself:
   - Where have I fallen short of what God wants for me?
   - Whom have I hurt?
   - What have I done that I knew was wrong?
   - What have I not done that I should have done?
   - Have I done penance and tried as hard as I could to make up for past sins?
   - Am I working to change my bad habits?
   - With what areas am I still having trouble?
   - Am I sincerely sorry for all my sins?
4. In addition to confessing your sins, you may wish to talk with the priest about one or more of the above questions.

Virtue

- The **theological virtues** of faith, hope, and love are gifts from God. These virtues help you live in a loving relationship with God.
- **Cardinal virtues** are the principal moral virtues that help you lead a moral life. These virtues are prudence (careful judgment), fortitude (courage), justice (giving God and people their due), and temperance (moderation, balance).

Prayer

The Sign of the Cross

In the name of the Father, and of the Son, and
   of the Holy Spirit. Amen.

The Lord's Prayer

Our Father,
   who art in heaven,
hallowed be thy name;
thy kingdom come;
thy will be done on earth
   as it is in heaven.
Give us this day our
   daily bread;
and forgive us our
   trespasses
as we forgive those who
   trespass against us;
and lead us not into
   temptation,
but deliver us from evil. Amen.

Hail Mary

Hail, Mary, full of grace,
   the Lord is with you!
Blessed are you among women,
   and blessed is the fruit of your womb, Jesus.
Holy Mary, Mother of God,
   pray for us sinners,
now and at the hour of our death. Amen.

Glory to the Father (Doxology)

Glory to the Father, and to the Son, and to the Holy Spirit:
   as it was in the beginning, is now, and will be for ever. Amen.

The Nicene Creed

I believe in one God,
the Father almighty,
maker of heaven and earth,
of all things visible and invisible.
I believe in one Lord Jesus Christ,
the Only Begotten Son of God,
born of the Father before all ages.
God from God, Light from Light,
true God from true God,
begotten, not made, consubstantial
    with the Father;
through him all things were made.
For us men and for our salvation
he came down from heaven,

At the words that follow up to and including and
    became man, *all bow.*

and by the Holy Spirit was incarnate
    of the Virgin Mary,
and became man.
For our sake he was crucified under
    Pontius Pilate,
he suffered death and was buried,
and rose again on the third day
in accordance with the Scriptures.
He ascended into heaven
and is seated at the right hand of the Father.
He will come again in glory
to judge the living and the dead
and his kingdom will have no end.
I believe in the Holy Spirit, the Lord, the giver of life,
who proceeds from the Father and the Son,
who with the Father and the Son is adored and glorified,
who has spoken through the prophets.
I believe in one, holy, catholic and apostolic Church.
I confess one Baptism for the forgiveness of sins
and I look forward to the resurrection
    of the dead
and the life of the world to come. Amen.

Act of Faith

O God, we firmly believe that you are one God in three divine Persons, Father, Son, and Holy Spirit; we believe that your divine Son became man and died for our sins, and that he will come to judge the living and the dead. We believe these and all the truths that the holy Catholic Church teaches because you have revealed them, and you can neither deceive nor be deceived.

Act of Hope

O God, relying on your almighty power and your endless mercy and promises, we hope to gain pardon for our sins, the help of your grace, and life everlasting, through the saving actions of Jesus Christ, our Lord and Redeemer.

Prayer

Act of Love

O God, we love you above all things, with our whole heart and soul, because you are all-good and worthy of all love. We love our neighbor as ourselves for the love of you. We forgive all who have injured us and ask pardon of all whom we have injured.

Act of Contrition

My God,
I am sorry for my sins with all my heart.
In choosing to do wrong
and failing to do good,
I have sinned against you
whom I should love above all things.
I firmly intend, with your help,
to do penance,
to sin no more,
and to avoid whatever leads me to sin.
Our Savior Jesus Christ
suffered and died for us.
In his name, my God, have mercy.

Prayer to the Holy Spirit

Come, Holy Spirit, fill the hearts of your faithful.
And kindle in them the fire of your love.
Send forth your Spirit and they shall be created.
And you will renew the face of the earth.
Let us pray.
Lord,
by the light of the Holy Spirit
    you have taught the hearts of your faithful.
In the same Spirit
    help us to relish what is right
    and always rejoice in your consolation.
We ask this through Christ our Lord. Amen.

Angelus

V. The angel spoke God's message to Mary,
R. and she conceived of the Holy Spirit.
    Hail, Mary. . . .
V. "I am the lowly servant of the Lord:
R. let it be done to me according to your word."
    Hail, Mary. . . .
V. And the Word became flesh,
R. and lived among us.
    Hail, Mary. . . .
V. Pray for us, holy Mother of God,
R. that we may become worthy of the promises of Christ.
Let us pray.
Lord,
fill our hearts with your grace:
once, through the message of an angel
you revealed to us the incarnation of your Son;
now, through his suffering and death
lead us to the glory of his resurrection.
We ask this through Christ our Lord.
R. Amen.

Prayer

Morning Prayer

God be in my head, and in my understanding;
God be in my eyes, and in my looking;
God be in my mouth, and in my speaking;
God be in my heart, and in my thinking;
God be at my end, and at my departing.
Amen.

Grace at Mealtime

Blessed are you, Lord.
You have fed us from our earliest days.
You give food to every living creature.
Fill our hearts with joy and delight.
Let us always have enough
and something to spare
for works of mercy
in honor of Christ Jesus, our Lord.
Through Christ may glory, honor, and power
be yours for ever and ever.
Amen.

Evening Prayer

Lord, from the rising of the sun to its
setting your name is worthy of all praise.
Let our prayer come like incense before
you. May the lifting up of our hands be
as an evening sacrifice acceptable to you,
Lord our God.
Amen.

Prayer Before Meditation

Blessed are you, Lord, God of all creation:
you manifest yourself when we are silent.

Faith Fact

There are many different ways we pray. As Catholics, we have common prayers of the Church that we learn and recite together, but we can also construct our own spontaneous prayers. Meditation, in which we simply focus our hearts and minds on God, is another good form of prayer. You may be hearing about meditation today as a means of relaxation and physical well-being. But meditation (to concentrate deeply on) and contemplation (to be completely in the presence of) are methods of prayers that have been used since the beginning of time. Two saints known for these types of prayer are John of the Cross and Teresa of Ávila.

© Our Sunday Visitor Curriculum Division

God's Presence

When we laugh,
You, God, are there.
When we fall,
You reach to lift us up.
When we struggle,
You cheer us on.
When we are sad,
You reach out to us.
Although we may not always see you, God,
You are always there.

Prayer for Our Lady of Guadalupe Day

(December 12)
Loving God,
you bless the peoples of the Americas
with the Virgin Mary of Guadalupe
as our patron and mother.
Through her prayers
may we learn to love one another
and to work for justice and peace.
Amen.

Lady of Guadalupe,	pray for us
La morena of Tepeyac,	comfort us
Mother of the Faithful,	defend us
Refuge of the oppressed,	strengthen us
Hope of the immigrant,	cheer us
Light of the traveler,	guide us
Friend of the stranger,	welcome us
Shelter of the poor and needy,	sustain us
Patron of the Americas,	unite us
Mother of many children,	watch over us
Star of the morning,	waken us to the coming of your Son, Jesus Christ, who arose from you the sun of justice and is Lord for ever and ever. Amen.

Prayer

Litany of St. Joseph

Lord, have mercy.	Lord, have mercy.
Christ, have mercy.	Christ, have mercy.
Lord, have mercy.	Lord, have mercy.
Good Saint Joseph,	pray for us.
Descendant of the House of David	pray for us.
Husband of Mary,	pray for us.
Foster father of Jesus,	pray for us.
Guardian of Christ,	pray for us.
Support of the holy family,	pray for us.
Model of workers,	pray for us.
Example to parents,	pray for us.
Comfort of the dying,	pray for us.
Provider of food to the hungry,	pray for us.
Companion of the poor,	pray for us.
Protector of the church,	pray for us.

Merciful God,
grant that we may learn from Saint Joseph
to care for the members of our families
and share what we have with the poor.
We ask this through Christ our Lord. Amen.

Faith Fact

A litany is a prayer with one line that is meant to be repeated over and over again so that those praying are caught up in the prayer itself.

How to Pray the Rosary

1. Pray the Sign of the Cross and say the Apostles' Creed.
2. Pray the Lord's Prayer.
3. Pray three Hail Marys.
4. Pray the Glory to the Father.
5. Say the first mystery; then pray the Lord's Prayer.
6. Pray ten Hail Marys while meditating on the mystery.
7. Pray the Glory to the Father.
8. Say the second mystery; then pray the Lord's Prayer. Repeat 6 and 7 and continue with the third, fourth, and fifth mysteries in the same manner.
9. Pray the Hail, Holy Queen.

The Mysteries of the Rosary

The Joyful Mysteries	The Luminous Mysteries
The Annunciation	The Baptism of Jesus
The Visitation	The Wedding at Cana
The Nativity	The Proclamation of the Kingdom
The Presentation in the Temple	The Transfiguration
The Finding in the Temple	The Institution of the Eucharist

The Sorrowful Mysteries	The Glorious Mysteries
The Agony in the Garden	The Resurrection
The Scourging at the Pillar	The Ascension
The Crowning with Thorns	The Descent of the Holy Spirit
The Carrying of the Cross	The Assumption of Mary
The Crucifixion and Death	The Coronation of Mary in Heaven

Eucharist Prayer

How holy this feast
in which Christ is our food:
his passion is recalled,
grace fills our hearts,
and we receive a pledge of the glory to come.

Thomas Aquinas

Prayer

The Way of the Cross

The First Station: *Jesus is condemned to death.* John 3:16
"For God so loved the world that he gave his only Son, so that everyone who believes in him may not perish but may have eternal life."

The Second Station: *Jesus bears his cross.* Luke 9:23
"Then he said to them all, 'If any want to become my followers, let them deny themselves and take up their cross daily and follow me.'"

The Third Station: *Jesus falls the first time.* Isaiah 53:6
"All we like sheep have gone astray; we have all turned to our own way, and the Lord has laid on him the iniquity of us all."

The Fourth Station: *Jesus meets his mother.*
Lamentations 1:12
"Is it nothing to you, all you who pass by? Look and see if there is any sorrow like my sorrow…"

The Fifth Station: *Simon of Cyrene helps Jesus carry his cross.* Matthew 25:40
"And the king will answer them, 'Truly I tell you, just as you did it to one of the least of these who are members of my family, you did it to me.'"

The Sixth Station: *Veronica wipes the face of Jesus.* John 14:9
"… 'Whoever has seen me has seen the Father'…"

The Seventh Station: *Jesus falls a second time.* Matthew 11:28
"Come to me, all you that are weary and are carrying heavy burdens, and I will give you rest."

The Eighth Station: *Jesus meets the women of Jerusalem.*
Luke 23:28
"But Jesus turned to them and said, 'Daughters of Jerusalem, do not weep for me, but weep for yourselves and for your children.'"

The Ninth Station: *Jesus falls a third time.* Luke 14:11
"For all who exalt themselves will be humbled, and those who humble themselves will be exalted."

The Tenth Station: *Jesus is stripped of his garments.*
Luke 14:33
"So therefore, none of you can become my disciple if you do not give up all your possessions."

Faith Fact

In the devotion known as the Way of the Cross, "stations" represent stops along the way of Jesus' journey from Pilate's court all the way to the tomb. Walking in a church from one station to the next and really focusing on each picture or image of the passion of Christ can inspire prayer from the heart.

The Eleventh Station: *Jesus is nailed to the cross. John 6:38*
"[F]or I have come down from heaven, not to do my own will, but the will of him who sent me."

The Twelfth Station: *Jesus dies on the cross. Philippians 2:7–8*
"…And being found in human form, he humbled himself and became obedient to the point of death—even death on a cross."

The Thirteenth Station: *Jesus is taken down from the cross. Luke 24:26*
"Was it not necessary that the Messiah should suffer these things and then enter into his glory?"

The Fourteenth Station: *Jesus is placed in the tomb. John 12:24*
"[Very truly, I tell you,] unless a grain of wheat falls into the earth and dies, it remains just a single grain; but if it dies, it bears much fruit."

Gloria

Glory to God in the highest,
and on earth peace to people of good will.
We praise you,
we bless you,
we adore you,
we glorify you,
we give you thanks for your great glory,
Lord God, heavenly King,
O God, almighty Father.
Lord Jesus Christ, Only Begotten Son,
Lord God, Lamb of God, Son of the Father,
you take away the sins of the world,
    have mercy on us;
you take away the sins of the world,
    receive our prayer;
you are seated at the right hand of the Father,
    have mercy on us.
For you alone are the Holy One,
you alone are the Lord,
you alone are the Most High,
Jesus Christ,
with the Holy Spirit,
in the glory of God the Father.
Amen.

Prayer

Memorare

Remember, most loving Virgin Mary,
never was it heard
that anyone who turned to you for help
was left unaided.

Inspired by this confidence,
though burdened by my sins,
I run to your protection
for you are my mother.

Mother of the Word of God,
do not despise my words of pleading
but be merciful and hear my prayer.
Amen.

Hail, Holy Queen

Hail, holy Queen, Mother of mercy,
hail, our life, our sweetness, and our hope.
To you we cry, the children of Eve;
to you we send up our sighs,
mourning and weeping in this land of exile.
Turn, then, most gracious advocate,
your eyes of mercy toward us;
lead us home at last
and show us the blessed fruit of your womb,
  Jesus:
O clement, O loving, O sweet Virgin Mary.
Salve, Regina

Holy, Holy, Holy Lord

In English
Holy, Holy, Holy Lord God of hosts.
Heaven and earth are full of your glory.
Hosanna in the highest.
Blessed is he who comes in the name of the Lord.
Hosanna in the highest.

In Latin
Sanctus, Sanctus, Sanctus
Dominus Deus Sabaoth.
Pleni sunt coeli et terra gloria tua.
Hosanna in excelsis.

Benedictus qui venit in nomine Domini.
Hosanna in excelsis.

Agnus Dei (Lamb of God)

In English
Lamb of God, you take away the sins of the world, have mercy on us.
Lamb of God, you take away the sins of the world, have mercy on us.
Lamb of God, you take away the sins of the world, grant us peace.

In Latin
Agnus Dei, qui tollis peccata mundi:
miserere nobis.
Agnus Dei, qui tollis peccata mundi:
miserere nobis.
Agnus Dei, qui tollis peccata mundi:
dona nobis pacem.

Faith Fact

As members of the Catholic Church, we ordinarily pray in the language that we speak, but we sometimes pray in Latin, the common language of the Church. The following are a couple of the common prayers of the Church in both English and Latin.

Words of Faith

absolution The forgiveness of sins in God's name through the Sacrament of Reconciliation. (207)

apostolic The mark of the Church which indicates that the teaching authority of the Church comes directly from Jesus and his chosen Apostles because the bishops of the Church are direct successors of the Apostles. (152)

bishop The leader of a particular diocese. Bishops have received the fullness of the Sacrament of Holy Orders. (163)

Body of Christ The Church. Jesus is the head, and his followers are the members. (163)

canonize The pope making a solemn declaration that a person is enjoying eternity with God and that his or her life can be a model for all Christians. (173)

cardinal virtues Virtues acquired by human effort and cooperation with God's grace. (99)

catechumen A "learner," or person preparing to celebrate the Sacraments of Initiation. (197)

charism This word comes from the Greek charismata, or "gifts of grace." A charism is a special power given by the Holy Spirit. (259)

chrism Sacred oil, made from olive oil and scented with spices, used for anointing in the Sacraments of Initiation. In Eastern Rite Churches Confirmation takes its name from this word and is known as *Chrismation*. (197)

consecration That part of the Eucharistic Prayer in which the words of Jesus are prayed over the bread and wine, and these elements become the Body and Blood of Christ. (245)

contrition Sincere sorrow for having sinned. (207)

conversion The process of turning away from sin and toward God and his ways. It is a response to God's love and forgiveness. (127)

Corporal Works of Mercy Actions that show justice, love, and peace, as Jesus did when caring for the physical needs of people. (281)

covenant A sacred agreement between God and his people. (65)

creation All things that exist, made from nothing by God and held together by God's love. (54)

disciple One who learns from and follows the example of a teacher. The disciples of Jesus are those who follow his teachings and put them into practice. (161)

divine God, like God, or of God. Sometimes God is referred to as *The Divine*. (117)

elect The candidates who have been approved by the community to receive the Sacraments of Initiation, usually at the Easter Vigil. The word *elect* means "chosen." (196)

eternal life Life forever with God for all who die in friendship with God. (269)

320

Eucharistic assembly The community of baptized people who gather to celebrate the Eucharist. (225)

evangelization Sharing the good news of Jesus in a way that invites people to accept the gospel. (281)

faith Both a gift given by God and your free choice to seek God and believe in him. (45)

fortitude The cardinal virtue that helps people act with courage to do what is right. Sometimes known as courage, this virtue is one of the gifts of the Holy Spirit. (99)

grace God's free, loving gift of his own life and help. It is participation in the life of the Holy Trinity. (45)

heaven The souls of the just experience the full joy of living in God's presence forever. (268)

hell Separation from God forever. (268)

holiness The quality of being sacred or belonging to God. (171)

Holy Trinity The mystery of one God in three Persons: Father, Son, and Holy Spirit. (81)

homily A talk given by the priest, deacon, or special speaker during Mass. The homilist interprets the readings and encourages the community to live faithfully. (235)

image of God The divine likeness in each person, the result of being created by God. (81)

immersed A person who is covered or surrounded by the water of Baptism is said to be immersed. Immersion may be full or partial. (197)

Incarnation The mystery that the Son of God took on a human nature in order to save all people. (117)

infallibility A gift of the Holy Spirit to the Church by which the pope and the bishops together declare definitively that a matter of faith or morals is free from error and must be accepted by the faithful. (163)

initiation The process of becoming a member of the Church. The Sacraments of Baptism, Confirmation, and Eucharist are Sacraments of Initiation, necessary for entering fully into the life of the Church. (196)

justice The cardinal virtue that means giving to God and to each person their due. We work for social justice on earth as a sign of the everlasting justice of God's reign. (99)

kingdom of God God's reign of justice, love, and peace. Jesus came to bring the kingdom of God which is both present now and yet to come. (125)

laity The name for members of the Church who are not priests or consecrated sisters or brothers.

liturgical assembly The community of believers who come together for public worship, especially in the Eucharist. (223)

liturgical year The Church's public celebration of the whole mystery of Christ in the liturgy through the feasts and seasons of the Church calendar. (173)

liturgy The official public worship of the Church. The word means "the work of the people." (91)

Liturgy of the Word The first main part of the Mass that begins with the first reading from the Bible and ends with the General Intercessions. (235)

magisterium The teaching office of the Church. (163)

marks of the Church The Church is one, holy, catholic, and apostolic. These marks, or characteristics, are signs to the world that God's reign is already present, though incomplete. (153)

miracles Signs and wonders of the divine power of Jesus that help you see the presence of the kingdom of God. (127)

missionary A person who answers a call from God to devote a period of his or her life to bringing Christ's message to people who do not know it. (279)

mortal sin The most serious form of personal sin, through which a person turns completely away from God. (189)

mystery A truth of faith that you cannot fully understand but that you believe because God has shown it to people in Scripture, in the life of Jesus, or in the teachings of the Church. (79)

ordained ministers Those who serve God and the Church through the Sacrament of Holy Orders as bishops, priests, and deacons. (259)

original sin The sin of the first humans, which led to the sinful condition of the human race from its beginning. (187)

pall A white cloth used to cover the coffin at a funeral Mass. It is a sign of the white garment of Baptism. The word *pall* means "cloak." (271)

parables Stories that make comparisons in order to teach something. Jesus used parables to teach about the kingdom of God. (125)

Paschal mystery Christ's work of redemption through his Passion, death, Resurrection, and Ascension. (137)

People of God The Church, called by Christ to share in his mission. (153)

personal sin The deliberate choice to think, say, or do something that goes against your relationship with God or goes against God's law. (189)

pope The successor of Peter, the bishop of Rome, and the head of the entire Church. (163)

prayer Talking to and listening to God. Prayer can be private or public; spoken, sung, or silent; formal or spontaneous. (89)

providence God's loving care for all things; God's will and plan for creation. (55)

prudence The cardinal virtue that helps a person choose what is morally right, with the help of the Holy Spirit and a correct conscience. (99)

Real Presence The true presence of Christ in the Eucharist under the appearance of bread and wine. (223)

reconciliation The sacrament that celebrates God's forgiveness of sin through the Church. This sacrament is also known as penance. The word *reconciliation* means "coming back together" or "making peace." (207)

Redeemer A title for Jesus, because by his death on the cross, he "bought back" the human race from the slavery of sin. (187)

religion The group of beliefs, prayers, and practices through which people express longing for God. (43)

religious life The lives of men and women in religious communities who make vows of poverty, chastity, and obedience as religious priests, sisters, brothers, monks, or friars. (259)

Resurrection Jesus' bodily rising from death to new life that will never end. Christ's Resurrection is the crowning truth of the Catholic faith. (136)

Rite of Christian Initiation of Adults, or RCIA, The process by which adults and some children become members of the Catholic Church through the Sacraments of Initiation. (197)

sacraments Effective signs of God's life, given by Christ to the Church. (65)

Sanctifier The Holy Spirit, who makes holy, or sanctifies, the Church. (171)

Scripture The holy writings of the Old and New Testaments, the written word of God. (235)

social justice The respect, rights, and conditions that must be provided by societies. (281)

sponsor A representative of the Christian community who supports an older child or adult celebrating the Sacraments of Initiation. (197)

stewardship The human response to God's many gifts. It includes respect for all life and responsible care for creation. (55)

temperance The cardinal virtue that helps people practice moderation, or balance, in their lives. (99)

Tradition The living process of handing on the message of Jesus through the Church, especially through its teachers. (235)

Transubstantiation The process by which the power of the Holy Spirit and the words of the priest transform the bread and wine into the Body and Blood of Jesus. (245)

venial sin A less serious personal sin that weakens but does not destroy a person's relationship with God. (189)

viaticum The Eucharist given to a person who is near death to sustain him or her on the journey to eternity. (271)

virtue The habit of doing good that helps you grow in love for God. (81)

vocation A particular way to answer God's call, whether as a lay person (married or single), a religious, or a member of the ordained ministry. (259)

vows Deliberate and free promises made to God and usually witnessed by the community. (259)

worship Public adoration and honor shown to God in prayer. (91)

Boldfaced numbers refer to pages on which the terms are defined.

A

absolution, **207**, 299, **320**
abstinence, 303
Act of Contrition, 210, 310
Advent, 12–15, 300, 302
Alighieri, Dante, 268
All Souls Day, 272, 302
altar servers, 226
anger, 190
anointing with oil, 36
Anointing of the Sick, Sacrament of, 65, 137, 208–209, 299, **320**
Apostles, 28, 31, 161, 162–163, 292, 295
Apostles' Creed, 84, 295
apostolic, 152, 153, **320**
archangels, 194
Ark of the Covenant, 88–89
Ascension, 302
Assumption of Mary, 172, 302
Athanasius, Saint, 86
Augustine, Saint, 50, 300

B

Baptism, 299
    of adults, 196–197
    anointing at, 36
    of Jesus, 16, 80
    liturgy of, 90
    Paschal mystery and, 137
    purpose of, 28, 117, 198–199, 280
    salvation and, 45
    symbols of, 65, 294
    vocations and, 259–260
Baptismal font, 138
Beatitudes, 305, 307
Benedict, Saint, 60
Bernadette, Saint, 298
bishop, 163, 164, 225, 261, 300, 302, **320**
body language, 92
Body of Christ, 23, 152–**153**, 222, **320**
    See also Church
body language, 92
Breaking of the Bread, 32
Buber, Martin, 124
bullying, 143–144

C

canon, 292
canonize, **173**, **320**
cantor, 226
cardinal virtues, 99–**101**, **307**, **320**
Casa Guadalupe, 252
catechist, **164**
catechumen, 45, 196–**197**, **320**
Catherine of Siena, Saint, 230
Catholic Social Services, 251, 252
Cecilia, Saint, 96
charism, 259, **320**
charity, 24, 81, 281
Charles de Foucauld, Blessed, 278
Chavez, Cesar, 180
choices, 102
choir, 226
chrism, 197, **320**
Christmas, 293, 300, 302
Christmas Season, 16–19
Church, 297
    as community, 222–224
    creeds of, 295
    leaders of, 225
    marks of, 152–153
    mission of, 259, 278–279, 280–281, 287
    outreach of, 215
    as place to seek God, 46
    precepts of, 304
    special language of, 164
    teachers of, 162–163
    visions of, 154
    work of, 127, 161–163
    worship of, 89
church community, 200
Clare of Assisi, Saint, 250
comforter, 272
community, 251, 262, 282
confession, *See* Reconciliation, Sacrament of
Confirmation, 36, 65, 90, 137, 197, 198, 299
conscience, 210, 307
consecration/consecrated, **245**, **320**
contrition, **207**, 310, **320**
conversion, **127**, 199, **320**
cooperation, 144
Corporal Works of Mercy, 251, 272, **281**, 305, **320**
courage (fortitude), 99, 101, 305
covenant, 64–**65**, **320**
creation, 54–56, 71, **320**
creed, 295–298
cross, 138, 296
Cyril of Jerusalem, Saint, 204

D

David, king of Israel, 88–89
Day, Dorothy, 286
deacon, 164, 225, 261, 297, 300, 302
Dead Sea Scrolls, 232–233
death and dying, 136–137, 187, 268–271, 298, 299
decision making, 102, 200
dignity, 282
disciple, 161, 280–**281**, **312**
disciples on road to Emmaus, 32
divine, 116–**117**, **320**
    law, 304
doctrine, 164
dogma, **164**
Douglass, Frederick, 160

E

Easter, 32–35, 300, 302
elect, 196, **320**
energy conservation, 71–72
eternal life, **269**–271, 296, 298, **320**
Eucharist, 298, 299
    Holy Spirit in, 296
    litany of, 248
    parish community and, 222–224
    Paschal mystery and, 137
    purpose of, 28, 127, 198, 242–245, 280
    strength from, 200
    symbols of, 65
    in your life, 246
Eucharistic assembly, 225, **313**
Eucharist Prayer, 317
euthanasia, 305
evangelization, 280–**281**, **321**
Evening Prayer, 312
evil, 186–187, 188
extraordinary minister of Holy Communion, 226

F

faith, **45**, 81, 82, **321**
family, 251, 282
fasting, 24, 303
Fatima, 8, 298
feast days
    of Christmas Season, 16
    Easter, 32
    for Mary, 8–11, 16, 173, 302
    Pentecost, 36
    readings for, 293
    of Saints, 20, 50, 60, 70, 86, 96, 106, 132, 142, 158, 168, 172–173, 204, 214, 230, 240, 250, 266, 276
foot washing, 28, 31
forgiveness, 27, 127, 188–189, 206–207, 210
fortitude (courage), 99, **321**
Francis Xavier, Saint, 266
Fruits of Holy Spirit, 305
funerals, 270–271

G

Gabriel, Angel, 11, 297
gestures, 92
gifts of Holy Spirit, 305
Gloria, 316
Glory to God, 54
God
    honoring of, 88–91
    how to seek, 46
    image of, 20, 23, 81, 116–117, 143, 306, 321
    kingdom of, 124–127, 313
    longing for, 43–45
    mystery of, 78–81
    names and titles of, 62
    signs of presence of, 62–65, 66, 91, 223
    Trinity of, 295
    Word of, 236
    your response to, 82
God's Presence, 313
good works, 171
Gospels, 234, 292, 293
grace, **45**, 127, 199, 306, 312, **321**
Great Commandment, 98–99, 304
greeter, 226
grief, 272

H

Hail, Holy Queen, 318
Healing, Sacraments of, 206–209, 299
heaven, 269, 298, **321**
Hebrew people, 62–64, 80, 98–99, 224, 276, 278
hell, 268–269, **321**
Hildegard of Bingen, Saint, 70
holiness, **171**–173, **321**
Holy Days of Obligation, 302
Holy, Holy, Holy Lord, 319
Holy Orders, 65, 137, 163, 261, 297, 299, 300
Holy Spirit
    Baptism and, 173
    Church and, 152–153
    as guide, 200, 210
    in liturgy, 91, 296
    Pentecost and, 36–39, 280
    as Person of the Trinity, 80–81, 295, 296
    work of, 36, 91, 163, 171, 279
Holy Trinity, 80–**81**, 90–91, 295, **321**
homily, 235, **321**
hope, 81, 82
human dignity, 107–108, 306
human rights, 143–144, 179–180, 282, 287

I

image of God, 23, **81**, 116–117, 306, **321**
Immaculate Conception, 172, 173, 298, 302
immersed, 197, **321**
Incarnation, 116–**117**, 296, **321**
infallibility, **163**, **321**
Initiation, Sacraments of, 196–199, 200, 299, **321**
Isidore, Saint, 258–259

J

Jerome, Saint, 240
Jesus Christ
    baptism of, 16, 80
    birth of, 16, 114–115
    choosing of Peter, 162
    commission to disciples, 161, 260
    as cornerstone, 152
    death, Resurrection, and Ascension of, 28, 32, 136–137, 296, 302
    Eucharist and, 245
    image of, 20, 23
    as image of God, 116–**117**
    Incarnation of, 116–117, 296, 321
    Last Supper of, 244
    in liturgy, 235
    mission of, 36
    names and titles of, 12, 116, 118, 136,

244, 296
  new covenant in, 64–65
  new life in, 28, 31, 187, 198, 270
  as Person of the Trinity, 80–81, 296
  sacraments and, 197–198, 299
  second coming of, 15, 136
  in synagogue, 279
  teachings of, 44, 124–127, 268
  works of, 91, 126–127, 260
John, Saint, 298
John the Baptist, Saint, 80
John Paul II, Pope, 305
John XXIII, Pope, 150
John Vianney, Saint, 214
Joseph, Saint, 16, 19, 298
judgment of nations, 269
justice, 99–100, 215–216, 281, 282, **321**

K

Katharine Drexel, Saint, 20
Keller, Helen, 42–43
kingdom of God, 124–127, **125**, **321**

L

Lamb of God, 319
laity (laypeople), **259**, **321**
lamentations, 190
Last Rites, 270, **321**
Last Supper, 64, 244
law, 304
lay people (laity), **259**, **321**
lectionary, **293**–294
Lent, 24–27, 296, 300, 302, 303
Leo XIII, Pope, 20
Litany of St. Joseph, 314
liturgical assembly, 222–**223**, 251, **322**
liturgical environment, 303
liturgical ministries, 225, 226
liturgical posture and gestures, 92
liturgical vestments, 302
liturgical year, 7–39, **173**, 293–294, 300–301, **321**
liturgy, 90–**91**, 293–295, 299–303, **314**
Liturgy of the Hours, 90, 300
Liturgy of the Word, 234–235, 293, **322**
living stones, 152
longing, gift of, 42–45
Lord's Day, 224–225
love, 27, 81, 82, 98–99, 117
Luke, Gospel of, 136

M

Magi, 16, 114–115
magisterium, **163**, **322**
Marguerite Bourgeoys, Saint, 132
María, Saint, 258–259
María de la Encarnación del Corazón de Jesús, Blessed, 122
marks of the Church, **153**, 171, **322**
marriage, 259, 261, 300
martyrs, 106, 134–135, 276, 295
Mary, Mother of God
  family life of, 16, 19
  feast days for, 8, 16, 173, 178, 302
  holiness of, 172
  names and titles of, 8, 174, 178
  obedience of, 297
  Rosary and, 174
Mass
  Eucharist in, 245
  on Holy Days of Obligation, 224, 302
  Liturgy of the Word in, 235, 293, 301
  outline of, 301
  signs of God in, 65
  strength from, 200
  as worship, 89–91
Mass of Christian burial, 271
Matrimony, Sacrament of, 65, 137, 261, 300
Mendes, Chico, 52–53
Memorare, 318
Michael, Archangel, 194
miracles, 126–**127**, **322**
mission, 36, 152–153, 278–279, 287
missionary, 216, 278–281, **279**, **322**
moral decisions, 102

morality, 304–307
Morning Prayer, 312
Morrison, Ana, 252
mortal sin, 188–**189**, **306**, **322**
Moses, 62–63
mourning, 272
mysteries, 78–81, 116, 136–137, 244–245
mystery, **79**, **322**

N

new life, 28, 31, 187, 197, 198
New Testament, 173, 235, 292–294
Nicene Creed, 295

O

O Antiphons, **12**
Old Testament, 89, 232–234, 235, 294
ordained ministers, **259**, 302, **322**
Order of Christian Funerals, 270, 298
Order of Christian Initiation, 196–197
Ordinary Time, 8–11, 20–23, 300, 302
original sin, 117, 136, **187**, 199, 270, **306**, **322**
Ozanam, Frederick, 288

P

pall, 271, **322**
Parable of the Two Sons, 206
Parable of the Sower, 125
parables, **125**, 128, **322**
parish community, 222–225
Paschal mystery, 136–**137**, 138, 223, 296, **322**
Passover meal, 64, 244
Patrick, Saint, 78–79
Paul, Saint, 187, 198, 224, 270
Paul Miki, Saint, 142
peace, 144
penance, See Reconciliation, Sacrament of
Pentecost, 36–39, 280
People of God, 152–**153**, **322**
  See also Church
personal sin, 188–**189**, **306**, **322**
Peter, Saint, 162
poor people, 287
pope, **163**, 164, 294, 297, **322**
postures, 92
praise, 88–91
prayer, 12, 46, 66, 89–**91**, 92, 174, 190, 294, 295, 301, 302, **322**
  See also individual prayers on pages 308–319 and at beginning and end of each lesson
Prayer Before Mediatation, 312
Prayer for Our Lady of Guadalupe Day, 313
precepts of the Church, 304
priest, 164, 225, 261, 296, 297, 300, 302, 307
providence, 54–**55**, **322**
prudence, 99–100, **322**

R

Rabut family, 216
reader, 226
Real Presence, **223**, **323**
reconciliation, 207, **323**
Reconciliation, Sacrament of, 65, 127, 137, 189, 206–207, 299, 304, 307
Redeemer, 187, **323**
religion, **43**, **323**
religious communities, 262
religious life, **259**, **323**
religious vocation, 262
respect, 143–144, 179–180, 282
Resurrection, 28, 136–137, **323**
rights, 143–144, 179–180, 282, 287
Rite of Christian Funerals, 270, 298
Rite of Christian Initiation of Adults, 196–**197**, **323**
Robert Bellarmine, Saint, 158
Romero, Archbishop Oscar, 134–135
Rosary, 8–11, 174, 298, 300
  How to Pray the Rosary, 317
  The Mysteries of the Rosary, 317

S

sacramental symbols, 294

sacraments, 65, 299, **323**
  creation and, 55
  of Healing, 206–209, 299
  of Initiation, 36, 196–199, 200, 299
  Jesus in, 296
  liturgy and, 90, 293
  matter and form of, 299
  mystery of God and, 80
  Paschal mystery and, 137
  purpose of, 127, 280
  Scripture and, 293
  of Service, 261–262, 300
  See also Baptism; Eucharist
saints, 170–173, 298
  See also individual names of saints
salvation, 28, 45, 171, 244, 296
Sanctifier, **171**, **323**
sanctoral cycle, 173
scribes, 98
Scripture, 46, 234–**235**, 292–294, **323**
Second Vatican Council, 150–152
sense of the faithful, 163
service, 200, 226, 262
Service, Sacraments of, 261–262, 300
Sign of the Cross, 81, 91, 295, 308
signs of God's love, 62–65, 66, 117, 126–127, 280
sin, 117, 136, 187–189, 199, 207, 210, 306, 307
slavery, 107–108
social justice, **281**, 282, 287–288, **323**
social sin, **306**
Society of St. Vincent de Paul, 287–288
Solemnity of the Epiphany, 16
solidarity, 215
sorrow, 190, 272
Spiritual Works of Mercy, 272, 305
sponsor, 196–**197**, **323**
Stephen, Saint, 276
stewardship, **55**, 56, 71, **323**
storytelling, 124–125
suffering, 215
Sunday Mass, 224, 293–294, 302
symbols of Paschal mystery, 138
synagogue, **278**–279

T

teacher, **164**
temperance, 99, 101, **323**
Ten Commandments, 81, 200, 304, 307
theological virtues, 307
The Way of the Cross, 315
Thomas Aquinas, Saint, 168
Thomas More, Saint, 106
Tradition, 234–**235**, **323**
Transubstantiation, **245**, **323**
Triduum, 28–31
Trinity. See Holy Trinity

U

unity, 153, 222–223

V

venial sin, **189**, **306**, **323**
Veuster, Damien de, 208–209
viaticum, 270–**271**, **323**
violence, 143–144
virtue, 81, **323**
virtues, **81**, 99–101, 307
vocation, 258–261, 262, **323**
vows, 259, **323**

W

woman at the well, 44–45
Word of God, 236
work, 179–180
worship, 88–**91**, **323**
  See also liturgy

Y

Yevtushenko, Yevgeny, 242

Illustration Credits

4-5 Jane Sanders; 16-17 Simone Boni; 24-25 Larry Schwinger
UNIT 1: 40 Dan Brown; 41 Dan Brown; 44 Corey Wolfe; 50 Lois Woolley; 53 Steve Dittberner; 54 Cathy Diefendorf; 60 Lois Woolley; 62 Chuck Gillies; 70 Lois Woolley
UNIT 2: 78 Sandy Rabinowitz; 86 Lois Woolley; 88 James Watling; 96 Lois Woolley; 98 Jeff Preston; 106 Lois Woolley
UNIT 3: 122 Lois Woolley; 125 Mike Jaroszko; 126 Tom Newsome; 132 Lois Woolley; 142 Lois Woolley
UNIT 4: 158 Lois Woolley; 160 Jeff Preston; 161 Jeff Preston; 162 Dean Kennedy; 168 Lois Woolley; 170 Lois Woolley; 171 Lois Woolley; 172 Jeff Preston; 178 Lois Woolley
UNIT 5: 184 Clint Hansen; 185 Clint Hansen; 186 Thea Kliros; 187 Shannon Stirnweis; 194 Lois Woolley; 204 Lois Woolley; 206 Shannon Stirnweis; 208 Matthew Archambault; 214 Lois Woolley
UNIT 6: 226 Kristen Funkhouser; 230 Lois Woolley; 232 Dominick D'Andrea; 233 Dominick D'Andrea; 240 Lois Woolley; 242 Jeff Preston; 244 Jack Pennington; 250 Lois Woolley
UNIT 7: 256 Greg Lafever; 257 Greg Lafever; 258 Greg Dearth; 260 Jeff Preston; 266 Lois Woolley; 269 Matthew Archambault; 276 Lois Woolley; 278 Ron Croci; 279 Jack Pennington; 286 Lois Woolley

Photo Credits

iii Richard Hutchings; 1 l PhotoLink/Photodisc/Getty Images; 1 r RubberBall Productions/Getty Images; 2 Ariel Skelley/CORBIS; 6 PhotoAlto/Creatas; 7 b Jon Smyth/SuperStock; 7 inset Father Gene Plaisted, OSC; 8 fg EPA/Landov; 8-9 bg Steve Vidler/SuperStock; 10-11 bg George Diebold/Getty Images; 11 fg Photodisc/Getty Images; 12 cl Photodisc/Getty Images; 12 cr Photodisc/Getty Images; 12 bl Photodisc/Getty Images; 12 br C Squared Studios/Photodisc/Getty Images; 13 t Photodisc/Getty Images; 13 tl Photodisc/Getty Images; 13 c Photodisc/Getty Images; 13 cl Corel; 14-15 bg Photos.com; 14-15 fg Myrleen Ferguson Cate/PhotoEdit; 15 inset Photodisc/Getty Images; 18-19 bg Ariel Skelley; 19 inset Photos.com; 20-21 Robert Lentz; 22-23 bg Alexander Walter/Getty Images; 23 inset Father Gene Plaisted, OSC; 26-27 bg Corel; 26-27 fg Myrleen Ferguson Cate/PhotoEdit; 27 inset Photodisc/Getty Images; 28-29 Laura James/Bridgeman Art Library; 30-31 Nancy Sheehan/PhotoEdit; 32-33 bg ASAP Ltd./Index Stock Imagery/Photolibrary; 32-33 fg Richard Hutchings; 34-35 Victor Englebert; 36-37 bg Corel; 36-37 fg Father Gene Plaisted, OSC; 38-39 David Young-Wolff/PhotoEdit; 40 c John Burcham/Getty Images; 40 r Jim Whitmer Photography; 42 Bettmann/CORBIS; 43 t Father Gene Plaisted, OSC; 43 b Myrleen Ferguson Cate/PhotoEdit; 45 Our Sunday Visitor Curriculum Division; 46-47 Ed McDonald Photography; 48 Myrleen Ferguson Cate/PhotoEdit; 50 Photodisc/Punchstock; 51 John Burcham/Getty Images; 52-53 Margarette Mead/Getty Images; 55 l Jeremy Frechette/Getty Images; 55 c Carol Havens/Corbis; 55 b Richard H Johnston/Taxi/Getty Images; 56 John Welzenbach; 58 Photodisc/Getty Images; 61 Jim Whitmer Photography; 64 Father Gene Plaisted, OSC; 66 James W. Porter/Corbis; 68 Rolf Bruderer/Corbis; 70 Laura Dwight/PhotoEdit; 71 t Owaki-Kulla/Corbis; 71 b Jeff Greenberg/Index Stock/Photolibrary; 72 bl Jim Cummins/Corbis; 72 br Matt Meadows; 73 t Fredrik Skold/The Image Bank/Getty Images; 73 b Photodisc/Getty Images; 76 l Jeff Greenberg/PhotoEdit; 76 c Sonny Senser; 76 r Richard Hutchings; 76-77 bg Jeff Greenberg/PhotoEdit; 80 Library of Congress; 81 George Doyle/Getty Images; 82 Sonny Senser; 84 Father Gene Plaisted, OSC; 86 Bill Wittman; 87 Sonny Senser; 89 Tony Freeman/PhotoEdit; 90 t Father Gene Plaisted, OSC; 90 c Michael Newman/PhotoEdit; 90 bl Taxi/Getty Images; 90 br Father Gene Plaisted, OSC; 91 cl Stephen McBrady/PhotoEdit; 91 c Father Gene Plaisted, OSC; 91 cr Father Gene Plaisted, OSC; 92 l Matt Meadows; 92 c Matt Meadows; 92 r Matt Meadows; 94 Gary A. Conner/PhotoEdit; 97 Richard Hutchings; 99 Myrleen Ferguson Cate/PhotoEdit; 100 Richard Hutchings; 101 Lisette Le Bon/SuperStock; 102 Ed McDonald Photography; 104 Jay Dickman/Corbis; 107 c Howard Davies/Corbis; 107 bl Torleif Svensson/Corbis; 107 br Frank Kroenke/Peter Arnold/Photolibrary; 108 Courtesy of American Anti-Slavery Group; 112 l Brand X Pictures/Punchstock; 112 c Lawrence Migdale/Stone/Getty Images; 112 r David Young-Wolff/PhotoEdit; 112-113 bg Brand X Pictures/Punchstock; 115 inset Jim Whitmer Photography; 116 Superstock/Getty Images; 117 J. Silver/Superstock; 118 t Sonny Senser; 118 b Sonny Senser; 120 Philippe de Champaigne/Superstock; 122 tl Myrleen Ferguson Cate/PhotoEdit; 122 Medioimages/Photodisc/Getty Images ; 123 Lawrence Migdale/Stone/Getty Images; 124 Sonny Senser; 127 cl Tony Freeman/PhotoEdit; 127 cr Jack Hollingsworth/Getty Images; 128 Ed McDonald Photography; 130 Myrleen Ferguson Cate/PhotoEdit; 132 Sonny Senser; 133 David Young-Wolff/PhotoEdit; 134-135 br Bettman/Corbis; 135 t Luis Galdamez/Reuters; 135 b Jim Whitmer Photography; 136 Bridgeman-Giraudon/Art Resource, NY; 138 Brand X Pictures/Punchstock; 140 Nathan Blaney/Getty Images; 142 David Young-Wolff/PhotoEdit; 143 Gabe Palmer/Corbis; 144 c Jeff Greenberg/PhotoEdit; 144 bl Michael Newman/PhotoEdit; 144 br Peace by Peace; 145 t Photodisc/Getty Images; 145 c Peace by Peace; 145 b Gabe Palmer/Corbis; 148 l Sonny Senser; 148 c Peter Beck/Corbis; 148 r Jim Whitmer Photography; 148-149 bg Sonny Senser; 150 bg Photodisc/Getty Images; 150 fg David Lees/Corbis; 151 bg Photodisc/Getty Images; 151 tl Bettman/Corbis; 151 tr Paul Schutzer/Time Life Pictures/Getty Images; 152 Ed McDonald Photography; 153 Jim Whitmer Photography; 154 Will Hart/PhotoEdit; 156 Herb Snitzer/Stock Boston; 158 Paul Barton/Corbis; 159 Peter Beck/Corbis; 161 Ed McDonald Photography; 163 Osservatore Romano/Pool/Reuters/Corbis; 164 Ed McDonald Photography; 166 Massimo Listri/Corbis; 169 Jim Whitmer Photography; 173 Father Gene Plaisted, OSC; 174 l Photodisc/Getty Images; 174 r Matt Meadows Photography; 176 Karen Callaway/Catholic News Service; 179 cl Echo/Getty Images; 179 bg James L. Amos/Corbis; 179 bl Will & Deni McIntyre/Corbis; 179 bc Richard Ransier/Corbis; 179 br Photodisc/Getty Images; 180-181 bg Emma Lee/Life File/Photodisc/Getty Images; 180 bl Arthur Schatz//Time Life Pictures/Getty Images; 180 br David Young-Wolff/PhotoEdit; 181 t Dwayne Newton/PhotoEdit; 181 c Jules Frazier/Photodisc/Getty Images; 184 c Sonny Senser; 184 r Ed McDonald Photography; 188 David Young-Wolff/PhotoEdit; 189 Myrleen Ferguson Cate/PhotoEdit; 190 Michael Newman/PhotoEdit; 192 Michael S. Yamashita/Corbis; 195 Sonny Senser; 196 Jim Whitmer Photography; 197 c Jim Whitmer Photography; 197 b Jim Whitmer Photography; 198 Our Sunday Visitor Curriculum Division; 199 t Bill Wittman; 199 c Father Gene Plaisted, OSC; 200 C/B Productions/Corbis; 202 Myrleen Ferguson Cate/PhotoEdit; 204 Ed McDonald Photography; 205 Ed McDonald Photography; 209 Society of the Sacred Heart General Archives, Rome, Italy; 210 bg Jack Holtel/Photographik Company; 210 fg Tony Freeman/PhotoEdit; 212 Father Gene Plaisted, OSC; 214 Joe Brooks Photography; 215 c Sébastien Cailleux/Sygma/Corbis; 215 bl John Van Hasselt/Corbis; 215 br Denny Allen/Getty Images; 216 c Sean Sprague; Property of/Permission from Maryknoll Lay Missioners; 216-217 b Pablo Corral V/Corbis; 217 t Powerstock/Index Stock/Photolibrary; 217 bc Houghton Mifflin Harcourt; 217 br Jack Holtel/Photographik Company; 220 l Tom Stewart/Corbis; 220 c Ed McDonald Photography; 220 r Ed McDonald Photography; 220-221 Tom Stewart/Corbis; 222-223 Jeff Greenberg/PhotoEdit; 224 c Stephen McBrady/PhotoEdit; 225 b Myrleen Ferguson Cate/PhotoEdit; 225 cl Bill Wittman; 225 cr Myrleen Ferguson Cate/PhotoEdit; 228 Jim Whitmer Photography; 230 Our Sunday Visitor Curriculum Division; 231 Ed McDonald Photography; 234 Stockbyte/Getty Images; 236-237 Myrleen Ferguson Cate/PhotoEdit; 238 Father Gene Plaisted, OSC; 241 Ed McDonald Photography; 243 Father Gene Plaisted, OSC; 245 Myrleen Ferguson Cate/PhotoEdit; 246-247 George Disario/Corbis; 248 Father Gene Plaisted, OSC; 251 c Jim Whitmer Photography; 251 bl Terry Vine/Stone/Getty Images; 251 br Alan Schein Photography/Corbis; 252 c Jim Whitmer Photography; 252 b Christian Michaels/Taxi/Getty Images; 253 Thinkstock/Getty Images; 256 c Father Gene Plaisted, OSC; 256 r Jim Cummins/Corbis; 259 c Myrleen Ferguson Cate/PhotoEdit; 259 b Ed McDonald Photography; 261 Michael Newman/PhotoEdit; 262 c Spencer Grant/PhotoEdit; 262 b Pablo Corral V/Corbis; 264 Mark C. Burnett/Stock Boston; 266 l David Young-Wolff/PhotoEdit; 266 cl Spencer Grant/PhotoEdit; 266 cr Jim Whitmer Photography; 266 r Elana Rooraid/PhotoEdit; 267 Father Gene Plaisted, OSC; 268 British Museum, London UK/Bridgeman Art Library; 270 Dennis MacDonald/PhotoEdit; 271 Father Gene Plaisted, OSC; 272 bl James Shaffer/PhotoEdit; 272-273 br Tony Freeman/PhotoEdit; 274 Daemmrich/Stock Boston; 277 Our Sunday Visitor Curriculum Division; 280 c Myrleen Ferguson Cate/PhotoEdit; 280 b Jeff Greenberg/PhotoEdit; 281 Myrleen Ferguson Cate/PhotoEdit; 282 cl Viviane Moos/Corbis; 282 cr Gerald Herbert/AP/WorldWide Photos; 282 bl Louise Gubb/Corbis/SABA; 284 Carsten Koall/Getty Images; 287 c Bill Wittman; 287 b Myrleen Ferguson Cate/PhotoEdit; 288 c Society of St. Vincent de Paul; 288 bl Society of St. Vincent de Paul; 288 br Bill Wittman; 289 t Comstock/Getty Images; 289 b Our Sunday Visitor Curriculum Division; 292 Richard Hutchings; 294 Alessandra Benedetti/Corbis; 295 Father Gene Plaisted, OSC; 296 PhotoSpin; 297 Richard Cummins/Superstock; 300 Steve Cole/Photodisc/Getty Images; 301 Father Gene Plaisted, OSC; 302 Bill Wittman; 303 Father Gene Plaisted, OSC; 305 KAI PFAFFENBACH/Reuters/Corbis; 306 Bill Wittman; 308-309 Thinkstock/Getty Images; 310-311 Thinkstock/Getty Images; 312-313 Thinkstock/Getty Images; 314-315 Thinkstock/Getty Images; 316-317 Thinkstock/Getty Images; 318-319 Thinkstock/Getty Images

Acknowledgments

For permission to reprint copyrighted material, grateful acknowledgment is made to the following sources:

Liveright Publishing Corporation: From "i thank You God for most this amazing" in *Complete Poems: 1904-1962* by E. E. Cummings, edited by George J. Firmage. Text copyright 1950; text copyright renewed © 1978, 1991 by the Trustees for the E. E. Cummings Trust. Text copyright © 1979 by George James Firmage.

Manna Music, Inc., 35255 Brooten Road, Pacific City, OR 97135 : Lyrics from "How Great Thou Art" by Stuart K. Hine. Lyrics copyright © 1953 by S. K. Hine; lyrics copyright renewed © 1981 by Manna Music, Inc.

OCP Publications, 5536 NE Hassalo, Portland, OR 97213: Lyrics from "Here I Am, Lord" by Dan Schutte. Lyrics © 1981 by OCP Publications.

G.P. Putnam's Sons, A Division of Penguin Young Readers Group, A Member of Penguin Group (USA) Inc., 345 Hudson Street, New York, NY 10014: "Everybody Says" from *Everything and Anything* by Dorothy Aldis. Text copyright © 1925-1927; text copyright renewed © 1953, 1954, 1955 by Dorothy Aldis.

Twenty-Third Publications, A Division of Bayard: From "God's Presence" in *500 Prayers for Catholic Schools & Parish Youth Groups* by Filomena Tassi and Peter Tassi. Text copyright © 2004 by Filomena Tassi and Peter Tassi.

United States Conference of Catholic Bishops, Inc., Washington, D.C.: English translation of "Hail, Holy Queen" (*Salve, Regina*), "Before a Time of Solitude" (Retitled: "Prayer before Meditation"), "Psalm-prayer" (Retitled: "Evening Prayer"), and "For the Day's Work at Home" (Retitled: "Morning Prayer") from *Catholic Household Blessings and Prayers.* Translation copyright © 1989 by United States Catholic Conference, Inc.

World Library Publications, www.wlpmusic.com: Lyrics from "Sing Praise to Our Creator" by Omer Westendorf. Lyrics copyright © 1962 by World Library Publications.